D1505582

DEFINING MOMENTS
ROE v. WADE

DEFINING MOMENTS
ROE v. WADE

Laurie Collier Hillstrom

CONTRA COSTA COUNTY LIBRARY

3 1901 04420 9130

Omnigraphics

P.O. Box 31-1640
Detroit, MI 48231

Omnigraphics, Inc.

Cherie D. Abbey, *Managing Editor*

Peter E. Ruffner, *Publisher*
Matthew P. Barbour, *Senior Vice President*

Elizabeth Collins, *Research and Permissions Coordinator*
Kevin M. Hayes, *Operations Manager*

Allison A. Beckett and Mary Butler, *Research Staff*
Cherry Stockdale, *Permissions Assistant*
Shirley Amore, Martha Johns, and Kirk Kauffman, *Administrative Staff*

Copyright © 2008 Omnigraphics, Inc.
ISBN 978-0-7808-1026-6

Library of Congress Cataloging-in-Publication Data

Hillstrom, Laurie Collier, 1965-
 Roe v. Wade / Laurie Collier Hillstrom.
  p. cm. -- (Defining moments)
 Summary: "Explores the history of abortion in America, describing the Roe v. Wade case, explaining the decision and its implications, and examining the continuing debate over abortion rights and its impact on American society and politics. Features include a narrative overview, biographical profiles, primary source documents, detailed chronology, glossary, annotated sources for further study, bibliography, and index"-- Provided by publisher.
 Includes bibliographical references and index.
 ISBN 978-0-7808-1026-6 (hardcover : alk. paper) 1. Abortion--United States--History. 2. Abortion--Law and legislation--United States. 3. Abortion--Moral and ethical aspects. I. Title.
 HQ767.5.U5H55 2008
 363.460973--dc22
                                                                                2008003524

All rights reserved. No part of this publication may be reproduced or transmitted in any form or by any means, electronic or mechanical, including photography, recording, or any other information storage and retrieval system, without permission in writing from the publisher.

The information in this publication was compiled from the sources cited and from other sources considered reliable. Additional copyright information can be found on the photograph credits page of this book. While every possible effort has been made to ensure reliability, the publisher will not assume liability for damages caused by inaccuracies in the data, and makes no warranty, express or implied, on the accuracy of the information contained herein.

This book is printed on acid-free paper meeting the ANSI Z39.48 Standard. The infinity symbol that appears above indicates that the paper in this book meets that standard.

Printed in the United States

TABLE OF CONTENTS

NARRATIVE OVERVIEW

BIOGRAPHIES

PRIMARY SOURCES

PREFACE

Throughout the course of America's existence, its people, culture, and institutions have been periodically challenged—and in many cases transformed—by profound historical events. Some of these momentous events, such as women's suffrage, the civil rights movement, and U.S. involvement in World War II, invigorated the nation and strengthened American confidence and capabilities. Others, such as the McCarthy era, the Vietnam War, and Watergate, have prompted troubled assessments and heated debates about the country's core beliefs and character.

Some of these defining moments in American history were years or even decades in the making. The Harlem Renaissance and the New Deal, for example, unfurled over the span of several years, while the American labor movement and the Cold War evolved over the course of decades. Other defining moments, such as the Cuban missile crisis and the terrorist attacks of September 11, 2001, transpired over a matter of days or weeks.

Although significant differences exist among these events in terms of their duration and their place in the timeline of American history, all share the same basic characteristic: they transformed the United States' political, cultural, and social landscape for future generations of Americans.

Taking heed of this fundamental reality, American citizens, schools, and other institutions are increasingly emphasizing the importance of understanding our nation's history. Omnigraphics' *Defining Moments* series was created for the express purpose of meeting this growing appetite for authoritative, useful historical resources. This series, which focuses on the most pivotal events in U.S. history from the twentieth century forward, will be of enduring value to anyone interested in learning more about America's past—and in understanding how those historical events continue to reverberate in the twenty-first century.

Each individual volume of *Defining Moments* provides a valuable resource for readers interested in learning about the most profound events in our nation's history. Each volume is organized into three distinct sections—Narrative Overview, Biographies, and Primary Sources.

- The **Narrative Overview** provides readers with a detailed, factual account of the origins and progression of the "defining moment" being examined. It also explores the event's lasting impact on America's political and cultural landscape.

- The **Biographies** section provides valuable biographical background on leading figures associated with the event in question. Each biography concludes with a list of sources for further information on the profiled individual.

- The **Primary Sources** section collects a wide variety of pertinent primary source materials from the era under discussion, including official documents, papers and resolutions, letters, oral histories, memoirs, editorials, and other important works.

Individually, each of these sections is a rich resource for users. Together, they comprise an authoritative, balanced, and absorbing examination of some of the most significant events in U.S. history.

Other notable features contained within each volume in the series include a glossary of important individuals, places, and terms; a detailed chronology featuring page references to relevant sections of the narrative; an annotated bibliography of sources for further study; an extensive general bibliography that reflects the wide range of historical sources consulted by the author; and a subject index.

Special Note about *Defining Moments: Roe v. Wade*

In keeping with the mandate of the *Defining Moments* series, we have made every effort to provide readers with an objective, historical overview of the Supreme Court's 1973 *Roe v. Wade* decision and its impact on the political, cultural, and social landscape of the United States. We recognize that many Americans have strong feelings about the abortion issue, and we have attempted to balance pro-choice and pro-life perspectives on the events covered in this volume.

Throughout the text, we have used the term "pro-choice" in reference to individuals and groups who support legalized abortion, and the term "pro-life" in reference to individuals and groups who oppose legalized abortion. We selected these terms—rather than the many other terms that are sometimes used to describe the divergent positions in the abortion debate—because they are the terms that the two sides most often use to describe themselves. In the Primary Sources section, the language reflects the wording of the original documents.

Acknowledgements

This series was developed in consultation with a distinguished Advisory Board comprising public librarians, school librarians, and educators. They evaluated the series as it developed, and their comments and suggestions were invaluable throughout the production process. Any errors in this and other volumes in the series are ours alone. Following is a list of board members who contributed to the *Defining Moments* series:

Gail Beaver, M.A., M.A.L.S.
Adjunct Lecturer, University of Michigan
Ann Arbor, MI

Melissa C. Bergin, L.M.S., NBCT
Library Media Specialist
Niskayuna High School
Niskayuna, NY

Rose Davenport, M.S.L.S., Ed.Specialist
Library Media Specialist
Pershing High School Library
Detroit, MI

Karen Imarisio, A.M.L.S.
Assistant Head of Adult Services
Bloomfield Twp. Public Library
Bloomfield Hills, MI

Nancy Larsen, M.L.S., M.S. Ed.
Library Media Specialist
Clarkston High School
Clarkston, MI

Marilyn Mast, M.I.L.S.
Kingswood Campus Librarian
Cranbrook Kingswood Upper School
Bloomfield Hills, MI

Rosemary Orlando, M.L.I.S.
Library Director
St. Clair Shores Public Library
St. Clair Shores, MI

Comments and Suggestions

We welcome your comments on *Defining Moments: Roe v. Wade* and suggestions for other events in U.S. history that warrant treatment in the *Defining Moments* series. Correspondence should be addressed to:

Editor, *Defining Moments*
Omnigraphics, Inc.
P.O. Box 31-1640
Detroit, MI 48231
E-mail: editorial@omnigraphics.com

HOW TO USE THIS BOOK

*D*efining *Moments: Roe v. Wade* provides users with a detailed and authoritative overview of the landmark 1973 Supreme Court decision that legalized abortion in the United States, as well as the principal figures involved in this pivotal episode in U.S. history. The preparation and arrangement of this volume—and all other books in the *Defining Moments* series—reflect an emphasis on providing a thorough and objective account of events that shaped our nation, presented in an easy-to-use reference work.

Defining Moments: Roe v. Wade is divided into three primary sections. The first of these sections, the **Narrative Overview**, provides a detailed, factual account of the *Roe v. Wade* case and decision. It explores the history of abortion in America, describes the early movements to reform anti-abortion laws, follows the *Roe v. Wade* case from its origins in Texas to its two hearings before the U.S. Supreme Court, explains the landmark 1973 decision and its implications, traces the rising power and influence of the pro-life movement, and examines the continuing debate over abortion rights and its impact on American society and politics.

The second section, **Biographies**, provides valuable biographical background on leading figures involved in the *Roe v. Wade* case and in the national debate over abortion rights. Individuals profiled include Supreme Court Justice Harry A. Blackmun, author of the majority opinion; Norma McCorvey, the pregnant woman who agreed to serve as a plaintiff in the case under the false name Jane Roe; Henry Wade, the Dallas district attorney who served as the defendant; and Sarah Weddington, the young attorney who successfully argued the case before the Supreme Court. Each biography concludes with a list of sources for further information on the profiled individual.

The third section, **Primary Sources**, collects essential and illuminating documents from the *Roe v. Wade* case and the larger battle over abortion rights.

This collection includes the National Organization for Women's 1967 call for the repeal of abortion laws; excerpts from the Supreme Court's majority opinion and dissenting opinions; Robert H. Bork's defense of the pro-life position; and the 2004 Democratic and Republican party platforms on abortion.

Other valuable features in *Defining Moments: Roe v. Wade* include the following:

- Attribution and referencing of primary sources and other quoted material to help guide users to other valuable historical research resources.

- Glossary of Important People, Places, and Terms.

- Detailed Chronology of events with a *see reference* feature. Under this arrangement, events listed in the chronology include a reference to page numbers within the Narrative Overview wherein users can find additional information on the event in question.

- Photographs of the leading figures and major events associated with the *Roe v. Wade* case and the abortion issue.

- Sources for Further Study, an annotated list of noteworthy works about the case.

- Extensive bibliography of works consulted in the creation of this book, including books, periodicals, Internet sites, and videotape materials.

- A Subject Index.

NARRATIVE OVERVIEW

PROLOGUE

⸻

In October 1972 Justice Harry A. Blackmun sat at his desk in the U.S. Supreme Court Building, thinking about how he should handle the opinion he had just been assigned to write. He had received the assignment from Chief Justice Warren E. Burger, a fellow Minnesota native who had been one of his closest friends since boyhood.

Blackmun knew it was somewhat unusual for a relatively inexperienced justice, like himself, to be asked to write the majority opinion in such an important case. He wondered why his friend had given him the assignment. Was it because Burger valued Blackmun's background in medical law, which he had gained as an attorney for the prestigious Mayo Clinic? Or because Burger knew that one of Blackmun's daughters had become pregnant at 19 and dropped out of college to marry the baby's father, only to go through a miscarriage and a divorce? Or did the chief justice simply believe that his friend's opinion would most closely reflect his own?

Blackmun had weighed in on a number of controversial cases since joining the Supreme Court in 1970. American society was in the midst of a period of great turmoil and change at that time. The Court had settled many important legal disputes that grew out of the civil rights movement, the women's liberation movement, and the anti-Vietnam War movement. But the current case presented many difficult, complex, emotionally charged questions, and Blackmun struggled to come up with answers. "It is not a happy assignment," he wrote in a note to himself.

Although Blackmun did not know it at the time, the opinion he was about to write would define his judicial career. When the Supreme Court announced the ruling on January 22, 1973, Blackmun became a hero to mil-

3

lions of feminists. But the decision outraged millions of other Americans, some of whom made Blackmun the target of hate mail and death threats.

Blackmun suspected that the Court's decision would create controversy, but he did not expect it to spark an all-out war that would fundamentally change American law, politics, society, and culture for generations to come. The case in question, though, was *Roe v. Wade,* and the opinion he wrote made abortion legal throughout the United States.

Blackmun spent the remainder of his long and distinguished career defending the opinion he wrote as a second-year justice. "*Roe against Wade* hit me early in my tenure on the Supreme Court. And people forget that it was a 7-2 decision. They always typify it as a Blackmun opinion," he remarked upon his retirement in 1994. "But I'll say what I've said many times publicly—I think it was right in 1973, and I think it was right today. It's a step that had to be taken as we go down the road toward the full emancipation of women."

As the United States marked the thirty-fifth anniversary of the landmark ruling in 2008, the nation remained as deeply and bitterly divided over the abortion issue as ever. Some Americans view the Supreme Court's decision in *Roe v. Wade* as a historic milestone that established important legal protections for women's rights and privacy rights. Other Americans view the ruling as a terrible tragedy that led to the deaths of millions of unborn children and to a decline of moral values in American society. Given the strength of these conflicting views, it is little wonder that the *Roe v. Wade* case remains one of the most controversial events in American history.

Chapter One

THE EARLY HISTORY OF ABORTION

Abortion is an option to which people of all times and places have resorted, with or without religious consent, legal approval, or medical supervision.

—Laurence H. Tribe, *Abortion: The Clash of Absolutes*

omen had abortions long before the 1973 Supreme Court decision in *Roe v. Wade* made the procedure legal in the United States. In fact, abortion has taken place around the world, in various cultures, since ancient times. The women of ancient Egypt, Greece, and Rome ate toxic substances derived from plants—such as silphium, Queen Anne's lace, pennyroyal, and acacia gum—to end unwanted pregnancies. Abortion was not generally considered a crime in these cultures, but a form of birth control.

Abortion was also practiced in America from the time that the earliest European settlers arrived. Although the legal status of abortion during the colonial period is unclear, because the issue was rarely contested in court, it is clear that many women had abortions. Some of the reasons they made this decision still apply three centuries later. Women in colonial America chose to end pregnancies that resulted from incest or rape, for instance, or that posed a threat to their mental or physical health. Some poor families made the decision to abort pregnancies out of concern that they could not afford to feed another child. In addition, many single women had abortions rather than face the shame of delivering a child out of wedlock.

During the 1700s, abortion was considered a private matter. Many women relied on methods passed down from friends and relatives to end a pregnancy. Others went to folk healers or midwives for help. Common abortion procedures during this time involved eating toxic plants like juniper and snakeroot, which Native Americans had traditionally used for that purpose, or douching with harsh chemicals like vinegar or brine.

The Concept of "Quickening"

After the Revolutionary War, the United States continued to follow English common law on abortion. This generally accepted code of conduct allowed women to have abortions up until the time that they could feel the fetus moving inside them. This stage of pregnancy was known as "quickening," and it typically occurred around the fourth month.

Many religious traditions believed that quickening was the point of development at which the fetus received a soul from God.

In this era, long before pregnancy tests became available, quickening provided the first indisputable evidence that a woman was pregnant. Many pregnant women experienced physical symptoms well before this time, including fatigue, nausea, weight gain, and a lack of menstrual periods. Until quickening occurred, however, these symptoms could be attributed to other health issues.

The concept of quickening played an important role in public attitudes about abortion in the late 1700s and early 1800s. Many religious traditions believed that quickening was the point of development at which the fetus received a soul from God. Likewise, early American legal thought defined quickening as the point when the fetus could be considered a human being. Therefore, if a woman took steps to end a pregnancy in its early months, before quickening occurred, the abortion was considered neither a sin nor a crime.

State Laws Regulate Abortion

In 1821 Connecticut became the first state to pass a law against abortion. The statute made it illegal for a woman to have an abortion after quickening had occurred. Before quickening, her decision to end a pregnancy was not considered abortion. Since it was nearly impossible to prove that quickening had occurred without the woman's cooperation, however, the Connecticut law was very difficult to enforce. In fact, abortion providers were only prosecuted under the law when a woman died or suffered serious health consequences from the procedure.

In 1828 Illinois, Missouri, and New York followed Connecticut's lead and outlawed abortion. These states, however, made no distinction between abortions that were performed before or after quickening occurred. Instead, all abortions were deemed illegal. The main purpose of these new state laws was to protect women, even in the early stages of pregnancy, from negligent conduct by abortion providers. Women were considered the victims of the crime, and they could not be prosecuted for seeking an abortion or for performing one on themselves.

Laws regulating abortion spread to more states throughout the 1830s and early 1840s. In 1845 New York revised its law so that a woman could be charged with a crime if she tried to obtain an abortion or attempted to perform one on herself. This new law was almost impossible to enforce, though, because few women were willing to provide evidence to incriminate themselves.

Abortion Remains Available

Partly due to the difficulty of enforcing laws against it, abortion continued to take place throughout the United States during the early 1800s. In fact, abortion started to become more visible during this period, even as an increasing number of states enacted measures to restrict or outlaw it.

A Massachusetts doctor named Charles Knowlton played an important role in making abortion a growing topic for public discussion and debate. In the 1840s, Knowlton became the country's best-known advocate of abortion rights. Knowlton justified abortion by saying that it was a necessary aid to family planning. He argued that American society would benefit if all parents were happy and healthy and all children were wanted and well-cared for. If having an additional child would create a burden, he said, the parents should be allowed to end the pregnancy.

As more Americans accepted Knowlton's views, women's health clinics opened in many cities around the country. Most of these clinics provided abortions, although they often disguised this fact in order to avoid conflict with state laws. Instead, the clinics claimed to treat diseases specific to women, which naturally included problems with the reproductive system. At the same time, many popular newspapers and magazines began featuring advertisements for mail-order drugs and potions that promised to clean out women's reproductive tracts and restore a normal menstrual cycle. Most of these products were actually abortifacients, or substances that induced abortion.

As the visibility and availability of abortion increased, so did the number of abortions performed. Some studies estimated that one abortion took place for every four live births by the mid-1800s. In addition, statistics showed that the fertility rate among American women declined by 50 percent between 1800 and 1900, from an average of 7 to 3.5 children. Although industrialization and other factors played a role in the decline, many historians believe that the statistics reflect an increasing reliance on abortion to limit family size.

Diverse Groups Oppose Abortion

Opponents of abortion watched these developments with mounting alarm. Determined to prevail, they launched new efforts to outlaw abortion during the second half of the nineteenth century, especially following the Civil War (1861-65).

Popular newspapers and magazines began featuring advertisements for mail-order drugs and potions that promised to clean out women's reproductive tracts and restore a normal menstrual cycle.

One of the main groups that opposed the practice was the American Medical Association (AMA), a professional organization for doctors that had been formed in 1847. The AMA argued that abortion posed extreme and unnecessary risks to women's lives and health. In those days, most surgical abortions were performed by midwives, and many women who underwent the procedure suffered from dangerous infections or other complications. Partly as a way to protect women, and partly as a way to give doctors greater control over the practice of medicine, the AMA lobbied state and federal governments to prohibit anyone but a licensed physician from performing an abortion.

Some early women's rights activists also opposed abortion. Susan B. Anthony, a leader in the movement to secure the right to vote for American women, echoed the AMA's position by citing concerns about women's health. But rather than outlaw abortion, Anthony wanted to make it unnecessary by changing the social circumstances that often drove women to seek abortions. She argued that women needed education to help them make informed decisions about family planning and prevent unwanted pregnancies. Anthony also claimed that a key to ending abortion was to grant women equal rights and opportunities in American society. She believed that women who were allowed to vote and hold jobs would be better equipped to support children.

This illustration from an 1867 edition of the *National Police Gazette* depicts an evil abortionist abandoning a dying woman who sought his services.

Other Americans opposed abortion on moral grounds. They argued that bearing children was a woman's fundamental duty and purpose, and they asserted that women who had abortions were selfishly refusing to accept their natural roles as wives and mothers. In this way, opposition to abortion was sometimes linked to a desire to keep women in a subservient, domestic position in American society. "The criminalization of abortion fit the overall gendering of law, in which male lawgivers asserted that women must be protected against their own weakness and immorality in having unwanted children and then seeking the assistance of abortionists," N.E.H. Hull and Peter Charles Hoffer wrote in *Roe v. Wade: The Abortion Rights Controversy in American History.* "Doctors and legislators agreed that the state must interpose itself between women and the dangers of such abortions."

Changing perspectives on the morality of abortion also led some religious and ethnic groups to condemn the practice in the late 1800s and early 1900s. The Catholic Church was the most influential of these organizations. It abandoned the concept of quickening in 1869 and declared instead that human life was sacred from the moment of conception. Catholic leaders soon joined the fight against abortion, calling it a moral evil.

Finally, some white Protestant leaders opposed abortion because they wanted to maintain a high birth rate among educated, middle-class women in their ranks. Taking notice of the vast numbers of immigrants pouring into the United States around the turn of the twentieth century, some white Anglo-Saxon Protestants worried about losing their majority status. These nativists did not try to restrict abortion among segments of the population that they considered inferior—including recent immigrants, African Americans, and Native Americans—but only among members of their own group. This selective opposition to abortion came to be seen as a tool by which they could maintain control over the country's racial and cultural makeup.

Abortion Becomes a Criminal Offense

With such diverse groups joining in opposition to abortion, anti-abortion laws were passed in many states during the years following the Civil War. By 1880, in fact, abortion was illegal in nearly every state. In some cases it was not only illegal to perform or have an abortion, but also to sell, advertise, or provide materials or information that could be used for that purpose. An increasing number of people were arrested and charged with abortion-related offenses, and those convicted faced harsher penalties.

A few states made exceptions that allowed abortion in certain circumstances, such as when the pregnancy resulted from rape or incest, when the mother's life was threatened by the pregnancy, or when the fetus was deformed. In general, however, abortion was difficult and risky to obtain by the end of the nineteenth century.

Despite all the efforts to outlaw the practice, however, abortions continued to take place into the twentieth century. In fact, studies estimated that one out of every three or four pregnancies ended in abortion in the early 1900s. This percentage increased significantly during the Great Depression of the 1930s, when economic hardship struck many American families and made it difficult for them to support additional children (see "Abortion during the Great Depression," p. 17). Due to the illegal nature of the practice, however, abortion once again became something that was done secretly. Women in rural areas used home remedies that were passed down through families to end unwanted pregnancies, while women in cities used the services of illegal abortion providers.

States Outlaw Birth Control

The expansion of laws restricting abortion in the late 1800s was part of a larger effort to improve the moral values of American society. In addition to abortion, artificial birth control became a target for reformers during this era. They argued that the availability of contraceptives—like the availability of abortion—encouraged women to behave in immoral and promiscuous ways. They charged that if women were free to have sex without worrying about becoming pregnant, then they would no longer be bound to cultural institutions like marriage and child-rearing. As historian Laurence Tribe explained in *Abortion: The Clash of Absolutes*, "A central theme throughout the history of abortion in the United States is that women who are able to control their reproductive destinies gain freedom to pursue personal missions other than the traditional one in the home." Although this idea appealed to some women, many people viewed it as a serious threat to the moral and social foundations of American life.

The leading figure in the fight against birth control was Anthony Comstock (see "Anthony Comstock: The 'Weeder in God's Garden,'" p. 12). Born in Connecticut in 1844 and raised as a devout Christian, Comstock took a job as a salesman in New York City following the Civil War. He was deeply troubled by some of the things he saw in the city, such as prostitution and pornography, which he considered to be immoral and obscene. He soon became convinced that the availability of contraceptives contributed to these problems, and he decided to try to outlaw their sale and use.

In 1872 Comstock wrote a proposal for a new law and took it to Washington, D.C. Officially called the "Act for the Suppression of Trade in, and

Anthony Comstock: The "Weeder in God's Garden"

One of the best-known crusaders against birth control, abortion, and the publication of sexually suggestive materials was Anthony Comstock. Born in New Canaan, Connecticut, on March 7, 1844, he was one of ten children in a family that was devoted to the Congregationalist Church. After completing his schooling, Comstock fought for the Union in the Civil War. He recalled being offended by the drinking, smoking, gambling, and swearing that he frequently witnessed among his fellow soldiers.

Once the war ended, Comstock moved to New York City. In 1868 he launched his career as a self-described "weeder in God's garden"—removing any negative influences before they could corrupt young people's moral values—by arranging the arrest of a well-known publisher of pornography. The publisher, Charles Conroy, was so enraged that he attacked Comstock and slashed his face with a knife. Comstock wore long sideburns for the rest of his life to cover the scar, but the incident only made him pursue his mission with greater determination.

In 1873 Comstock and his supporters formed the Society for the Suppression of Vice and took their fight against obscenity to Washington, D.C. They succeeded in convincing the U.S. Congress to pass the sweeping anti-obscenity law that became known as the Comstock Act. The law prohibited anyone from sending a wide variety of materials through the mail, including nude photos, suggestive literature, and educational information about sex, birth control, or abortion. After the law passed, Comstock

Circulation of, Obscene Literature and Articles for Immoral Use," but better known as the Comstock Act, it was passed by the U.S. Congress on March 3, 1873 (see "The Comstock Law Bans Birth Control and Abortion," p. 170). Hull and Hoffer claimed that it "was in its time and remains to this day the nation's most sweeping intrusion of government into private conduct."

The law made it illegal for anyone to sell, publish, or possess a wide variety of materials that Comstock and his supporters considered obscene. This included all printed information about sex, sexually transmitted diseases, became a special agent for the U.S. Postal Service. This position gave him authority to inspect any piece of mail and arrest anyone who mailed something that he found offensive.

Comstock's activities extended to censoring the work of writers and artists, which earned him many critics among liberal intellectuals. In fact, the famous playwright George Bernard Shaw coined the term "comstockery" to describe overbearing censorship of various forms of artistic expression. Perhaps Comstock's most controversial attempt at censorship came in 1913, when he tried to force an art gallery to stop showing a painting called *September Morn* by the French artist Paul Chabas. The painting showed a nude woman, discreetly covered, standing in a mountain lake watching a sunrise. Public outrage over Comstock's efforts generated a great deal of attention for the painting, which became one of the most widely reproduced works of its era.

Still, Comstock's anti-obscenity crusades had a significant impact in their day. He oversaw the destruction of 50 tons of books—including many medical textbooks on anatomy—and 4 million photographs that he considered offensive. He once boasted that the number of people he helped convict on obscenity charges would fill 60 railroad cars. Comstock also expressed pride in the fact that several people whose activities he exposed went on to commit suicide, including Madam Restell, a provider of abortion services and contraceptive devices. Comstock himself died on September 21, 1915, in New Jersey. Some of his anti-obscenity laws remained in place until the *Roe v. Wade* decision of 1973.

birth control, and abortion. The Comstock Act also made it illegal to provide any "instrument... drug or medicine, or any article whatever, for the prevention of conception, or for causing unlawful abortion." It became a criminal offense to send contraceptive devices through the U.S. mail or to transport them across state lines. The law effectively prohibited Americans from using or even talking about birth control.

Shortly after the Comstock Act became the law of the land, twenty-four states passed their own statutes prohibiting the distribution and use of con-

Women's rights advocate Margaret Sanger (left) sits in a courtroom with her sister Ethel Byrne in January 1917. Sanger was prosecuted by local authorities after she opened the nation's first birth control clinic in Brooklyn, New York.

traceptives. Connecticut passed one of the most restrictive laws in the country. The leader of Connecticut's anti-birth control movement was Phineas T. Barnum, the famous circus showman and politician who was also a vocal opponent of alcohol use. Under Barnum's law, it became illegal for a doctor in Connecticut to discuss birth control with a patient. It also became illegal for a married couple to use birth control in the privacy of their own home. The state's residents could go to jail for these offenses. Although police did not often enforce Barnum's anti-contraceptive measures, the law remained in place for the next eighty years.

Reformers Fight for Access to Contraception

The efforts to outlaw birth control led by Comstock, Barnum, and others came under heavy criticism in the early twentieth century. During this time, many American women fought to gain the right to vote so that they could help shape the future direction of the country. They also challenged other laws and social customs that they felt prevented them from achieving equal rights and opportunities in American life. Campaigns to repeal state laws against birth control became a leading focus of these women's rights groups.

The leader in the fight to legalize contraception was Margaret Sanger (see Sanger biography, p. 146). Born in 1879, Sanger became concerned about the issues of birth control, pregnancy, child-bearing, and abortion in the early 1900s through her work as a nurse. She was frequently called upon to treat women who were suffering dangerous health complications as a result of illegal abortions. Some of these women had attempted to perform abortions on themselves, while others had sought the services of untrained abortionists. Most of Sanger's patients were so poor and desperate that they were willing to risk their lives rather than bear more children.

Sanger sympathized with her patients' situations, and she expressed deep anger that risky abortions had become America's primary means of family planning. She felt strongly that these women needed access to contraceptives to prevent unwanted pregnancies. "Mothers were denied by law knowledge to prevent conception," Sanger wrote in *My Fight for Birth Control*. "This was so outrageous, so cruel, so useless a law that I could not respect it. I longed to prove its bad effects, to show up its destructive force on women's and children's lives." Sanger soon gave up her job as a nurse and launched a new career as an activist in the movement to legalize birth control.

As she worked to change the law, Sanger also defied it by publishing information about birth control. In direct violation of the Comstock Act, for instance, she circulated a pamphlet called *Family Limitation* that discussed various methods for preventing pregnancy. In 1914 she began publishing *The Woman Rebel*, a magazine that promoted the idea that women could only advance in American society if they were allowed to control their own bodies. In 1916 Sanger opened the first birth control clinic in the United States. Even though her actions led to her arrest a short time later, she helped open dozens more clinics in various cities over the next twenty years. Her goal, as she wrote in the *North American Review,* was to enable "American mothers ... to choose the time and conditions best suited for fulfillment of the maternal function."

The Birth Control Movement Gains Support

The efforts by Sanger and other activists to legalize birth control gained support throughout the 1920s. American women won the right to vote at the start of that decade, and the nation's attitudes about sexuality began to shift and become more progressive. Many people started discussing and using birth control, even though it was still illegal.

The organization that Sanger founded in 1921, the American Birth Control League, expanded to include chapters in states across the country during these years. The Connecticut chapter was started by activists Kit Hepburn (mother of the famous actress Katharine Hepburn) and Sallie Pease in 1923. The members of this group worked to overturn their state's strict laws against

Pro-choice activists Kit Hepburn (left) and Margaret Sanger (right) discuss a birth control bill with Congressman Walter Pierce at a 1934 meeting.

contraceptive distribution and use. In 1935 Hepburn and Pease opened the Hartford Maternal Health Center. This center provided married couples with information about birth control and fitted women for diaphragms, in direct violation of the Barnum laws. The clinic received so much support from Hartford residents, however, that police and prosecutors refused to take action against it for several years. Still, Hepburn and Pease were unable to convince the Connecticut legislature to overturn the Barnum laws.

The ongoing efforts to legalize contraception received an important boost in the 1930s from the American Medical Association. In the early 1930s, a number of studies suggested a connection between the number of children in a family and the likelihood that the family lived in poverty. In gen-

Abortion during the Great Depression

Facing poverty and hardship during the Great Depression of the 1930s, many desperate women used abortion to limit the size of their families. Middle-class women could often afford to pay a doctor or midwife to perform an abortion. Poor women, on the other hand, often resorted to attempting the procedure themselves.

Edward Keemer was an African-American doctor who worked at Freedman's Hospital in Washington, D.C., during the Depression era. As he recalled in his autobiography, his job involved treating hundreds of women who suffered terrible complications from botched abortion attempts. Keemer found this situation so upsetting that he eventually began providing illegal abortions himself.

I had treated a woman whom we had rushed hemorrhaging into the emergency room. She still had the straightened-out coat hanger hanging from her vagina. Some obtained rubber urinary catheters and died from air embolisms or infection. Over the years, I was to encounter hundreds of other women who had resorted to imaginative but deadly methods of self-induced abortion before they came to me. Some would swallow quinine or turpentine. Others would insert a corrosive potassium permanganate tablet into their vaginas. I recalled a sixteen-year-old girl who died after douching with a cupful of bleach.

Source: Edward Keemer, *Confessions of a Pro-Life Abortionist*. Detroit: Velco Press, 1980.

eral, the studies found that families with fewer children tended to enjoy a higher standard of living and better health. Such research helped convince the AMA to abandon its opposition to birth control in 1935.

The following year, the U.S. Court of Appeals decision in the case *U.S. v. One Package* made it legal for doctors to import contraceptive devices from overseas and to transport them across state lines. The ruling acknowledged that doctors had a responsibility to promote the health and well-being of their patients. After seeing evidence about the potential dangers of pregnancy and

This 1941 photograph shows two women installing a Planned Parenthood exhibit titled "Every Baby Wanted and Loved."

the relative safety of using contraception, the court determined that doctors must be allowed to prescribe contraception in order to meet this responsibility. The court ruling also said that birth control had social value, and that providing information about it was not obscene. Although laws against contraception remained in place in many states, the *One Package* decision gave new hope to the activists working to legalize birth control across America.

Changes in the Twentieth Century

The movement to legalize birth control was closely tied to efforts to legalize abortion. After all, both issues centered on the question of whether women had the legal and moral right to control their reproductive capacity.

Many reformers viewed the fight for access to birth control as a way to make public discussion of abortion more socially acceptable.

The first half of the twentieth century saw a number of developments in the fields of science and medicine that affected the parallel debates over birth control and abortion. For instance, scientists increased their knowledge of human development. Once they learned that the growth of a fetus is a continuous process that begins at conception, they abandoned the idea that quickening marked a distinctive stage of development.

Medical research also led to the introduction of more effective contraception in the mid-twentieth century. Birth control options expanded to include condoms, diaphragms, spermicidal creams, and eventually "the pill." As a wider variety of birth control methods became available, the Roman Catholic Church emerged as the most powerful opponent of legalized contraception. Church leaders argued that God intended people to engage in sexual intercourse for the purpose of procreation, and that artificial efforts to prevent conception violated natural law. They also claimed that the availability of birth control made it easier for men and women to engage in immoral sexual relations.

Beginning in the middle of the twentieth century, abortion also became significantly safer—at least when it was performed by a trained physician. Medical research led to the development of antibiotics that greatly reduced the risk of dangerous infections during such procedures. Doctors also gained a better understanding of anatomy and made use of improved surgical techniques. As a result, the mortality rate associated with abortion declined from 100 out of every 100,000 women in 1955 to three out of every 100,000 women in 1972.

These developments encouraged a number of states to change their anti-abortion laws in the 1950s. Many states passed exceptions that allowed doctors to perform abortions under specific circumstances, such as when continuing a pregnancy posed a threat to the life or health of the mother. But the wording of the new laws was often vague and confusing, so many doctors remained hesitant to provide abortions. In fact, the number of legal abortions performed in U.S. hospitals actually declined between 1945 and 1960. Women continued to seek abortions during this time, however, even if that meant resorting to risky illegal procedures.

Chapter Two

THE RISE OF THE FEMINIST AND ABORTION-REFORM MOVEMENTS

⬥

No woman can call herself free who does not own and control her body. No woman can call herself free until she can choose consciously whether she will or will not be a mother.

—Margaret Sanger

A s America entered the second half of the twentieth century, both abortion and birth control remained illegal in many states. Reproductive rights activists first concentrated on increasing access to birth control, which they viewed as less controversial than abortion. The 1936 *One Package* decision had overturned federal laws that prohibited Americans from obtaining and using contraceptives. Yet many state laws banning birth control remained on the books, and some continued to be enforced into the 1950s. Connecticut's laws, which had originated with circus showman P.T. Barnum in the 1870s, were the strictest in the nation.

The American Birth Control League began fighting to repeal the Barnum laws in the 1920s. The activists faced powerful opposition, however, in the form of Roman Catholic members of the state legislature. Over the years, the birth-control advocates experienced a number of setbacks in court as well, as judge after judge refused to overturn the state's wide-reaching anti-obscenity acts, which also outlawed birth control and abortion.

In 1941 the American Birth Control League merged with another organization to become the Planned Parenthood Federation of America, and the local chapter opposing the Barnum laws became the Planned Parenthood League of Connecticut (PPLC). After struggling unsuccessfully for several

21

years, the organization got a new leader in 1953: Estelle Griswold (see "Birth Control Advocate Estelle Griswold," p. 23). She increased the PPLC's membership, improved its finances, and launched a referral service to help Connecticut residents go to birth control clinics in neighboring New York and Rhode Island.

Griswold eventually became convinced that the Connecticut legislature would never lift the ban on birth control. She decided that the PPLC's best hope to change the law rested with the courts. With the help of Dr. Charles Lee Buxton, chairman of the Department of Obstetrics and Gynecology at Yale University, Griswold launched a legal challenge against the old Barnum laws.

Buxton v. Ullman Attacks the Birth Control Ban

In 1958 the PPLC filed a lawsuit against Abraham S. Ullman, the state attorney for the New Haven district, on behalf of Buxton and several married couples who were his patients. The female spouses had health problems that could make pregnancy dangerous for them. Under Connecticut law, Buxton was not allowed to prescribe birth control for these patients, even though he felt it was necessary to protect their health.

Two attorneys helped prepare the PPLC's lawsuit, Fowler Harper and Catherine Roraback. They argued that the Barnum laws violated the rights of Dr. Buxton and his patients, especially their right to privacy in making a personal medical decision about whether to use contraceptives. "When the long arm of the law reaches into the bedroom and regulates the most sacred relations between man and wife, it is going too far," Harper explained in *The Case of* Roe v. Wade.

Even though privacy is not one of the specific rights guaranteed to American citizens under the Constitution, Harper and Roraback claimed that the U.S. Supreme Court had established its existence in several earlier decisions. In a famous 1928 opinion, for example, Justice Louis Brandeis stated that the framers of the Constitution meant to give the American people "the right to be let alone—one of the most comprehensive rights and the right most valued by civilized men." Similarly, the 1925 Court decision in *Pierce v. Society of Sisters* had declared parents' decisions about raising and educating their children to be private, and therefore beyond the realm of government control.

The case of *Buxton v. Ullman* made its way through the court system in Connecticut, with the doctor and his patients losing each round. The U.S.

Birth Control Advocate Estelle Griswold

Estelle Trebert Griswold was born on June 8, 1900, in Hartford, Connecticut. After marrying Richard Griswold, she moved with him to Washington, D.C., in 1927. For the next dozen years she studied medicine and worked as a medical technologist. During the 1940s she worked with several international relief organizations, helping poor and displaced persons in South America and the Caribbean.

After witnessing the effects of extreme poverty and overpopulation, Griswold became convinced that increasing access to birth control could help solve these problems. She returned to Connecticut and joined the Planned Parenthood League, becoming its executive director in 1953. Outraged by the old Barnum laws that made it illegal to distribute and use contraceptives in her home state, Griswold organized a referral service to help women visit birth control clinics in neighboring states.

In 1961 Griswold decided to challenge the Barnum laws by opening a PPLC birth control clinic in New Haven. She was promptly arrested, tried, and fined $100, but she appealed her conviction all the way to the U.S. Supreme Court. The Court's historic 1965 decision in *Griswold v. Connecticut* not only legalized the use of contraception by married couples, but also established a new constitutional right to privacy. Griswold died on August 13, 1981, and was buried in Wethersfield, Connecticut.

Supreme Court finally heard the case in March 1960. Once again, Harper argued that the Barnum laws violated his clients' right to privacy in the most personal areas of their lives.

Three months later, five of the nine justices voted to dismiss the case on a technicality, without issuing a ruling. The Court said Harper had failed to prove that the doctor and his patients had suffered immediate harm due to the Barnum laws. After all, the plaintiffs had never been charged with a crime. In fact, no one had been prosecuted for prescribing or using birth control in Connecticut for many years. In the Court's view, this turned the case of *Buxton v. Ullman* into a theoretical question, and the justices preferred not to rule on such questions. "For the bench, the consistency of the law and the limitations on what courts could do were more important issues than the theoretical or potential harms that some laws might work on women and men," N.E.H. Hull and Peter Charles Hoffer explained in *Roe v. Wade: The Abortion Rights Controversy in American History*.

Still, Harper's arguments seemed to have an impact on some of the justices. Justice John Marshall Harlan disagreed with his colleagues' decision to dismiss the case. In an angry dissenting opinion, he called the Barnum laws "obnoxiously intrusive" and "an intolerable and unjustifiable invasion of privacy in the conduct of the most intimate concerns of an individual's private life." Griswold and the PPLC were encouraged by his words. They felt that the Court might rule in their favor if they presented the issue again as part of a stronger case.

Griswold v. Connecticut and the Right to Privacy

Shortly after the *Buxton v. Ullman* case was dismissed, Griswold launched a new case that she hoped would overcome the Supreme Court's procedural concerns. The PPLC opened a birth control clinic in New Haven, in direct violation of the Barnum laws. Unlike the maternal health clinics that had quietly provided Connecticut women with contraceptive information in earlier decades, the new clinic made no secret about its purpose. In fact, Griswold held a press conference to announce its opening. She and the other activists wanted the state to shut down the clinic so that the PPLC could demonstrate harm from the Barnum laws.

As Griswold and her allies had hoped, state authorities wasted little time in moving against the New Haven clinic. In fact, the state shut down the facility within a week after it opened and placed Griswold under arrest. In 1962 a Connecticut court convicted Griswold of providing birth control information and materials in violation of state law. She appealed her conviction all the way to the U.S. Supreme Court, which heard arguments in the case of *Griswold v. Connecticut* in 1965. By this time, Fowler Harper had died of prostate cancer, so his colleague Tom Emerson presented the PPLC's case before the Court.

Emerson argued that the Barnum laws violated Connecticut citizens' right to privacy in marital relations. He acknowledged that the Constitution did not explicitly list privacy among the people's rights, but he claimed that privacy was protected under the Ninth Amendment (see "The Foundations of Privacy in the U.S. Constitution," p. 169). This article in the Bill of Rights says that "the enumeration in the Constitution of certain rights, shall not be construed to deny or disparage others retained by the people." In other words, the Ninth Amendment says that citizens have rights and liberties that may not be spelled out in the Constitution. One of these rights, Emerson argued, involved freedom from government interference in a citizen's home, marriage, and family.

The Supreme Court announced its decision in the case of *Griswold v. Connecticut* on June 7, 1965. The justices ruled 7-2 in favor of Griswold, overturning her conviction as well as Connecticut's Barnum laws. In effect, the ruling legalized the distribution and use of birth control—at least by married couples (the Supreme Court legalized the use of birth control by unmarried people with its 1972 decision in *Eisenstadt v. Baird*). It also established an individual's right to privacy in reproductive decisions.

Justice William O. Douglas wrote the majority opinion in the case, and the Court also issued three concurring and two dissenting opinions. These

Estelle Griswold, seen here standing outside a Planned Parenthood clinic in New Haven, Connecticut, was a leader in the fight to legalize birth control.

opinions showed some disagreement among the justices about whether the Constitution supported a citizen's right to privacy. Douglas suggested that privacy was protected through "penumbras" or shaded borders around the Bill of Rights, while other justices felt the right resided elsewhere in the document. Justice Hugo Black, on the other hand, argued in his dissent that the Constitution did not support a "broad, abstract, and ambiguous concept" of privacy. Although he found the Barnum laws "viciously evil," he explained that he could not declare them unconstitutional.

Supreme Court Justice William O. Douglas wrote the majority opinion in the landmark *Griswold v. Connecticut* case.

The Court's decision was also condemned in other quarters. Some legal scholars felt that the Supreme Court had overstepped its authority in the *Griswold v. Connecticut* decision. They complained that the Court had invented a new right that simply did not exist in the Constitution. Many citizens expressed concern that the legalization of birth control would encourage women to behave in a promiscuous manner. But many other people celebrated the ruling as an important victory for women. Margaret Sanger, who had opened the nation's first birth control clinic fifty years earlier, died a year later knowing that her life-long goal had finally been achieved.

Changing Views on Abortion

Once the Supreme Court legalized the use of birth control with its 1965 *Griswold* decision, some activists argued that the Court had also given American women the right to choose not to reproduce. They asserted that women should be allowed to exercise this right even after they had become pregnant, by choosing to have an abortion. They believed that the right to privacy in reproductive decisions should also extend to abortion.

Many activists who supported abortion rights believed that the time was right to go on the offensive. In addition to the *Griswold* case, a number of factors had contributed to a dramatic shift in public attitudes toward abortion in the early 1960s. The women's liberation movement had made it more acceptable for women to discuss matters concerning their sexuality. In addition, rising concerns about world overpopulation had led many people to think more carefully about whether to have a baby. Finally, several events that received prominent news coverage during the early 1960s helped increase public acceptance of abortion as an option that should be available to women.

One of these events was the highly publicized case of Sherri Finkbine, a 29-year-old mother of four and the star of "Romper Room," a children's TV program broadcast from Phoenix, Arizona. In 1962, Finkbine was pleased to learn that she was expecting her fifth child. She had trouble sleeping during the early months of her pregnancy, however, so she took a tranquilizer that her husband had brought back from England a year earlier. As it turned out, the tranquilizer contained a drug called thalidomide. When expectant mothers took this drug in the early months of pregnancy, it had the potential to cause severe deformities in the fetus. Thalidomide was linked to birth defects in thousands of babies born in Europe, Australia, and Canada in the early 1960s.

When Finkbine read newspaper reports about the risks of taking thalidomide in early pregnancy, she immediately contacted her doctor. He showed her pictures of deformed fetuses in a medical journal and recommended that she have an abortion. Finkbine soon learned that abortion was illegal in her home state of Arizona except when the procedure was deemed necessary to save the mother's life. She appeared before a panel of three doctors to explain her situation, and she told them that carrying the baby to term could have a negative effect on her mental health. Finkbine expected the doctors to grant their approval for a therapeutic abortion, as they had done in many similar cases in the past.

In the meantime, hoping to prevent other women from taking thalidomide during pregnancy, Finkbine described her situation to a newspaper reporter. The story quickly traveled across the country, and the publicity led to delays in approval of the abortion procedure. When a lawsuit brought by Finkbine and her husband failed to convince the Phoenix hospital board, the desperate couple finally obtained an abortion in Sweden, where the procedure was legal. Just as they had feared, the fetus was badly deformed.

Many Americans followed the Finkbine case in the news, and it generated a great deal of public discussion about abortion. A Gallup poll taken shortly after the couple obtained an abortion overseas found that 52 percent of the respondents approved of their decision, 32 percent disapproved, and 16 percent had no opinion. Many people expressed sympathy for the couple's plight, but others—including radio broadcasters representing the Roman Catholic Church—accused them of committing murder.

Shortly after the Finkbine case became news, thousands of other American women found themselves facing a similar situation. An epidemic of rubella, or German measles, swept across the country between 1962 and 1965. When a woman contracted the disease during pregnancy, it had the potential to cause blindness, deafness, and mental retardation in the fetus. The measles outbreak resulted in approximately 15,000 babies born with birth defects. This tragic situation helped convince many people that abortion should be an option under certain circumstances.

Reforming Criminal Abortion Laws

The Finkbine case and the measles outbreak helped raise public awareness of the inconsistent and outdated nature of many state anti-abortion laws. Most of these laws had been put in place decades earlier to protect women from untrained abortion providers and dangerous abortion methods. The laws sought to ensure that abortions were performed by licensed physicians in safe and sanitary conditions. Many states only allowed abortions under certain circumstances and required women to get approval from a hospital review panel or county health board.

As the Finkbine case illustrated, however, hospital boards were often influenced by outside factors in deciding whether or not to approve a request for an abortion. As a result, the laws were often applied inconsistently. Wealthy, urban women were often able to find sympathetic doctors to support claims that they needed a therapeutic abortion to protect their mental or physical health. But the abortion requests of poor and rural women were often denied, which led many to resort to illegal or self-induced abortions.

The American Law Institute (ALI)—an organization of top lawyers, law professors, and judges—recognized the confusing and contradictory state of anti-abortion laws in the late 1950s. According to Hull and Hoffer, the ALI felt these laws were "so vague and varied, and so often disregarded, [that they] brought all law into disrespect." In 1959 the organization recommended that all state anti-abortion laws include exceptions for three specific cases: when the pregnancy resulted from rape or incest; when carrying the baby to term posed a threat to the physical or mental health of the mother; or when there was reason to believe that the fetus possessed grave physical or mental defects.

The ALI's recommendations did not have the weight of law, but they did hold some influence with lawmakers, especially when state legislatures started feeling pressure from the public and the media to reform anti-abortion laws. Once the Finkbine case and the measles outbreak put the issue into the news, it received increased public attention throughout the mid-1960s. In 1965, for instance, the CBS television network broadcast a documentary called "Abor-

As her daughter Lucy looks on, television personality Sherri Finkbine packs a suitcase in July 1962 in preparation for a trip to Sweden to obtain a legal abortion.

tion and the Law," and the *New York Times* printed an editorial that stressed the need for reform. In 1967 the American Medical Association added its voice to the calls for reform of anti-abortion laws. The AMA argued that doctors must be allowed to use their clinical judgment—without fear of arrest and prosecution—in deciding whether a patient should have an abortion.

Around this time, state courts started overturning anti-abortion laws that they found vague or unfair. For example, the California Supreme Court ruled in favor of Dr. Leon Belous, who had been arrested for referring one of his patients to another doctor for an abortion. Similarly, a judge in the District of Columbia dismissed the case against Dr. Milan Vuitch, an admitted abortion provider, on the grounds that his patients had a right to privacy in reproductive decisions.

The reformers' main intention was to give doctors the right to perform abortions when they decided it was medically necessary, rather than to give women the right to decide for themselves whether to have an abortion.

In the wake of these court cases, 28 state legislatures considered reform measures in 1967. Twelve of these states actually adopted reforms by 1970. Most of the reforms took the approach suggested by the ALI, creating specific exceptions when abortion would be allowed by law. The reformers' main intention in passing these laws was to give doctors the right to perform abortions when they decided it was medically necessary, rather than to give women the right to decide for themselves whether to have an abortion. Therefore, the changes did not go far enough to please some supporters of abortion rights.

Feminists Speak Out about Abortion

Another important factor in raising public awareness of the impact of anti-abortion laws was the women's liberation movement that began during the 1960s. Growing numbers of women, calling themselves "feminists," started to break out of traditional roles and seek equal rights and opportunities in American society. All across the country, they participated in rallies, marches, and protests designed to bring attention to issues that concerned women.

Influenced by the women's movement, growing numbers of women attended college and took jobs outside of the home. Many women launched careers in male-dominated fields and demanded to be paid the same salaries as their colleagues. As more career opportunities opened up, many women decided to postpone marriage and child-rearing. These factors contributed to a decline in the fertility rate of American women from an average of 3.7 children in the mid-1950s to 1.8 children by the mid-1970s.

The introduction of the birth control pill in 1960—along with improvements in other contraceptive methods, like the intrauterine device (IUD)—

helped create a sexual revolution among American women during this time as well. Many women viewed these options as putting them on equal footing with men, because they gained the freedom to engage in sexual activity without worrying about unwanted pregnancy. Enthusiasm about "the pill" was so great that approximately 80 percent of fertile adult women reported trying it by 1970.

In this atmosphere of increasing openness about women's sexuality, many feminists began speaking out in favor of legalizing abortion. By the late 1960s, as many as 1.2 million American women had abortions each year. Most of these were illegal abortions, and the safety and effectiveness of the procedure depended greatly on the patients' resources. Desperate women who could not afford to pay up to $1,000 for a safe, medical abortion either sought the services of untrained abortionists or attempted to perform the procedure themselves. Countless women ended up in emergency rooms afterward with life-threatening infections and other health complications.

"I had an abortion when I was newly out of college, and had told no one," wrote Gloria Steinem. "If one in three or four adult women shares this experience, why should each of us be made to feel criminal and alone?"

The women's liberation movement encouraged many women to share their experiences with illegal abortions. In New York City, for instance, a feminist group called the Redstockings organized "speak outs" where women told personal stories about having abortions. Gloria Steinem, a leader in the women's rights movement and co-founder of *Ms.* magazine, remembered the feeling of empowerment she got from attending such a meeting. "I had had an abortion when I was newly out of college, and had told no one," she wrote in her autobiography, *Outrageous Acts and Everyday Rebellions.* "If one in three or four adult women shares this experience, why should each of us be made to feel criminal and alone? How much power would we ever have if we had no power over the fate of our own bodies?"

Growth of the Repeal Movement

Although a number of states took steps to reform their anti-abortion laws in the late 1960s, the changes did not always make it easier for women to obtain legal abortions. In fact, many of the new laws established strict requirements that still prevented most women from legally ending unwanted pregnancies. In Georgia, for instance, a woman seeking an abortion had to prove she was a resident of the state and get the approval of three individual

As president of the National Organization for Women, feminist author Betty Friedan emerged as a nationally recognized leader of the movement to repeal abortion laws across the United States.

doctors and a hospital review board. The California legislature put similar restrictions in place when it adopted abortion reforms in 1967. The following year, according to Hull and Hoffer, only 2,000 legal abortions were performed in the state, compared to an estimated 100,000 illegal abortions.

Such statistics convinced many feminists that legislative reform would never give women full access to safe, legal abortions. Some activists decided that the only solution was to work toward the repeal of all state and federal laws against abortion. "The idea of repealing abortion laws was consistent with the view that women had a right to a legal and safe abortion," Tribe wrote. "For many women, more reform of abortion laws was not enough, for it would simply mean that (primarily male) physicians would have wider latitude to make a decision that these women believed was the business only of the pregnant woman. The necessity of a doctor's approval, even under reformed abortion laws, reinforced the traditional role of the woman as dependent, without control over her future."

A number of women's rights organizations joined the movement to repeal anti-abortion laws across the country. One of these groups was the National Organization for Women (NOW), which had been formed in 1966 by feminist author Betty Friedan to "take action to bring women into full participation in the mainstream of American society now." The following year, NOW members held a debate on abortion at their national meeting. They voted to add an amendment supporting a woman's right to control her reproductive decisions to NOW's "Women's Bill of Rights" (see "NOW Calls for the Repeal of Abortion Laws," p. 171).

In 1968 Planned Parenthood—which had long been concerned with such issues as birth control and overpopulation—joined NOW in calling for the repeal of all anti-abortion laws. The following year, abortion-rights activist Lawrence Lader founded a new organization, NARAL (originally the National Association for the Repeal of Abortion Laws, and after 1973 the National Abortion Rights Action League), specifically to promote repeal.

As the repeal movement got underway, various groups openly defied existing anti-abortion laws. For example, a group of twenty-one Protestant ministers formed the Clergy Consultation Service to help women obtain safe abortions. The members operated a referral service that circumvented state anti-abortion laws by sending women to legitimate abortion providers in other states or overseas. The clergymen even advertised their services in the

New York Times. Within a short time, they offered referrals in numerous cities across the country.

These developments heartened supporters of a woman's "right to choose" whether to end a pregnancy, who described their position as "pro-choice" rather than "pro-abortion." But the movement to repeal abortion laws also encountered firm resistance in the late 1960s. The Roman Catholic Church stated its profound opposition to abortion, for instance, and other anti-abortion groups formed and started to organize protests. These groups called themselves "pro-life" to emphasize their commitment to defending the unborn.

One of the leaders in this early stage of the pro-life movement was John C. Willke (see Willke biography, p. 163), a doctor from Cincinnati, Ohio, who helped found the National Right to Life Committee. Willke fought to shift the focus of the abortion debate from the rights of the pregnant woman to the rights of the fetus. He published and distributed informational brochures, such as *A Handbook on Abortion* and *Life and Death,* that included graphic details about the procedure and color photographs of aborted fetuses. Willke's campaign helped defeat repeal efforts in Michigan, North Dakota, and other states. It also provided an early glimpse of the emotionally charged debates over abortion that would grip the nation in the 1970s.

Chapter Three

ROE v. WADE

—◁◁◁◁ᒐᐰ▷▷▷—

This certainly … is a matter which is of such fundamental and basic concern to the woman involved that she should be allowed to make the choice as to whether to continue or to terminate her pregnancy.

—Sarah Weddington, oral argument before the U.S. Supreme Court in *Roe v. Wade,* December 13, 1971

The movement to repeal anti-abortion laws achieved an important victory in 1970, when Hawaii became the first state to legalize abortion. New York followed a short time later, passing a referendum that allowed women to have abortions anytime within the first 24 weeks of pregnancy. Alaska and Washington soon liberalized their statutes as well, eliminating criminal penalties for abortions performed in the early stages of pregnancy.

The changes in these states reflected a general shift in public opinion toward reform or repeal of abortion laws. The women's rights movement had succeeded in convincing many people that women needed greater control over their reproductive lives in order to achieve equality in American society. Events in the news—such as the risk of birth defects associated with the drug thalidomide or the measles epidemic—had led many other people to favor expanding the exceptions under which abortion would be allowed. Some people, influenced by battles over civil rights and social justice, decided that it was unfair to restrict poor and minority women's access to safe abortions when wealthy white women had the resources to flout the law.

As a result of these various factors, the percentage of Americans who said they approved of "liberalizing the abortion laws" increased from 15 percent in 1968 to 40 percent the following year. By 1972, a Gallup poll found that 73 percent of respondents agreed that the decision to have an abortion should be left "solely to the woman and her physician."

Alarmed by this trend, pro-life activists became more vocal in their opposition to abortion reform. They argued that a fetus was a unique human being from the moment of conception and thus had a right to life that should be protected by law. Members of the pro-life movement particularly opposed "abortion on demand," or the idea that a pregnant woman had a right to an abortion for any reason. They believed that the fetus's rights must be weighed against those of the pregnant woman, and they felt that choosing abortion was the moral equivalent of committing murder. The efforts of the pro-life movement were rewarded in a number of states. Although several states legalized abortion in the early 1970s, abortion repeal measures were voted down in 13 states in 1971 alone.

Many states also stepped up their enforcement of abortion laws around this time. As a result, the nation saw a surge in the number of court cases dealing with abortion. For example, Jane Hodgson became the first doctor arrested for performing an abortion in Minnesota, where the procedure was illegal except when necessary to save the life of the mother. After treating many patients for complications from illegal abortions, Hodgson had decided to challenge the law in 1971. She agreed to perform an abortion on a mother of three children who had contracted rubella early in her pregnancy. The doctor was convicted of a felony, but she remained free while her case went through a long series of appeals. Hodgson's conviction was finally overturned in 1973, following the U.S. Supreme Court's decision in a similar case: *Roe v. Wade*.

Challenging Abortion Law in Texas

Sarah Weddington (see Weddington biography, p. 159), the attorney who argued the *Roe v. Wade* case before the Supreme Court, recalled years later that the historic lawsuit got started at a garage sale in September 1969. A committed supporter of the women's rights movement, Weddington had recently earned a law degree from the University of Texas. She and a group of fellow graduate students held the garage sale to raise money for the Women's Liberation Birth Control Information Center, a campus organization that helped women obtain contraceptives. Although the center did not advertise the fact, its volunteers also operated a referral service that advised women where to get safe abortions.

At that time, abortion was illegal in Texas except when a doctor deemed it necessary to save the life of the mother. The Texas law, which dated back to 1854, established a penalty of two to five years in prison for anyone who performed, attempted to perform, or furnished the means for an abortion. The punishment was doubled if the abortion was performed without the woman's consent, and the charge was increased to murder if the woman died as a result of the abortion. Importantly, the statute only included criminal penalties for abortion providers. The pregnant woman could not be charged with a crime for seeking or having an abortion.

Weddington began working with the referral service after she had an illegal abortion. She had become pregnant in 1967, while she was attending law school and dating her future husband, Ron Weddington. After deciding that they were not ready to have a baby at that point in their lives and relationship, the couple decid-

Sarah Weddington was the lead attorney arguing the pro-choice position in the *Roe v. Wade* case.

ed to seek an abortion. Since it was illegal in Texas, they arranged for an abortion in Mexico. Abortion was illegal there, too, but many practitioners were willing to break the law for a fee. These illegal services were not regulated, however, so women who traveled to Mexico for an abortion faced some risks. "I was one of the lucky ones," Weddington recalled in her autobiography, *A Question of Choice*. "The doctor was pleasant and seemed competent.... I know there were countless others living out their own private scenes when abortion was illegal. Some of them were not as lucky as I; they ended up in awful places, they were operated on by people with no medical skills." The fear and shame Weddington felt during this experience left her with a deep interest in legalizing abortion.

At the garage sale, fellow referral service volunteers expressed concern about whether they could be prosecuted under Texas law for providing women with information about where to obtain safe abortions. Weddington agreed to research the question. Her research uncovered the 1965 Supreme Court decision in *Griswold v. Connecticut*, which had established a right to privacy that protected a couple's decision to use birth control. Weddington wondered whether this right might also extend to other reproductive decisions, such as abortion. She found support for this idea in an article that appeared in the *Loyola University Law Review*. Written by former Supreme Court Justice Tom C. Clark, who had voted with the majority in the *Griswold* case, the article argued that "abortion falls within that sensitive area of privacy—the marital relation."

In December 1969, Weddington presented her ideas to one of her law school classmates, Linda Coffee (see "*Roe* Attorney Linda Coffee," p. 39). Despite earning the second-highest score on the Texas bar exam, Coffee had found it difficult to find a job after graduation. Few large Texas law firms were interested in hiring a female attorney in those years. Coffee ended up spending a year working as a law clerk for Sarah T. Hughes, one of the first women to become a federal circuit court judge. In this position, Coffee learned a great deal about the workings of the federal court system. She also became active in the movement to gain equal rights and employment opportunities for women.

Weddington asked Coffee about the possibility of challenging the Texas anti-abortion law in federal court. Looking back on her own experience, Weddington expressed the hope that a successful lawsuit would allow women facing a similar situation to have a safe, legal abortion in Texas. Coffee agreed to help with the lawsuit. The lawyers' first task involved finding a plaintiff—a person who had been directly affected by the law and was willing to go to court to challenge it. The American justice system does not allow people to sue simply because they disagree with a law. To bring a case to court requires a plaintiff who has been charged with a crime or is able to claim that they have suffered harm as a result of a law.

A Fateful Meeting

In the fall of 1969, when she found out she was pregnant for the third time, Dallas resident Norma McCorvey (see McCorvey biography, p. 138) was 21 years old and divorced. She had a five-year-old daughter who was being raised by her mother and stepfather, and she had given up another child for adoption. Since McCorvey was struggling to support herself, she felt that she could not afford to have a baby. She wanted to have an abortion, but she was prevented from doing so by Texas law, and she did not have enough

Roe Attorney Linda Coffee

Linda Nellene Coffee was born in 1942 in Houston, Texas. She grew up in Dallas, where her father worked as a research chemist and her mother worked as a legal secretary. Always an outstanding student, Coffee earned her undergraduate degree from Rice University. She then enrolled in law school at the University of Texas, where she became one of only five women in her class.

After earning her law degree and passing the bar exam in 1968, Coffee had trouble finding a job. Few law firms were willing to hire female attorneys at that time. Coffee spent a year serving as a law clerk for Judge Sarah T. Hughes, one of the most prominent female judges in the country. Afterward, she finally went to work for a small corporate law firm.

A committed feminist, Coffee also tried to secure equal rights and employment opportunities for women as a member of the Women's Equity Action League. She believed that women needed the ability to control their reproductive capacity in order to achieve true equality with men.

In 1969 a former law school classmate, Sarah Weddington, contacted Coffee about challenging Texas's anti-abortion law in federal court. Coffee eagerly agreed to help develop the case. She found a pregnant woman who was denied an abortion under the law, Norma McCorvey, and convinced her to serve as a plaintiff under the fictional name Jane Roe.

Coffee and Weddington first filed the case of *Roe v. Wade* in Texas in 1970. It eventually went all the way to the U.S. Supreme Court. In 1973 the two lawyers won a landmark ruling that invalidated most state laws restricting abortion. A short time later Coffee sued a Dallas hospital for refusing to provide abortion services.

As the years passed, Coffee left the public eye and led a quiet life as a bankruptcy attorney. In 1998 she told CNN that "I'm somewhat surprised there is so much debate [about abortion]. I would have guessed the question of abortion would be pretty passé by now. I thought there would be more progress in birth control."

In 1969 Norma McCorvey agreed to be the anonymous "Jane Roe" in the landmark *Roe v. Wade* case. She is shown here twenty years later (at left) at a pro-choice rally in Washington, D.C.

money to travel to a state or country where abortion was legal.

After trying and failing to obtain an illegal abortion in Texas, McCorvey eventually contacted an attorney to arrange to put her baby up for adoption. This attorney suggested that she call Coffee and Weddington, who were looking for someone in her situation to participate in a lawsuit. McCorvey agreed to meet them at Colombo's Pizzeria in Dallas in January 1970.

At this fateful meeting, Coffee and Weddington described their plans to challenge the Texas anti-abortion law. Even if they eventually succeeded in overturning the law, they explained, the legal proceedings would almost certainly take too long for McCorvey to have a legal abortion in Texas. If she agreed to become a plaintiff, it meant that she would have to carry her baby to term. Still, the lawyers noted, McCorvey had a chance to help other women avoid a similar situation in the future. A successful lawsuit would give all Texas women the right to terminate their pregnancies in a safe medical environment.

Longing to do something important in her life, McCorvey agreed to serve as a plaintiff. Weddington and Coffee knew that their lawsuit would be controversial and would attract a great deal of media coverage. In order to conceal McCorvey's identity and protect her from unwanted attention, they decided to give the plaintiff a false name, Jane Roe. They filed the lawsuit against Henry Wade (see Wade biography, p. 156), the Dallas County district attorney who was responsible for enforcing the Texas anti-abortion law in that area. The case thus became known by the legal shorthand title of *Roe v. Wade*.

Shortly after they filed the lawsuit, Weddington and Coffee anxiously debated whether McCorvey had the legal standing necessary to serve as a plaintiff. If the court decided that McCorvey had not suffered harm under the law, the case would be dismissed. The lawyers worried about the plaintiff's standing for two reasons. First, it was clear that McCorvey would give birth before the case was heard. Since she would no longer be pregnant when the court date arrived, the defendant (Wade) might argue that she could not demonstrate harm under the law. Weddington and Coffee addressed this problem by changing their lawsuit to a class action, meaning that McCorvey represented not only her own interests but those of an entire class of people—namely, all pregnant women in Texas.

The second issue involved the fact that the Texas law did not make it a crime for a pregnant woman to seek or have an abortion. The focus of the law was on abortion providers, not women looking to end their pregnancies. Since McCorvey did not run the risk of prosecution under the law, the lawyers felt that it might be more difficult for her to demonstrate harm. Weddington and Coffee soon found a way to overcome this problem, as well. They allowed two other parties to join in the lawsuit as plaintiffs. One of these parties was a doctor, James H. Hallford, who was subject to prosecution under Texas law if he performed an abortion. The other party was a married couple, John and Mary Doe. The wife suffered from a physical condition that made pregnancy dangerous to her health. If she did happen to become pregnant, she wanted to be able to have a legal abortion, but she would be unable to do so because the Texas statute did not make an exception for the mother's health. Weddington and Coffee filed the Does' part of the lawsuit as a class action on behalf of all married couples in the state.

Taking the Case to Court

Federal courts generally only agree to hear challenges to state laws when there is reason to believe that the state law may conflict with a provision of the U.S. Constitution. Although the states have fairly broad authority to make laws within their borders, they are still governed by the federal Constitution, which is the highest law in the United States. In bringing their lawsuit to federal court, Weddington and Coffee had to charge that the Texas anti-abortion law violated the Constitution in some way.

The lawyers decided to attack the law on the basis of the Ninth and Fourteenth Amendments to the Constitution (see "The Foundations of Privacy in the

U.S. Constitution, p. 169). The Ninth Amendment, which was applied success-fully in *Griswold*, says that citizens have rights that are not specifically defined in the Constitution. Weddington and Coffee argued that the Ninth Amendment protected a right to privacy in reproductive decisions, and that the Texas law denied women the right to decide whether or not to have children. The Four-teenth Amendment includes provisions that grant all citizens equal protection under the law and require laws to be clearly written. The lawyers argued that the Texas law was unconstitutionally vague because it did not provide doctors with guidelines to determine whether a pregnancy threatened a woman's life. This argument had been used successfully in the past by doctors accused of perform-ing illegal abortions.

Henry Wade appointed two assistant district attorneys on his staff, John Tolle and Jay Floyd, to defend the Texas law in court. Tolle was Roman Catholic and shared his church's view of abortion as a moral evil. He and Floyd centered their arguments around the idea that the fetus was a person, and thus had a right to life under the Constitution. They said that this right was more important than a woman's right to privacy. Tolle and Floyd argued that the law in question was valid because the state of Texas had a compelling interest in defending the legal rights of the fetus. The defense also claimed that, by including an exception when the pregnancy threatened the mother's life, the law balanced the rights of the fetus and the pregnant woman.

The two sides in *Roe v. Wade* presented their arguments at the Fifth Circuit Court in Dallas on May 23, 1970. They appeared before a panel of three respect-ed federal judges: Sarah T. Hughes, for whom Coffee had clerked; William McLaughlin Taylor; and Irving Goldberg. The primary plaintiff, Norma McCor-vey, did not attend the trial because she and her attorneys wanted to protect her anonymity. Earlier in the legal proceedings, Tolle had asked that the defense be allowed to question Jane Roe. He wanted to make sure that she was a real person who was pregnant and wanted an abortion. Judge Hughes denied the request, however, and instead let McCorvey testify to the facts of the case in writing and submit her answers to the court.

After hearing the arguments on both sides, the three judges adjourned to consider the case. They announced their decision a few weeks later, on June 17. The circuit court ruled in favor of the plaintiffs, stating that "the Texas abortion laws must be declared unconstitutional because they deprive single women and married couples, of their right, secured by the Ninth Amend-ment, to choose whether to have children."

When Dallas County District Attorney Henry Wade declared his intention to ignore a federal court ruling and continue prosecuting people under Texas's 1854 anti-abortion law, the U.S. Supreme Court stepped in.

Weddington and Coffee were pleased that the judges agreed with their argument that the Texas anti-abortion laws violated the U.S. Constitution. They were also happy that the court made its determination based on a woman's right to choose an abortion, rather than based on vagueness of the statute or some other technical issue. But the lawyers had hoped that the judges would go a step further and issue an injunction, or court order, to force the state to stop its enforcement of the law. Weddington and Coffee believed that an injunction would allow women in Texas to have legal abortions.

The judges explained their decision not to issue an injunction by saying that Texas rarely enforced the criminal penalties in the law, so the plaintiffs were unlikely to suffer immediate harm that could be prevented by a court order. The defendant in *Roe*, District Attorney Henry Wade, responded by declaring the state's intention to ignore the circuit court ruling. While his

43

attorneys appealed the decision, Wade said that he planned to continue to prosecute people under the 1854 law.

Preparing for the U.S. Supreme Court

The circuit court's refusal to issue an injunction did have one positive outcome for Weddington and Coffee, however. It enabled the lawyers to bypass other legal channels and appeal the ruling directly to the U.S. Supreme Court. As the ultimate interpreter of the Constitution, the Court had the power to overturn not only the Texas law, but all state laws prohibiting abortion. The lawyers filed a written petition that explained the constitutional issues involved in *Roe v. Wade* and formally asked the Supreme Court to hear the case.

Weddington and Coffee knew that their case had only a slight chance of being granted a hearing. After all, the Supreme Court received over 6,000 requests for review each year, and the justices typically only granted a hearing to around 100 cases that presented important questions of federal law. In addition, the lawyers were aware that several similar cases were making their way through the federal court system at that time. It was possible that the Court might decide that one of those cases better addressed the central issues of abortion law.

On May 21, 1971, though, the U.S. Supreme Court announced its decision to hear arguments in the case of *Roe v. Wade*, along with a companion case from Georgia, *Doe v. Bolton*. In contrast to *Roe*, the *Doe* case concerned a state law that had been updated a few years earlier. Although Georgia allowed abortion, it placed strict limitations on the procedure. A woman seeking an abortion had to prove that she was a resident of the state, obtain permission from three doctors, and have the procedure at an approved facility.

Doe v. Bolton originated in April 1970, when an Atlanta hospital refused to perform an abortion on a 22-year-old woman known in court records as Mary Doe. Doe was in the process of divorcing an abusive husband and had given up custody of three previous children. When she was unable to obtain a legal abortion under Georgia law, she filed a lawsuit in U.S. District Court against Georgia Attorney General Arthur Bolton. The lower court issued a ruling that was very similar to the one issued by the three judges in Dallas. Many observers believed that the Supreme Court agreed to hear *Roe* and *Doe* together because they provided examples of old and new abortion laws.

Once the Supreme Court agrees to hear a case, the two sides must present their arguments in the form of written documents called briefs. Other interested parties are also allowed to submit documents—known as *amicus curiae* or "friend of the court" briefs—supporting one side or the other. Weddington and Coffee received 42 briefs that favored a woman's right to choose abortion, prepared by such prominent organizations as Planned Parenthood, the National Organization for Women, and the American College of Gynecologists and Obstetricians. One of these briefs, known as the "woman's brief," was signed by dozens of notable women in the fields of science, medicine, history, and sociology.

Wade's attorneys also received *amicus curiae* briefs supporting their argument that the fetus was a person entitled to the state's protection. The defense briefs were filed by such prominent organizations as the National Right to Life Committee and the Texas Diocese of the Roman Catholic Church. All together, the various briefs presented to the Supreme Court in the case made a pile more than a foot thick.

> *Once the Supreme Court agrees to hear a case, the two sides must present their arguments in the form of written briefs. All together, the various briefs presented to the Court in the* Roe v. Wade *case made a pile more than a foot thick.*

The briefs provide the Supreme Court justices with most of the information they need to reach a decision. As a result, each side in a case is granted only 30 minutes to present oral arguments before the Court. Although the attorneys must be ready to speak for the entire time, their prepared remarks are usually interrupted by questions from the justices. The justices might ask questions to clarify issues raised in the briefs, to debate specific points of law, or even to try to persuade other justices to share their views of the case.

Arguing the Case

The U.S. Supreme Court was scheduled to hear the cases of *Roe v. Wade* and *Doe v. Bolton* on December 13, 1971. Weddington and Coffee felt optimistic about their chances for a favorable ruling. Four of the justices they expected to hear the case (William Brennan, William O. Douglas, John Marshall Harlan, and Byron White) had voted to overturn state laws against birth control in *Griswold v. Connecticut*, which had also hinged on a right to privacy in reproductive decisions. They felt confident that at least one of the Court's new members—former civil rights attorney Thurgood Marshall, who became

The resignations of two Supreme Court justices in 1971 gave Republican President Richard M. Nixon an opportunity to nominate conservative replacements who opposed abortion.

the first African-American justice when he was appointed by President Lyndon Johnson in 1967—would rule in their favor as well. If all of these justices voted in their favor, that would give the plaintiffs a 5-4 victory.

This scenario changed in September 1971, however, when two Supreme Court justices (John Marshall Harlan and Hugo Black) retired suddenly due to poor health. Although the retiring justices had split on the *Griswold* decision, Weddington and Coffee knew that Republican President Richard Nixon would try to replace them with jurists who shared his conservative views. Accordingly, the lawyers felt that arguing before the remaining seven justices would give them the best chance to win. Wade's attorneys, on the other hand, preferred to delay the proceedings in hopes of getting a more favorable ruling from a full nine-member Court.

The Court denied several defense motions for delays, however, and the remaining seven justices heard the cases on schedule in December. Once the proceedings opened, Weddington was the first to present her oral arguments. She began by relating how the case had progressed up to that point and answering questions about how previous Court rulings might apply to it. Then she described, based in part on her own experiences, the impact of the Texas law on women. "I think it's without question that pregnancy to a woman can completely disrupt her life," she stated. "It disrupts her body, it disrupts her education, it disrupts her employment, and it often disrupts her entire family life."

Justice Potter Stewart complimented Weddington on her "eloquent policy argument" but reminded her that the Court did not involve itself in matters of policy. He then asked her to clarify exactly what part of the Constitution she felt supported a woman's right to abortion. Weddington initially based her argument on the equal protection clause of the Fourteenth Amendment, claiming that the Texas law was vague and created confusion about when abortion was allowed. She then brought up the Ninth Amendment, which had been used to establish a right to privacy in the *Griswold* case. When Weddington went on to mention the First, Fourth, Fifth, and Eighth Amendments, Justice Stewart teased, "And anything else that might obtain?" Forgetting her formal court manners for a moment, Weddington replied, "Yeah, right."

Justice Byron White asked Weddington a series of questions about the legal rights of the fetus, and whether she felt a woman should be able to choose abortion in the late stages of pregnancy. Weddington responded by claiming that the fetus did not have legal rights under U.S. law, because the Constitution "attaches protection to the person at the time of birth. Those persons born are citizens." She did grant, however, that the state might have a stronger interest in protecting the fetus as the pregnancy progressed, partly due to the "emotional response to a late pregnancy ... by persons considering the issue outside the legal context."

After Weddington's time expired, attorney Jay Floyd stood up to speak on behalf of Henry Wade and the state of Texas. He started off by arguing that Roe lacked legal standing to challenge the Texas law because she was no longer pregnant (Norma McCorvey had given birth and given the baby up for adoption). Justice Stewart dismissed this idea and insisted that the class action was still valid because "there are, at any given time, unmarried pregnant females in the state of Texas."

Floyd went on to challenge Weddington's claim that women had a constitutional right to choose to terminate a pregnancy. "I think she makes her choice

Some observers felt that Wade's legal team struggled to answer sharp questions from Thurgood Marshall and other Supreme Court justices.

prior to the time she becomes pregnant. That is the time of the choice," he declared. "Once a child is born, a woman no longer has a choice; and I think pregnancy makes that choice as well." Justice Stewart rejected this reasoning and responded, "Maybe she makes her choice when she decides to live in Texas."

The justices asked Floyd a number of questions about the state's interest in outlawing abortion. The lawyer replied that the idea behind the Texas law was to protect the fetus's right to life. "I would think that even when this statute was first passed, there was some concern for the unborn fetus," he stated. Then the justices asked why, if the fetus was a person with legal rights, the state law did not consider women who had abortions guilty of murder. Floyd conceded that he did not know the answer to that question. Finally, Justice Thurgood Marshall inquired about the exact point when life began according to the state of Texas. When Floyd answered, "Mr. Justice, there are unanswerable questions in this field," Marshall replied, "I appreciate it."

Next the Court heard oral arguments in the companion case of *Doe v. Bolton*. Attorney Margie Pitts Hames represented Mary Doe, the Georgia woman who was denied an abortion. She argued that the various requirements of the Georgia law were so "cumbersome, costly, and time-consuming" that it was virtually impossible for women to obtain abortions in the state. Dorothy Beasley, the lawyer representing Bolton, countered that the state of Georgia recognized the fetus as a "human entity" worthy of consideration under the law.

Deciding Not to Decide

Observers of the Supreme Court proceedings in the case of *Roe v. Wade* generally felt that Weddington had done a good job of addressing the justices' questions. Many people noted, however, that Weddington had made a more convincing argument about the effects of the Texas law than about the constitutional basis for overturning it. Most courtroom observers also felt that Floyd had seemed unprepared and had struggled in his responses to the justices' questions. Beasley received much higher marks for her defense of the Georgia statute.

Once the oral arguments concluded, the justices met to discuss *Roe v. Wade* in a private conference. Chief Justice Warren Burger outlined the issues involved in the case, and then each of the other six justices offered their opinions in order of seniority. An early poll indicated that a majority of the justices were prepared to overturn the Texas law. Burger assigned Justice Harry Blackmun (see Blackmun biography, p. 125), a close personal friend who had joined the Court the previous year, to write the majority opinion. Some of the other justices were upset that Burger did not assign the task to someone with more seniority.

Chief Justice Warren Burger (shown here) assigned Justice Harry Blackmun to write the majority opinion in the *Roe v. Wade* case.

Blackmun struggled with the opinion for weeks. When he finally circulated a draft to his colleagues, it largely avoided addressing the central issues of the case. Rather than endorsing a woman's right to choose abortion, or recognizing the state's interest in protecting the fetus, the opinion rested on a technical issue. Blackmun recommended overturning the Texas law based on its vagueness. His reasoning failed to convince the other justices, who were reluctant to sign on to the opinion.

Faced with opposition to his ideas, Blackmun suggested that the Court delay issuing a ruling until President Nixon appointed two new justices. At that point, *Roe v. Wade* could be reargued before a full Court. "On an issue so sensitive and so emotional as this one, the country deserves the conclusion of a nine-man, not a seven-man court, whatever the ultimate decision may be," Blackmun wrote in a memo to his colleagues. All of the other justices agreed

The U.S. Supreme Court in 1973

The U.S. Supreme Court underwent major changes both before and during its two hearings of the *Roe v. Wade* case. From 1953 until 1969, the Court had been led by Chief Justice Earl Warren, a liberal jurist who believed that the Court had a duty to step in as needed to protect the civil rights of individuals and minorities. The Warren Court made a number of historic rulings, including the 1954 *Brown v. Board of Education* decision that ended segregation in the nation's public schools. Critics considered the Warren Court overly activist and claimed that it improperly took over the law-making role that belonged to elected legislators.

Upon taking office in 1969, President Richard Nixon vowed to undo the Warren Court's years of judicial activism. If any of the sitting Supreme Court justices gave up their lifetime appointments, he promised to replace them with jurists who believed in basing their rulings on a literal reading of the Constitution. The president soon had an opportunity to make important changes to the Court by appointing four new justices. In June 1969 Nixon appointed Warren E. Burger to replace the retiring Earl Warren as chief justice. After seeing two other nominations blocked from confirmation by the Senate, Nixon successfully appointed Harry A. Blackmun to replace the retiring Justice Abe Fortas in June 1970. Both of these men were considered politically conservative.

In September 1971, just a few months before the Supreme Court heard initial arguments in *Roe v. Wade,* Justices Hugo Black and John Marshall Harlan retired due to failing health. Since there were only seven sitting justices when the case was argued, the Court decided to ask the two sides to reargue the case before the full court after two new justices joined.

to reargue the case except for William O. Douglas, the most liberal member of the Court. Knowing that Nixon's appointments could change the outcome, Douglas argued strongly in favor of issuing a ruling. Ultimately, though, the Supreme Court announced its decision to hear *Roe v. Wade* a second time on October 12, 1972.

Nixon appointed Lewis Powell, a moderate, in 1971 and William Rehnquist, a conservative, in 1972. Despite the president's conservative influence, however, the Court voted to legalize abortion by a margin of 7-2.

The following is a list of the Supreme Court justices who heard *Roe v. Wade,* along with information about their appointments, their political leanings, and their rulings in the case:

- Chief Justice Warren E. Burger, appointed by Nixon in 1969, conservative, issued concurring opinion in *Roe v. Wade;*

- Justice Harry A. Blackmun, appointed by Nixon in 1970, moderate, author of majority opinion;

- Justice William Brennan, appointed in 1956 by Dwight D. Eisenhower, liberal, joined majority opinion;

- Justice William O. Douglas, appointed in 1939 by Franklin D. Roosevelt, liberal, issued concurring opinion;

- Justice Thurgood Marshall, appointed by Lyndon Johnson in 1967, liberal, joined majority opinion;

- Justice Lewis F. Powell, Jr., appointed by Nixon in 1971, moderate, joined majority opinion;

- Justice William H. Rehnquist, appointed by Nixon in 1972, conservative, issued dissenting opinion;

- Justice Potter Stewart, appointed by Eisenhower in 1959, moderate, issued concurring opinion;

- Justice Byron White, appointed by John F. Kennedy in 1962, moderate, issued dissenting opinion.

Rearguing the Case

In the meantime, Nixon appointed two new justices to fill the vacancies on the Supreme Court: Lewis Powell, a prominent southern lawyer and former president of the American Bar Association; and William Rehnquist, a conservative attorney in the U.S. Department of Justice (see "The U.S.

Supreme Court in 1973," p. 50). They both participated in the reargument of *Roe v. Wade*.

Many observers noted that the delay gave both sides in the case time to sharpen their arguments. Weddington started out by explaining the Texas law's continuing impact, noting that 1,600 women had left the state to obtain legal abortions in New York since the case had last been argued. She went on to discuss the constitutional basis for her argument that a woman had a right to terminate an unwanted pregnancy without interference by the state. Weddington then faced a number of questions about whether the fetus had rights that must be balanced against those of the mother. She replied that no law or previous court case had granted rights to the unborn, and she pointed out that the equal protection clause of the Fourteenth Amendment applied only to "persons born or naturalized in the United States." Therefore, she insisted, the only considerations in the case were the woman's fundamental rights and the state's lack of compelling interest for regulation. Weddington did acknowledge, though, that "I would have a very difficult case" if it were somehow established that the fetus was a person with rights.

Given Floyd's poor performance in the initial argument of the case, Wade appointed Robert C. Flowers to act as the lead attorney for the state of Texas in the reargument. Flowers began by arguing that the state had an interest in protecting the rights of the fetus. "It is impossible for me to trace, within my allocated time, the development of the fetus from the date of conception to the date of its birth," he stated. "But it is the position of the State of Texas that, upon conception, we have a human being; a person, within the concept of the Constitution of the United States, and that of Texas, also." Once again, the justices made extensive inquiries about when life begins, and whether that could best be determined by medical, legal, philosophical, or religious authorities.

After Flowers concluded his argument, the Court allowed Weddington to make a statement with the four remaining minutes of her time allotment. "We do not ask this Court to rule that abortion is good, or desirable in any particular situation," she declared. "We are here to advocate that the decision as to whether or not a particular woman will continue to carry or will terminate a pregnancy is a decision that should be made by that individual; that, in fact, she has a constitutional right to make that decision for herself; and that the State has shown no interest in interfering with that decision." Once the case was submitted, everyone involved on both sides settled back to wait for a decision.

Chapter Four

THE LANDMARK DECISION AND ITS IMPLICATIONS

━━◦❦◦━━

We, therefore, conclude that the right of personal privacy includes the abortion decision, but that this right is not unqualified and must be considered against important state interests in regulation.

—Justice Harry A. Blackmun, announcing the U.S. Supreme Court decision in *Roe v. Wade*, January 22, 1973

Afterwards the reargument of *Roe v. Wade*, the nine justices of the U.S. Supreme Court held a private conference to discuss their views of the case. As before—despite the appointment of two new justices by President Richard Nixon—the majority expressed a willingness to overturn the Texas anti-abortion law. Chief Justice Warren Burger once again assigned Justice Harry Blackmun to prepare the majority opinion.

The majority opinion is the document that explains the Court's decision. At least five of the nine justices must agree with the decision for it to become the opinion of the Court. Justices who agree with the majority opinion are still allowed to prepare concurring opinions, which are documents that describe their individual reasoning or make comments about specific points of law. Justices who do not agree with the majority opinion are allowed to explain their findings and objections in dissenting opinions. All of these documents are released together by the Court and become part of the legal record.

Even though the majority favored overturning the Texas law, Blackmun knew that his colleagues differed in their reasoning. He set out to craft an opinion that would balance the competing interests and gain the support of his fellow justices. In preparation for this task, Blackmun had spent much of the summer between the argument and reargument of *Roe v. Wade* at home in Minnesota, where he had worked for nine years as an attorney for the prestigious Mayo Clinic. He used the facility's vast medical library to conduct research on fetal development and abortion.

Despite his extensive study of the subject, Blackmun still struggled to prepare an opinion that would unite the Court. After five weeks of writing and rewriting, he finally sent a 48-page draft to his colleagues on November 22, 1972. Based on his medical research, Blackmun proposed dividing a typical nine-month pregnancy into trimesters, or three-month periods. During the first trimester (the first three months following conception), he suggested that the decision to terminate a pregnancy should be left to a woman and her doctor. During the second trimester, Blackmun said that the state's interest in regulating abortion should be limited to protecting the mother's health. During the third trimester, the draft opinion said that the state could restrict abortion in order to protect the life of the fetus.

Gaining a Majority

Blackmun's original draft won the support of liberal Justices William O. Douglas and Potter Stewart. Surprisingly, one of Nixon's new appointees, Justice Lewis Powell, immediately joined the majority opinion as well. Powell viewed *Roe v. Wade* as a case about women's rights. "The concept of liberty was the underlying principle," he noted. He felt that the decision to terminate a pregnancy was a highly personal one that rightfully belonged to the woman involved.

Justice Thurgood Marshall liked Blackmun's approach, but he wanted the point at which the state was allowed to regulate abortion moved back later in pregnancy. He argued that the state's interest in protecting the fetus only became compelling when the fetus became viable, or able to survive outside of its mother's body. "Drawing the line at viability accommodates the interests at stake better than drawing it at the end of the first trimester," he wrote in a memo to Blackmun. Once Blackmun agreed to change the point that the state could begin restricting abortion to 28 weeks, Marshall signed on to the opinion.

Justice William Brennan soon became the sixth supporter of Blackmun's opinion. Like Marshall, Brennan wanted to prohibit states from restricting abortion until the late stages of pregnancy. He asserted that state abortion laws

This 1970 editorial cartoon from the *Washington Star* depicts Justice Harry Blackmun joining the Supreme Court, which is swamped with cases dealing with such controversial issues as abortion, segregation, and capital punishment.

had historically been enacted for the purpose of protecting the health and welfare of the pregnant woman. He felt that this state interest did not become compelling enough to justify restricting abortion until late in pregnancy.

Blackmun's opinion thus received the support of six members of the Supreme Court. Justices William Rehnquist and Byron White (see "Justice Byron R. White," p. 60) indicated that they planned to dissent, or disagree, with the majority. Blackmun waited to hear how Chief Justice Warren Burger would vote. Some observers wondered whether Burger intentionally delayed his vote so that the Court's decision would not be announced until after President Nixon took office for a second term on January 20, 1973. Nixon had spoken out against abortion during his 1972 re-election campaign, declaring that "unrestricted abortion policies, abortion on demand, I cannot square with my belief in the sanctity of human life—including the life of the yet unborn." The president thus seemed likely to be embarrassed by the fact that three of his four Supreme Court appointees had voted to legalize abortion. In the end, though, Burger decided to join the majority and explain his reasoning in a concurring opinion.

> *"We forthwith acknowledge our awareness of the sensitive and emotional nature of the abortion controversy," wrote Justice Harry Blackmun in his majority opinion. "Our task, of course, is to resolve the issue of constitutional measurement free of emotion."*

Announcing the Decision

The U.S. Supreme Court announced its decision in *Roe v. Wade* and released a final, revised version of Blackmun's majority opinion on January 22, 1973, the Monday after Nixon's inauguration (see "Justice Harry A. Blackmun Announces the Court's Decision," p. 174). Instead of reading the entire 51-page document to the assembled reporters, Blackmun read an 8-page summary of the Court's findings. Blackmun's opening statement showed that the Court recognized the strong feelings involved in the debate over abortion. "We forthwith acknowledge our awareness of the sensitive and emotional nature of the abortion controversy, of the vigorous opposing views, even among physicians, and of the deep and seemingly absolute convictions that the subject inspires," he stated. "Our task, of course, is to resolve the issue of constitutional measurement free of emotion."

Blackmun went on to explain the Court's finding that the constitutional right to privacy in reproductive decisions, which had been established in the

1965 birth-control case *Griswold v. Connecticut,* "is broad enough to encompass a woman's decision whether or not to terminate her pregnancy. The detriment that the State would impose upon the pregnant woman by denying this choice altogether is apparent." Although this ruling meant that states could no longer outlaw abortion entirely, Blackmun insisted that the Court did not support abortion on demand at any point in pregnancy. "The Court's decisions recognizing a right of privacy also acknowledge that some state regulation ... is appropriate," he explained. "The State may properly assert important interests in safeguarding health, in maintaining medical standards, and in protecting potential life. At some point in pregnancy, these respective interests become sufficiently compelling [to regulate] the factors that govern the abortion decision."

In the opinion itself, Blackmun began by noting that the laws making abortion a crime in the states of Texas and Georgia had been passed more than a century apart. He pointed out that medical knowledge had advanced significantly during this period, as had American legal and social ideas about race, poverty, and population issues.

The majority opinion went on to address some of the technical legal issues involved in the cases, including the plaintiffs' standing. Then, based on his research, Blackmun covered the history of legal and medical thought about abortion. He pointed out that doctors in ancient Greece had performed abortions, and that English common law considered the fetus a part of its mother's body until the time of birth. Blackmun noted that laws prohibiting abortion did not appear in the United States until the middle of the nineteenth century, and that these early statutes were intended to protect women from medical practices that posed a threat to their health. Blackmun concluded that "a woman enjoyed a substantially broader right to terminate a pregnancy [early in the nation's history] than she does in most states today," even though twentieth-century medical advances had made abortion less dangerous than carrying a pregnancy to full term.

The Trimester Formula

The majority opinion also discussed the right to privacy that the Court drew from the Ninth and Fourteenth Amendments to the Constitution. Blackmun wrote, however, that a woman's right to privacy in reproductive decisions did not provide her with an absolute right to abortion. Instead, he argued that this right must be balanced against the state's interest in protecting the fetus, which increased as the pregnancy progressed. Blackmun said that it was not the Court's place to decide the point at which life begins. Rather, he offered the trimester formula as a legal guideline to show when the state's interests became compelling and justified restrictions on abortion.

Under this formula, the state could not restrict abortion during the first trimester, and the only restrictions allowed during the second trimester were for the purpose of protecting the mother's health. During the third trimester, as the fetus reached the stage of viability, the state could restrict or even outlaw abortion, except when it was deemed medically necessary to preserve the life or health of the mother.

Blackmun's trimester formula did not follow a legal precedent or have a basis in constitutional law. It was a creative solution that tried to balance the competing interests and legal rights of the woman and the fetus. Roe's attorney, Sarah Weddington, had made it possible for the Court to impose such a solution by seeking an injunction to force Texas to stop enforcing its abortion law. When a plaintiff requests an injunction, judges have the power to come up with an equitable remedy, or a solution that the court feels is fair to all parties involved in the case. "Equitable remedies need not have precedent in the language of the law or the prior ruling of courts," N.E.H. Hull and Peter Charles Hoffer explained in *Roe v. Wade: The Abortion Rights Controversy in American History.* "Such relief must only be narrowly tailored to do justice, and that is what Blackmun intended."

Some legal experts compared Blackmun's trimester formula to the remedies federal judges used to enforce the Supreme Court's 1954 *Brown v. Board of Education* ruling, which had banned segregation in the nation's public schools. When some school districts were slow to comply with the ruling, federal judges came up with a plan to integrate schools by busing minority children into white districts.

Other Justices Have Their Say

Although six other justices joined Blackmun's majority opinion, three chose to expand upon it by writing concurring opinions. Chief Justice Burger wrote that he would have preferred for a woman to obtain the approval of two doctors before undergoing an abortion. The language of the majority opinion said only that the abortion decision should be left to the woman "in consultation with her doctor" during the first trimester. Nevertheless, Burger also declared that the Court's decision in *Roe* did not allow for "abortion on demand."

Justice Douglas used his concurrence to discuss the constitutional right to privacy that he had first outlined in the *Griswold* decision. He described privacy as the freedom to control one's personality, make basic decisions about one's personal life, and avoid bodily restraint and compulsion. He argued that state laws banning abortion amounted to government compulsion for a woman to remain pregnant and give birth to a child. He also said that these laws ignored the psychological effects of unwanted pregnancy. Justice Stewart, in his concurring opinion, explained his view that the Constitution's guarantee of liberty needed to change with the times. In the context of the women's rights movement of the 1970s, he claimed that it applied to freedom of choice in reproductive issues.

In a somewhat unusual move that some observers considered confrontational, Justices Rehnquist and White read their dissenting opinions immediately following Blackmun's summary of the majority opinion (see "Justice William H. Rehnquist Dissents," p. 186, and "Justice Byron R. White Dissents," p. 190). White strongly disagreed with the Court's ruling that the Constitution supported a right to abortion. He argued that state legislatures must be allowed to regulate abortion, because they were in the best position to weigh the "relative importance of the continued existence and development of the fetus on the one hand against a spectrum of possible impacts on the mother on the other hand." White was particularly critical of the majority opinion because he felt that it sanctioned abortion on demand. "The Court for the most part sustains this position," he wrote. "During the period prior to the time the fetus becomes viable, the Constitution of the United States values the convenience, whim, or caprice of the putative mother more than the life or potential life of the fetus."

In contrast, Rehnquist's dissent focused more on technical issues of law. For instance, he disputed Roe's standing in the case, arguing that since she was not pregnant at the time of the hearing, the Court should not have provided a remedy. Rehnquist also claimed that the right of privacy did not apply to a woman's decision to have an abortion because the doctor and fetus were also involved. Finally, Rehnquist pointed out that several states had already passed anti-abortion laws when the Fourteenth Amendment was ratified in 1868. According to Rehnquist, this timing proved that the framers of the amendment did not intend for it to prevent states from restricting abortion.

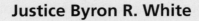

Justice Byron R. White

U.S. Supreme Court Justice Byron White— author of one of the two dissenting opinions in the *Roe v. Wade* case—was born on June 8, 1917, in Fort Collins, Colorado. His father, Alpha A. White, managed a lumber company and also served as the mayor of Wellington, Colorado. His mother was Maude Burger White.

White attended the University of Colorado and became a star running back on the football team. After earning his bachelor's degree in economics in 1938, he joined the Pittsburgh Pirates (now the Steelers) and led the National Football League (NFL) in rushing yards during his rookie season. White took the 1939 season off to attend Oxford University in England as a Rhodes Scholar, then returned to play two more NFL seasons for the Detroit Lions. He led the league in rushing for a second time in 1940.

White combined his NFL career with studies at Yale Law School. He interrupted both in order to serve as an intelligence officer in the U.S. Navy during World War II. When the war ended, White completed his law degree, finishing at the top of his class at Yale in 1946. He also married Marion Stearns that year, and they eventually had two children. In 1946-47 White served as a law clerk for Fred Vinson, the Chief Justice of the U.S. Supreme Court.

Abortion Becomes Legal

As soon as the Supreme Court announced its decision in *Roe v. Wade*, it became the law of the land. Abortion was legal across the country. All state laws that banned abortion or restricted it during the first trimester became invalid. The decision affected the laws of nearly every state. Even New York, which allowed unrestricted access to abortion during the first 24 weeks of

White then returned to Denver and entered private practice with a flourishing business law firm. In 1960 he became chairman of the Colorado campaign to elect Democratic Senator John F. Kennedy as president of the United States. After winning the election, Kennedy rewarded White with a position as deputy attorney general in his administration. White thus became the second-highest-ranking member of the U.S. Department of Justice, under Attorney General Robert F. Kennedy. In May 1961 he led 400 federal marshals into Selma, Alabama, to protect demonstrators in the civil rights movement.

In 1962, upon the retirement of Justice Charles Evans Whittaker, President Kennedy appointed White to the U.S. Supreme Court. Although White was only 44 years old and had no judicial experience, his sharp legal mind and personal integrity had impressed many members of the Kennedy administration. Over the next seven years, as Chief Justice Earl Warren led the Court in a number of liberal decisions, White became known as a moderate. He favored clear but limited government powers and resisted broad interpretations of the Constitution.

Although White voted to strike down a state ban on birth control in the 1965 case *Griswold v. Connecticut,* he wrote a strongly worded dissent a few years later in *Roe v. Wade.* Calling it "an exercise in raw judicial power," White remained critical of the *Roe* decision throughout the remainder of his 31-year term. Upon his retirement in 1993, President Bill Clinton appointed Ruth Bader Ginsburg to replace him. White died in Denver on April 15, 2002, at the age of 84. The NFL Players Association presents an annual award for humanitarian work in his honor, and the federal courthouse in Denver is named after him.

pregnancy, had to adjust its statute to meet the new 28-week standard. Many other states had to revise their laws to comply with the Supreme Court's ruling in the companion case *Doe v. Bolton,* which had disallowed specific restrictions on abortion, like residency requirements.

Women's rights and abortion rights activists were delighted with the decision. Many expressed surprise that the Supreme Court had gone so far as

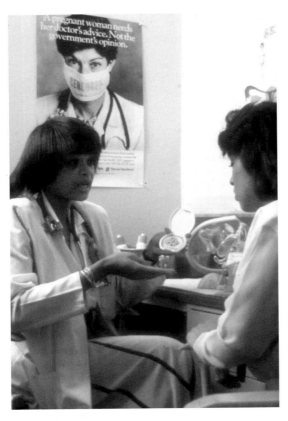

In the wake of the 1973 *Roe v. Wade* decision legalizing abortion in the United States, family planning clinics—like this Planned Parenthood center in Austin, Texas—opened across the country.

to remove all restrictions on abortions performed during the first trimester. "It scaled the whole mountain," Planned Parenthood of America attorney Harriet Pilpel said of the ruling. "We expected to get there, but not on the first trip." Lawrence Lader, founder of the National Abortion Rights Action League (NARAL), described the decision as "a thunderbolt."

Sarah Weddington—who had used the fame and connections she had gained from the *Roe* case to win a seat in the Texas House of Representatives during the fall 1972 elections—viewed the ruling as a victory for women's rights. "The Court's decision was an opportunity for all women. The battle was never 'for abortion'—abortion was not what we wanted to encourage. The battle was for the basic right of women to make their own decisions," she wrote in her autobiography. "The Court's decision in *Roe* was a declaration for human liberty, and was faithful to the values of the nation's founders. They had created a country where the government would not be allowed to control their most private lives."

Weddington expressed surprise about the trimester formula that Blackmun included in the decision. She felt that the author of the majority opinion may have wanted to provide details about what the Court would consider acceptable restrictions on abortion, in order to avoid an endless stream of cases dealing with that issue. Weddington still recognized, though, that the ruling would create controversy. She worried about the majority's decision to link abortion rights to viability of the fetus, because this meant that abortion could be restricted in earlier stages of pregnancy as medical technology advanced. She also noted that some abortion rights supporters might object to the Court not granting a woman complete control over her decision to terminate a pregnancy, but rather saying that she should make the decision "in consultation with her doctor."

Despite such concerns, most abortion rights activists applauded the *Roe v. Wade* ruling and set about the task of ensuring that American women had widespread access to legal abortion services. Organizations like Planned Parenthood opened new clinics and began offering safe, low-cost medical abortions in addition to birth control and family planning information. Several African-American groups launched referral services to provide poor and minority women with increased access to abortion providers.

Rise of the Pro-Life Movement

Although the Supreme Court's decision to legalize abortion was popular in some quarters, it generated a great deal of controversy in others. For instance, a number of constitutional law scholars criticized the ruling. They claimed that the Court had overstepped the bounds of its authority by creating "a new and formidable set of rights without express and substantive enabling language in the Constitution," according to Hull and Hoffer. Some legal experts felt that the sweeping nature of the ruling forced the American people to accept major social changes for which they were not yet ready. They expressed concern that the Court's action would deepen the national divide over the abortion issue. Others felt that the weak constitutional basis for the ruling would encourage future challenges. Finally, some scholars argued that the legality of abortion was a matter that should be decided by the states rather than imposed by the Supreme Court. They argued that the decision ignored widespread public disapproval of abortion, as evidenced by the defeat of repeal referenda in several states during the 1972 elections.

In addition to those who questioned the legal reasoning behind the *Roe* decision, many people opposed the ruling on moral grounds. Anti-abortion activists expressed sadness, outrage, and disbelief upon learning that the Supreme Court had overturned state laws restricting abortion. Many of these activists viewed abortion as the equivalent of murder, and they were appalled that it was now legal in the United States. John Cardinal Krol, president of the National Catholic Conference, described the ruling as an "unspeakable tragedy" in the *New York Times*, and said that the Supreme Court had "opened the doors to the greatest slaughter of innocent life in the history of mankind."

In the immediate aftermath of the *Roe* decision, the Roman Catholic Church took a leading role in organizing the opposition. The Church encouraged priests to speak out against abortion during Mass and to deny communion to Catholics who had abortions or supported abortion rights. The Church also forbade doctors in 600 Catholic hospitals across the country from performing abortions and lobbied for the addition of a Human Life Amendment to the U.S. Constitution.

Opposition to legalized abortion also provided a rallying point for evangelical Protestants. Many Christian fundamentalists viewed the Supreme Court's decision as a moral evil that threatened to destroy traditional family values. Leaders of the evangelical movement, like the Reverend Jerry Falwell, then decided to move beyond preaching against abortion and become more politically active. Falwell, who had already achieved a national reach with his "Old Time Gospel Hour" radio program, founded the Moral Majority in 1979. This Christian organization pushed for changes that would reflect its members' conservative religious beliefs and values on abortion and other social issues.

A number of other anti-abortion groups were founded in the aftermath of the *Roe* ruling, while those that had existed beforehand generally became more visible and increased their membership. Such organizations as Americans United for Life, the National Right to Life Committee, Operation Rescue, the Army of God, and the Lambs of Christ collectively referred to themselves as the pro-life movement for their desire to protect the unborn.

Working to Overturn *Roe*

Pro-life groups pursued several different legal and political strategies to try to reverse or at least limit the effects of the *Roe* decision. At the same time, they declared their intention to work toward the passage of a new amendment to the U.S. Constitution that specifically banned abortion. But although changing the Constitution offered pro-life activists the most permanent solution to the abortion issue, new amendments are typically very difficult to pass. A proposed amendment must receive the votes of two-thirds majorities in both houses of the U.S. Congress before it is sent to the states for ratification. Then it must be approved by voters in three-quarters of the 50 states before it can take effect. Despite the length and uncertainty of the ratification process, however, pro-life forces promoted amendments that would have granted legal rights to the fetus or outlawed abortion.

Introducing constitutional amendments also provided pro-life groups with a way to gauge the views of members of Congress about the abortion issue. This information proved helpful in implementing a second strategy for overturning the *Roe* decision: electing pro-life representatives to serve in state and federal governments. Abortion opponents especially hoped to elect pro-life presidents, who they felt would be likely to appoint federal judges willing to overturn *Roe*. They also supported the campaigns of pro-life members of Congress in hopes of gaining the passage of anti-abortion legislation.

In 1979 evangelist Jerry Falwell founded the Moral Majority, a conservative Christian organization dedicated to ending abortion and defending traditional "family values."

Finally, as they worked toward the long-term goal of outlawing abortion, pro-life groups also pursued a strategy of making legal abortions more difficult to obtain. They promoted a variety of state laws restricting abortion in ways that the *Roe* ruling had not directly addressed, including mandatory 24-hour waiting periods, clinical record-keeping requirements, and parental or spousal consent laws. Although the Supreme Court eventually struck down most of the laws that restricted access to abortion during the first trimester, pro-life activists continued working to erect barriers to prevent women from having abortions. For instance, they had considerable success in convincing hospitals across the country not to offer the procedure. By 1977, according to Rickie Solinger in *Pregnancy and Power,* 80 percent of public hospitals and 70 percent of private hospitals in the United States did not permit abortions in their facilities.

Abortion on TV

One of the earliest demonstrations of the growing power of the pro-life movement came in August 1973, when the Roman Catholic Church led a coalition of other groups in a boycott of the CBS television network. CBS had announced plans to broadcast a rerun of a controversial episode of the hit situation comedy "Maude," in which the title character decided to have an abortion.

"Maude" ran on CBS from 1972 to 1978. The main character—an independent, outspoken, politically and socially liberal feminist named Maude Findlay (played by Beatrice Arthur)—was first introduced on the groundbreaking series "All in the Family." Like that show, "Maude" used comic situations as a way to explore controversial social and political issues of the times. For example, various episodes covered topics like race relations, gender roles, alcoholism, depression, birth control, and divorce.

The two-part episode dealing with the abortion issue first aired in November 1972, two months before the Supreme Court decision in *Roe v. Wade* legalized abortion throughout the United States. The storyline begins when Maude—who is 47 years old, married to her fourth husband, and the mother of an adult daughter—finds out that she is pregnant. She finds the news very upsetting and feels that having a baby is not safe or wise at her age. After consulting with her husband and daughter, Maude makes the difficult decision to have an abortion, which is legal in her home state of New York.

Abortion Becomes a Political Issue

Recognizing the strength of opposition to legalized abortion, political conservatives in the Republican Party began reaching out to religious conservatives following the *Roe* decision. Although these two groups held opposing views on some social issues, they shared strong pro-life views. The alliance between Republicans and fundamentalist Christians of the Religious Right helped turn abortion into a major issue in American politics. "Thus *Roe*, a legal decision meant to take abortion out of politics, had not only thrust abor-

"Maude" thus became the first prime-time American television series to deal with the abortion issue. The episode was controversial when it first aired, and CBS received thousands of letters of protest from angry viewers who felt it promoted abortion. Once the *Roe* decision was announced in January 1973, however, millions more Americans became concerned about the issue. When the network made plans to broadcast the episode again over the summer, the pro-life movement organized a boycott.

By threatening not to buy their products, pro-life groups convinced all major national advertisers not to place commercials on the controversial episode of "Maude." The groups, joined by an organization called Stop Immorality on Television (SIT), also convinced 39 of the CBS network's 217 local affiliate stations not to air the episode. Their ultimate goal was to force CBS to cancel the program, but the network refused. After all, "Maude" ranked among the most popular shows on television at that time.

Concerns about "Maude" and other shows dealing with controversial topics did have an effect on the networks, however. By the time the series concluded in 1978, prime-time TV programming had shifted away from social and political commentary and toward more traditional, family-oriented topics. Furthermore, very few TV series have dealt with the abortion issue since that time. "Unlike such once-taboo issues as date rape, gay relationships, and teenage sex, abortion on television remains an aberration," Kate Arthur wrote in the *New York Times*. "[It] is the very rare character who actually has one; what's even more rare is that she doesn't regret it afterward."

tion back into politics but made abortion into the central domestic political issue for the next quarter century," Hull and Hoffer wrote.

Politicians responded to the increasing strength and visibility of the pro-life movement by introducing bills and amendments designed to restrict or outlaw abortion. Just eight days after the *Roe* decision was announced, for instance, U.S. Representative Lawrence Hogan of Maryland proposed a Constitutional amendment to define a fetus as a person under the Fourteenth Amendment. The next day, Senator James F. Buckley introduced a Right to

Pro-choice activists like these demonstrators at the 1976 Democratic National Convention opposed any efforts to weaken abortion rights.

Life Amendment to outlaw abortion. However, these and later draft amendments did not receive the votes needed to be sent to the states for ratification.

In the three years following the *Roe* decision, more than 50 bills intended to ban or limit abortion were introduced in the U.S. Congress. State legislatures considered more than 400 similar bills during this time, and a number of the bills restricting abortion became law. These laws created a patchwork of regulations that generally made it more time-consuming and expensive for women to have abortions. For example, some new state laws required married women to obtain the consent of their spouses. Others required minors to obtain the consent of a parent before having an abortion. Finally, some laws were passed that prohibited the use of public funds to provide abortion services to poor women. In the 1976 case *Planned Parenthood v. Danforth*, the Supreme Court overturned a series of state restrictions aimed at limiting access to abortion. That same year, however, the Court decided in *Maher v. Roe* that states could legally refuse to provide public funding for abortions for poor women.

Shortly after the *Maher* decision was announced, Henry Hyde—a conservative Republican congressman from Illinois—led an effort to ban all federal funding for abortion. During debate over an appropriations bill to establish a new budget for the Department of Health, Education, and Welfare (HEW), Hyde added wording to prevent HEW from providing abortions to poor women on Medicaid. Before this time, the government-sponsored health care program known as Medicaid had paid for around one-third of all legal abortions performed in the United States, or about 300,000 annually. "For opponents of abortion, a ban on all Medicaid-funded abortions was thought to represent one of the most effective means of reducing the number of abortions short of overturning *Roe*," Laurence Tribe explained in *Abortion: The Clash of Absolutes*. "It would constitute an important moral statement by the federal government and provide a means of showing politicians that the pro-life movement could flex its muscle in Congress on an issue of substance."

The original Hyde amendment banned all government funding for abortion, even if a doctor deemed the procedure medically necessary. The U.S. Senate added exceptions that allowed a poor woman to receive a Medicaid-funded abortion if her pregnancy resulted from rape or incest or posed a threat to her life. Although President Gerald Ford vetoed that version of the HEW appropriations bill, Congress overrode his veto and the funding ban became law.

In 1980 the Supreme Court heard a challenge to the law in *Harris v. McRae*. The Court upheld the funding ban, saying that state and federal governments did not have to pay for abortions in order to comply with *Roe*. "Although government may not place obstacles in the path of a woman's exercise of her freedom of choice, it need not remove those not of its own creation," Justice Potter Stewart wrote. "Indigency [poverty] falls in the latter category." In effect, the Court said that *Roe* had not established a constitutional right to abortion, but had only protected women from "unduly burdensome interference with [their] freedom to decide" whether to terminate a pregnancy.

> *In upholding a ban on federal funding for abortion, Justice Potter Stewart wrote that "although government may not place obstacles in the path of a woman's exercise of her freedom of choice, it need not remove those not of its own creation," such as poverty.*

The issue of public funding for abortion generated strong feelings on both sides. Pro-life activists argued that their tax money should not be spent on abortion, which they considered morally wrong. They also believed that withholding Medicaid funding would prevent some women from having abortions, and therefore save the lives of some babies.

Abortion rights activists, on the other hand, argued that the American political system did not allow citizens to direct their tax dollars only to programs they personally favored. They pointed out that many Americans opposed the Vietnam War, for example, but that a portion of their taxes went toward paying for that war anyway. Abortion rights supporters also claimed that denying public funding for abortion amounted to discrimination against poor women. They also worried that the Hyde amendment would endanger women's lives by forcing them to resort to cheap but dangerous abortion methods.

Despite the heated debate, some politicians viewed the funding ban as an appealing middle ground on the abortion issue. They claimed that the federal government could stay out of the abortion controversy by neither banning nor funding abortion.

Abortion in the 1976 Presidential Election

The abortion issue also played a role in the 1976 presidential campaign. "It did not take *Roe* to make politicians' views on abortion crucial to their chances of election and reelection," Hull and Hoffer noted, "but *Roe* gave focus and urgency to the political efforts of both sides." The growing pro-life

Abortion first emerged as a major campaign issue during the 1976 presidential election, which Democratic nominee Jimmy Carter (shown at left) eventually won.

movement proved to be particularly effective in promoting candidates who shared their views.

Gerald Ford, who had taken office in 1974 following President Nixon's resignation, received the Republican nomination. He personally opposed abortion except in limited circumstances, but he did not favor an outright ban. Instead, he supported a constitutional amendment that would return the power to regulate abortion to state legislatures. His wife Betty shed some doubt on his commitment to the pro-life cause, however, by speaking out in favor of abortion rights.

In the meantime, the support of pro-life groups helped Georgia Governor Jimmy Carter, a born-again Christian, win the Democratic nomination.

71

Carter personally opposed abortion and supported the ban on federal funding, but he too stopped short of calling for a constitutional amendment to overturn the *Roe* decision. After defeating Ford in the general election, Carter pleased many of his supporters by appointing Joseph Califano, a pro-life Catholic, as secretary of HEW. In the years following the 1976 presidential election, the abortion issue assumed an even more prominent role in American politics.

Chapter Five

THE COURT LIMITS ROE'S REACH

My Administration is dedicated to the preservation of America as a free land, and there is no cause more important for preserving that freedom than affirming the transcendent right to life of all human beings, the right without which no other rights have meaning.

—President Ronald Reagan, "Abortion and the Conscience of the Nation," *Human Life Review,* Spring 1983

Following the election of pro-life Democrat Jimmy Carter as president of the United States in 1976, Republican leaders began to place a greater emphasis on their party's opposition to abortion. At a time when only 20 percent of voters identified themselves as Republicans, many insiders felt that the party could expand its reach by demonstrating a strong commitment to the pro-life position. Specifically, the Republicans hoped to attract support in the 1980 elections from moderate Catholics in the Northeast and conservative Christians from the South and West.

As part of this strategy, the Republicans chose Ronald Reagan—a famous actor who had gone on to serve as governor of California—as their presidential nominee. While most candidates before him had taken a cautious stand on the abortion issue, Reagan strongly opposed abortion from the start of his campaign. He described the Supreme Court's ruling in *Roe v. Wade* as "an abuse of power" and called for a constitutional amendment to reverse the decision. Reagan also promised to cut taxes, reduce the size of the federal government, and bring the nation back to a position of world leadership.

Reagan's opposition to abortion helped him gain the support of the pro-life movement, including the National Right to Life Committee and the Moral Majority. Many other voters were drawn to his optimistic vision for the country's future. He ended up winning the presidency by a large margin, while the defeat of several prominent pro-choice Democrats also helped the Republicans take control of the U.S. Senate. The election results boosted the morale of pro-life activists and gave them new hope for ending legal abortion in the United States.

Changes to the Supreme Court

Throughout his presidential campaign, Reagan had promised to appoint pro-life judges to positions on the federal bench. Like many pro-life activists, Reagan believed that changing the ideological makeup of the judiciary—and especially the Supreme Court—could eventually lead to the reversal of *Roe*. Only one new justice had joined the Supreme Court in the nine years since President Nixon had made the last of his four appointments. In 1975 President Ford had appointed John Paul Stevens to fill the seat of William O. Douglas, who had decided to retire. Although Stevens was not nearly as liberal as Douglas, he turned out to be less conservative than many people expected. In fact, the independent-minded Stevens preserved the 7-2 majority that supported the *Roe* decision.

Shortly after taking office in 1981, Reagan got his first opportunity to replace one of the justices who comprised that majority. Upon the retirement of Potter Stewart, he followed through on a campaign promise to appoint the first female justice to the Supreme Court. His nominee was Sandra Day O'Connor (see "Justice Sandra Day O'Connor," p. 76), a conservative Republican who had served in the Arizona state senate. Some pro-life activists opposed the choice because, while in office, O'Connor had once voted to repeal a strict anti-abortion law. She still won confirmation fairly easily, however, after expressing her view that the role of the courts was to interpret rather than make law.

In 1983, on the tenth anniversary of the *Roe* ruling, Reagan explained his pro-life views in a lengthy essay entitled "Abortion and the Conscience of the Nation." It was very rare for a sitting president to publish his personal opinion on such a controversial issue while in office. During the 1984 presidential elections, a number of prominent pro-choice organizations campaigned against Reagan. The National Abortion Rights Action League (NARAL) pointed out to voters that five of the remaining Supreme Court justices who had formed the majority in *Roe* were over 75 years old. If Reagan won reelection, they warned, he might be able to appoint enough pro-life justices to overturn the decision. Despite such efforts, however, Reagan easily defeated the Democratic candidate, former vice president Walter Mondale, in the general election.

William Rehnquist, who wrote a dissenting opinion in *Roe v. Wade*, succeeded Warren Burger as chief justice of the Supreme Court in 1986.

As predicted, Reagan appointed two more Supreme Court justices during his second term. When Chief Justice Warren Burger stepped down in 1986, the president elevated William Rehnquist, author of one of the dissenting opinions in *Roe,* to chief justice. Rehnquist had been the most consistently conservative member of the Court. A number of Democratic senators joined pro-choice groups in opposing his confirmation. They claimed that Rehnquist was "too extreme" to hold such a powerful position. He won confirmation anyway, however, and Reagan succeeded in placing one of *Roe's* leading critics in charge of the Court. The president then appointed Antonin Scalia, a conservative legal scholar, to fill Rehnquist's position as associate justice.

Two Sides Debate over Bork

The following year another member of the *Roe* majority, Justice Lewis Powell, announced his retirement. Reagan immediately nominated Robert Bork (see Bork biography, p. 129), a conservative federal judge and an outspoken critic of the *Roe* decision, to the Supreme Court. During testimony before Congress in 1981, Bork had made no secret of his desire to overturn the ruling: "*Roe v. Wade* is, itself, an unconstitutional decision, a serious and wholly unjustifiable usurpation [claiming] of state legislative authority," he declared.

In light of Bork's well-known opinions about abortion (see "Robert H. Bork Defends the Pro-Life Position," p. 195), the pro-choice movement

Justice Sandra Day O'Connor

Sandra Day O'Connor was born March 26, 1930, in El Paso, Texas. She was the first of three children born to Harry and Ada Mae Day. She grew up on her family's cattle ranch in rural southeastern Arizona. Their home had no electricity or running water for the first few years of her life. Sandra helped with a variety of ranch tasks as a child, from riding horses and branding steers to driving tractors and fixing farm equipment.

Since educational opportunities were limited in their rural area, Sandra's parents sent her away to school in El Paso. She lived with her grandmother while attending Radford School, a private all-girls academy, and Austin High School. An excellent student, she went on to study economics at Stanford University, earning a bachelor's degree in 1950. A legal dispute involving her family's ranch gave Sandra an interest in law. She completed her law degree at Stanford in 1952, graduating third in a class of 102 students (the top student in her class was future Chief Justice William Rehnquist).

Despite her strong performance in law school, Sandra had trouble finding a job as a lawyer. Few law firms were willing to hire female attorneys in those days. In 1953 she married a law school classmate, John Jay O'Connor. When her husband was drafted into the U.S. Army, she accompanied him to Frankfurt, Germany. The couple returned to the United States three years later and settled in Phoenix, Arizona. They had three sons over the next five years. O'Connor did some legal and volunteer work during this time, but she mostly concentrated on raising her children.

O'Connor returned to full-time employment in 1965 as an assistant attorney general for the state of Arizona. She also became active in Republican Party politics. In 1969 the state senator for her district resigned to take a job in Washington, D.C., and Governor Jack Williams appointed O'Connor to fill the seat. She was elected to the position in 1970 and

launched an intensive effort to block his confirmation by the Senate. It was joined by many civil rights and women's rights groups, who worried that Bork would disregard *Griswold* and other rulings that had established a constitutional right to privacy. But the Reagan administration and the pro-life reelected in 1972. During her second term, she became the first woman in the country to serve as the majority leader in a state legislature.

O'Connor decided not to seek reelection in 1974. Instead, she campaigned successfully to become a judge in the Maricopa County Superior Court. Five years later she was appointed to the Arizona Court of Appeals. In 1981, upon the retirement of Justice Potter Stewart, President Ronald Reagan nominated O'Connor to serve on the U.S. Supreme Court. During his election campaign, Reagan had promised to select a woman if he got the opportunity to fill any vacancies on the Court. Some critics claimed that O'Connor lacked experience and constitutional knowledge, while others questioned her views on abortion and women's rights. Nevertheless, she was confirmed unanimously in the Senate to become the first female justice in the 191-year history of the Supreme Court.

During her early years on the Court, O'Connor often voted with the more conservative justices, like Rehnquist. As time went on, however, she increasingly showed an independent streak, especially on cases involving women's rights. By 1990 she had emerged as an unpredictable "swing voter" who decided each case based on practical applications of the law. In 1992 O'Connor joined forces with fellow justices Anthony Kennedy and David Souter to form a moderate or centrist group on the Court. In the case of *Planned Parenthood v. Casey,* the three justices voted to reaffirm the right to abortion that had been established in *Roe v. Wade,* but they also voted to uphold a variety of state restrictions on access to abortion.

O'Connor continued to seek compromises and build coalitions through the remainder of her service on the Court. She announced her retirement in 2005, and President George W. Bush appointed Samuel Alito to replace her. O'Connor published an autobiographical book about her childhood, *Lazy B: Growing Up on a Cattle Ranch in the American Southwest.* She also wrote a children's book called *Chico,* which was published in 2005.

movement expressed strong support for the nominee. Bork's confirmation hearings turned into a bitter, highly publicized battle that exposed the nation's deep divisions over the abortion issue. In the end, the Senate voted against Bork's confirmation.

When President Ronald Reagan (left) nominated Robert Bork (right) for the Supreme Court, Bork's views on abortion became the central focus of his confirmation hearings.

Reagan's second choice to fill the vacancy on the Supreme Court was Douglas Ginsburg, another conservative federal judge. But Ginsburg was forced to withdraw his name from consideration after opponents raised questions about his personal conduct. The president's third choice, Anthony Kennedy, finally won confirmation. Although he refused to comment on *Roe* directly, Kennedy did express support for privacy rights during his confirmation hearings. "The concept of liberty in the Due Process Clause [of the Fourteenth Amendment] is quite expansive, quite sufficient, to protect the values of privacy that Americans legitimately think are part of their constitutional heritage," he stated.

A Conservative Backlash against Women's Liberation

The election of Reagan in 1980 brought a surge in political power and influence for the pro-life movement. With a president in office who shared their conviction that abortion was a moral evil, many activists felt confident that they could reduce the American people's acceptance of the practice. They began working to pass new laws limiting abortion, and they believed that these laws would be upheld by pro-life judges appointed by Reagan. As the makeup of the Supreme Court changed, they hoped that new justices would eventually overturn *Roe* and allow states to outlaw abortion.

The election of Reagan also signaled a return to traditional, conservative values in the United States. Between the civil rights movement, the women's liberation movement, and protests against the Vietnam War, the 1960s and 1970s had seen a great deal of social upheaval. Many people viewed the "Reagan Revolution" as a rejection of some of the more extreme changes that had occurred during that time.

During the 1970s, for instance, feminists had fought for passage of a constitutional amendment banning discrimination on the basis of sex. The Equal Rights Amendment (ERA) passed Congress in 1972, and by 1980 it had been ratified by 35 states (out of a total of 38 needed to add it to the Constitution). After Reagan received the Republican nomination, however, he dropped support for the ERA from the party's platform. Religious and political conservatives opposed the amendment, claiming that it would erase distinctions between the sexes and force schools, sports teams, and the military to integrate the genders. Pro-life groups also helped defeat the amendment as it reached the deadline for ratification in 1982.

> *The failure of the Equal Rights Amendment was widely interpreted as evidence of a social backlash against the women's rights movement.*

The failure of the ERA was widely interpreted as evidence of a social backlash against the women's rights movement. Although feminism had produced important gains for women in American society—including expanded educational and work opportunities—critics claimed that the increased power and independence of women also had many negative effects. They blamed women's liberation for an overall decline in family values, which they saw reflected in social trends like sex outside of marriage, single motherhood, illegitimate children, divorce, and abortion. Some conservatives felt that American society was more stable and wholesome when women were subordinate to men and played traditional roles as wives and mothers. In this way, abortion became a part of a bigger debate over the appropriate roles and behavior of women.

A Radical Shift in the Pro-Life Movement

Heartened by the election of Reagan and the new emphasis on conservative values, the pro-life movement entered the 1980s with a great deal of optimism. Membership in existing organizations like the National Right to Life Committee increased, and a number of new groups were founded, including the Pro-Life Action League, Human Life International, Operation Rescue, and Rescue America. Some of these groups worked to change state and federal laws to limit abortion. Others opened clinics, sometimes called "problem pregnancy centers," in cities across the country. Although these clinics often resembled abortion clinics—and even placed ads under "abortion" in the phone book—they did not

The Mainstream Pro-Life Movement

Although the violent acts of anti-abortion extremists generated a great deal of media attention in the 1980s, their radical views and tactics represented only a small segment of the pro-life movement. The vast majority of activists in the mainstream of the movement condemned the use of violence and instead pursued change through peaceful protests and political pressure. "We unequivocally reject the use of violence in the pro-life cause as contrary to the central moral principles of our movement," a coalition of pro-life leaders wrote in "The America We Seek: A Statement of Pro-Life Principle and Concern." "We have worked within the democratic process to advance the protection of all innocent human life, and we will continue to do so."

Instead of focusing their attention on the clinics where abortions were performed, many pro-life activists worked toward eliminating the circumstances that often drove pregnant women to seek abortions. For example, they supported prenatal care to ensure healthy mothers and babies, marriage and family counseling to help build loving homes for children, affordable day care to allow single mothers to support their children, and assistance to help women in crisis find alternatives to abortion.

provide abortion services. Instead, they actively tried to discourage women from terminating their pregnancies. Toward this end, counselors typically showed patients pictures of fetal development or aborted fetuses. They also offered them assistance in continuing their pregnancies or placing their babies for adoption.

Despite such efforts, around 1.5 million legal abortions took place each year in the United States during the 1980s. Studies estimated that one out of every four pregnancies ended in abortion. Some people were alarmed by what they viewed as a significant increase in abortions since the *Roe* decision, but others claimed that the figures were actually very similar to the number of illegal abortions that had taken place annually before 1973.

By the mid-1980s, a number of pro-life activists expressed frustration at their lack of legal or political progress toward ending abortion. They also felt

Some pro-life activists also supported sex education and birth control to prevent unwanted pregnancies. Others, concerned that these options encouraged immoral sexual behavior, promoted abstinence instead.

In her book *Pregnancy and Power,* Rickie Solinger quoted the mission statement of a local Right to Life chapter in Pekin, Illinois, which outlines this broader perspective on preventing abortion: "Most women seek abortions because they are in social or economic difficulties. To merely oppose abortion and do no more is not only useless, but frankly immoral. Anyone active in the pro-life movement should be equally as active in a wide variety of social actions. Correcting social injustice is a most important aspect of the entire abortion problem."

One organization dedicated to social change as a means of reducing abortion is the Common Ground Network for Life and Choice. It was founded in 1992 by opponents in the Supreme Court case *Webster v. Reproductive Health Services*: Andrew F. Pudzer, a pro-life activist who had helped draft the Missouri law at issue; and B.J. Isaacson-Jones, the pro-choice executive director of Reproductive Health Services, the family planning clinic that sued to overturn the law. The two activists joined forces in hopes of finding new ways to help women find alternatives to abortion and to heal the bitter divisions that the issue created.

angry about what they saw as America's acceptance of the feminist agenda and rejection of traditional moral values. A few pro-life groups turned away from politics and shifted their focus toward direct action aimed at preventing abortions. For instance, pro-life demonstrators set up picket lines outside of abortion clinics to discourage patients from entering. They also blockaded clinic entrances and harassed doctors and other staff members.

Some members of the pro-life movement grew increasingly confrontational in their efforts to stop abortion. Joseph Scheidler, a former Benedictine monk, was a frequent participant in anti-abortion protests during the 1980s. He founded an aggressive, military-style group called Friends for Life that became known as the "green berets" of the pro-life movement (after the elite, highly trained special forces unit of the U.S. Marine Corps). Friends for Life

Operation Rescue founder Randall Terry, seen here at a 2004 anti-abortion protest, first launched his confrontational pro-life activities in the late 1980s.

displayed a willingness to use outrageous and even illegal tactics to draw attention to their cause. At one protest, for example, they carried human fetuses in jars that had been stolen from a research laboratory. In 1983 Scheidler published a pamphlet called *Closed: 99 Ways to Stop Abortion,* which described a variety of methods for intimidating patients and doctors at abortion clinics.

Another prominent leader of the confrontational branch of the pro-life movement during the 1980s was Dr. Bernard Nathanson. The physician and co-founder of NARAL rejected his former pro-choice position and became a vocal opponent of abortion during this time. In 1984 Nathanson produced and narrated a controversial documentary film called *The Silent Scream.* It generated a great deal of publicity by showing actual ultrasound footage of a fetus during an abortion. At one point in the procedure, when the fetus opened its mouth, Nathanson's voice-over described it as screaming.

Probably the best-known anti-abortion protester during this period was Randall Terry (see Terry biography, p. 152). After joining a number of pickets and protests organized by other pro-life groups, Terry founded Operation Rescue in 1987. This group adopted massive resistance techniques that had been used during civil rights and Vietnam War protests in an effort to "rescue" babies from abortion. For instance, they set up human blockades of abortion clinics that often resulted in the arrest of large numbers of protesters. Although many people with pro-life views distanced themselves from Operation Rescue and other radical groups, others were drawn to their charismatic leaders and uncompromising approach to the abortion issue.

Anti-Abortion Protests Turn Violent

A small segment of the pro-life movement resorted to violence as a means to end abortion. These extremists usually attacked abortion clinics, which they viewed as evil institutions where unborn children were legally murdered. The attacks were intended to shut down the clinics by destroying facilities, frightening away potential patients, and intimidating staff members. The clinics also represented reproductive rights in the minds of many pro-choice activists, so violent and destructive acts aimed at clinics also served a symbolic purpose.

The first instances of anti-abortion violence occurred in the late 1970s. A Planned Parenthood clinic in St. Paul, Minnesota, reported an arson attack in 1977, and a Women for Women clinic in Cincinnati, Ohio, reported a bombing the following year. The violence escalated over the next decade, until the radical fringe became the most visible segment of the pro-life movement. Between the first attack in 1977 and the end of the Reagan administration in 1988, according to Hull and Hoffer, 77 bombings, 117 arson attacks, 231 robberies, and 224 acts of vandalism occurred at abortion clinics across the country. Abortion providers also received 216 bomb threats, 65 death threats, and 162 pieces of hate mail during this time.

The Reverend Michael Bray became known for promoting the destruction of facilities and the use of violence toward staff members to force abortion clinics out of business. He published a pamphlet called *A Time to Kill* that included instructions on how to use pipe bombs and arson attacks to shut down clinics. He also detailed methods for harassing, intimidating, assaulting, and kidnapping clinic workers. Bray eventually spent time in prison for his activities.

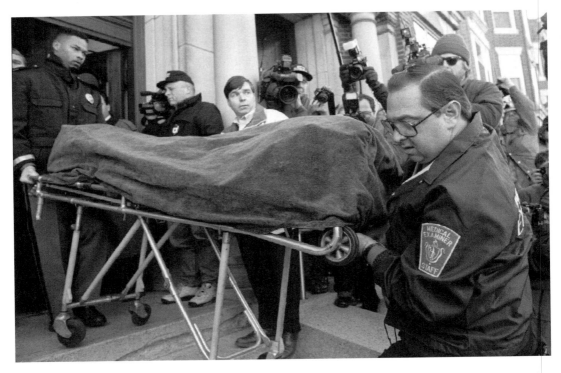

Massachusetts medical examiners remove the body of a woman shot at a Planned Parenthood clinic in suburban Boston in 1994.

Bombings at abortion clinics reached a new high in 1984. The *New York Times* described the wave of anti-abortion violence as a form of domestic terrorism. Many pro-choice activists criticized the Reagan administration's response to the bombings. These and other critics asserted that the administration tolerated the violence because of its pro-life stance. They became even more upset when the president waited three days to condemn a Christmas Day bombing that destroyed an abortion clinic in Pensacola, Florida.

The indifferent government reaction to the violence convinced many abortion-rights groups to dedicate large portions of their budgets to protecting clinic facilities and workers. "Just a few years after the legalization of abortion, human rights groups and feminist organizations that supported reproductive freedom were reeling and on the defensive," Rickie Solinger wrote in *Pregnancy and Power.* "The Hyde Amendment and *Harris v. McRae* demonstrated the government's willingness to turn reproductive freedom into a service-for-purchase. When communities and law enforcement agencies around the country passively tolerated clinic violence, women's reproductive 'choice' was weakened further."

New State Laws Limit Abortion

Encouraged by the Reagan administration's pro-life policies and judicial appointments, activists pushed state legislatures to pass new laws restricting abortion during the 1980s. Many states put new regulations in place that generally made it more costly, complicated, and time-consuming for women to obtain abortions. Some of these statutes were similar to ones that had already been struck down by the Supreme Court, while others were even more restrictive. Some state lawmakers openly defied provisions of the *Roe* decision, in hopes that legal battles over the legislation would eventually give the Court an opening to reconsider its ruling.

The restrictions imposed in these anti-abortion statutes varied widely. Many states restricted the locations where legal abortions could be performed. Some limited the procedure to hospitals, where it was more expensive than in clinics, while others banned public hospitals from providing abortions. Many other states placed new requirements on women, such as mandatory 24-hour waiting periods or the consent of a parent or spouse. Still other states tried to discourage doctors from performing abortions by requiring them to complete birth and death certificates for each aborted fetus or forcing them to distribute materials about fetal development and the potential health risks associated with abortion. The federal government, meanwhile, extended the ban on public funding for abortion to cover women who received medical care through the Indian Health Service, the U.S. military, the Peace Corps, and federal prisons.

Many cases involving state restrictions on abortion made their way to the U.S. Supreme Court in the 1980s. The cases fell into four general categories: denial of funding for abortion; limitations on access to abortion; restrictions on the information doctors could provide about abortion; and restraints on anti-abortion protesters. The Court had previously allowed state and federal governments to ban public funding for abortion. Up to this point, though, the Court had struck down most other laws that were intended to limit access to or information about abortion services.

In the 1983 case *Akron v. Akron Center for Reproductive Health,* for instance, the justices voted 6-3 to invalidate a series of abortion restrictions passed in Akron, Ohio. The Akron ordinance included a 24-hour waiting period, parental notification for minors, a mandatory speech by doctors about the dangers of abortion and the availability of adoption, and a procedure for the disposal of fetal remains. The Court found that these restrictions were illegal because they were clearly intended to discourage women from exercising their right to abortion. In a key dissent, however, Justice O'Connor made it clear that she did not approve of the trimester formula that Justice Blackmun had outlined in *Roe.* Instead, she proposed allowing the states to adopt restrictions as long as they did not pose an "undue burden" on a woman's right to choose abortion.

The Court reached a similar conclusion in the 1986 case *Thornburgh v. American College of Obstetricians and Gynecologists.* In a narrow 5-4 decision, the justices invalidated a series of Pennsylvania restrictions on abortion. The law in question had required doctors to perform tests to determine whether the fetus was viable, and if so, to use abortion methods that made a live birth possible and to have a second doctor present to care for the fetus. It also required doctors to provide information about fetal development, and hospitals to compile detailed reports about the abortions performed. The Court found that the Pennsylvania law violated the right to privacy of both women and doctors. The justices again said that states could not enact laws with the main purpose of interfering with a woman's right to choose abortion.

Webster v. Reproductive Health Services

Thornburgh was the last major abortion-related decision rendered by the Burger Court. The chief justice stepped down at the end of that session and was replaced by Rehnquist. Reagan's appointments of Scalia and Kennedy shifted the Court even further to the right over the next year. In 1988 the pro-choice movement received another blow when Republican George H. W. Bush, who had served as vice president under Reagan, was elected president of the United States. Although Bush had expressed support for abortion rights during the 1970s as a congressman from Texas, he adopted a strong pro-life position during his presidential campaign. As a result of all these changes, both pro-choice and pro-life supporters awaited new Supreme Court rulings with great nervousness.

The next major abortion case to reach the Court was *Webster v. Reproductive Health Services*. It concerned a Missouri law that contained 20 separate provisions, 7 of which were openly intended to discourage women from having abortions. Among these were a provision that prohibited public hospitals and their employees from performing abortions except when necessary to save the mother's life. Since poor women made up the majority of patients in these facilities, the law acted to restrict their ability to have abortions. The law also required doctors to test the fetus for viability if the woman was more than 20 weeks pregnant. The test of fetal lung development, called amniocentesis, posed risks to the mother's health. Finally, the state legislature added a preamble to the law that said human life began at conception and defined the fetus as a person with legal rights.

A lower court found the Missouri law unconstitutional and struck down the restrictions. The state, represented by attorney general William Webster,

As various states placed new restrictions on abortion, the pro-choice movement organized a series of rallies and campaigns to spread its message.

appealed the ruling. In asking the U.S. Supreme Court to hear the case, Webster referred to the "undue burden" standard that O'Connor had proposed to replace Blackmun's trimester formula. Webster argued that the various provisions of the Missouri law did not pose an undue burden on the right to choose an abortion as established in *Roe v. Wade*. But if the Court did find that the Missouri law conflicted with the *Roe* decision, Webster said, then the justices should reverse *Roe*. "The state was asking the Court to allow the state's rules under *Roe* or to throw out *Roe*," Hull and Hoffer explained. "Missouri's tactic raised the stakes of winning and losing for everyone."

When the Supreme Court agreed to grant Missouri's request for a review of the *Webster* case, leaders of the pro-choice movement expressed great concern. They recognized that the Court had become significantly more conservative under Reagan, and they openly worried that the new justices might overturn *Roe*. "Pro-choice groups had been more or less quiescent in the years following *Roe* because they relied on the federal judiciary to continue to support *Roe's* basic holding. But as the antiabortion drumbeat grew and the makeup of the federal bench was steadily transformed, they were awakening to altered circumstances," Barbara Hinkson Craig and David M. O'Brien wrote in *Abortion and American Politics*. "What had seemed impossible in the years immediately following *Roe*, namely, that that decision would not stand, now did not seem such a remote eventuality."

NARAL, now led by Kate Michelman (see Michelman biography, p. 143), launched a national advertising campaign in hopes of mobilizing pro-choice voters in support of abortion rights. The organization placed full-page ads in newspapers across the country that showed a picture of a coat hanger (an object that was sometimes used to perform illegal abortions) with the message: "For most of our daughters this looks like a coat-hanger. Let's keep it that way." It also ran a series of television commercials with the slogan, "Who decides?" Over the years, pro-life groups had often suggested that the decision about whether to legalize abortion should have been made by state legislatures rather than the Supreme Court. The NARAL ads said that the real question was whether the decision should be made by politicians or by the women whose lives would be directly affected. The advertising campaign helped raise awareness of the threat to *Roe*. An estimated 600,000 pro-choice activists participated in the March for Women's Lives in Washington, D.C., on April 9, 1989.

"Pull This One Thread"

As the two sides prepared to argue the *Webster* case before the Supreme Court, interested parties submitted a record 78 amicus curiae briefs. These briefs represented the opinions of thousands of individuals and more than 300 organizations and demonstrated the high level of public concern about the case. Oral arguments finally took place on April 26, 1989. Attorney Frank Susman appeared on behalf of Reproductive Health Services, the oldest abortion clinic in Missouri, while Webster once again presented the state's case. The Court also granted ten minutes to the Bush administration to present its views on the case. Charles Fried, a Harvard Law professor who had served as U.S. attorney general under Reagan, appeared for the federal government.

During oral arguments, Webster downplayed the controversial provisions in the Missouri law and tread lightly with regard to *Roe*. For instance, he argued that the preamble—which said life began at conception—was unenforceable and did not attempt to establish new rights. Webster claimed that the viability tests did not create an undue burden because they were not mandatory and carried no penalty. Finally, he pointed out that Missouri's ban on public funding for abortion had already been upheld in previous Supreme Court rulings.

When Fried stood up to present the Bush administration's position, however, he directly asked the Court to reconsider its decision in *Roe*. He claimed that overturning *Roe* would not affect other rulings based on a constitutional right to privacy, such as the *Griswold* decision legalizing the use of contraceptives. "We are not asking the Court to unravel the fabric ... of privacy rights which this Court has woven [in previous cases]," he stated. "Rather, we are asking the Court to pull this one thread."

> *"We are not asking the Court to unravel the fabric . . . of privacy rights which this Court has woven," declared Charles Fried. "Rather, we are asking the Court to pull this one thread."*

"A Chill Wind Blows"

As the justices prepared to announce their decision on July 3, a large crowd waited anxiously outside the Supreme Court Building to hear whether abortion would remain legal in the United States. Pro-life leaders felt hopeful when they learned that Chief Justice Rehnquist—a longtime critic of *Roe*—had written the majority opinion. But it turned out to contain a confusing mixture of good and bad news for both sides in the abortion debate. A fractured Court upheld most of the Missouri restrictions but declined to reconsider the *Roe* ruling.

The *Webster* ruling consisted of five separate opinions. Only Kennedy and White joined Rehnquist's opinion, which mostly offered a point-by-point discussion of why they decided that various provisions of the Missouri law were allowable under the Constitution. The opinion also criticized Blackmun's trimester formula and argued that states should have more power to regulate abortion throughout pregnancy. "We do not see why the State's interest in pro-

Justice Antonin Scalia is an outspoken critic of the *Roe v. Wade* decision who has repeatedly expressed his opinion that it should be overturned.

tecting potential human life should come into existence only at the point of viability, and that there should therefore be a rigid line allowing state regulation after viability but prohibiting it before viability," Rehnquist wrote.

O'Connor and Scalia both issued concurring opinions, but the reasoning cited by the two justices could not have been more different. O'Connor, perhaps feeling social pressure as the only woman on the Court, stressed the fact that she did not want to overturn *Roe*. She argued that abortion should remain legal as part of a woman's right to privacy in reproductive decisions. But she also continued to express doubts about the trimester formula and once again proposed replacing it with an undue burden test. Scalia, on the other hand, argued strongly in favor of overturning *Roe*. He also expressed impatience with O'Connor's opinion, which he said "cannot be taken seriously."

Blackmun authored a scathing dissent, which was joined by Brennan and Marshall. He expressed bitter feelings about the majority's disregard for *Roe* as a settled legal precedent. He angrily claimed that the *Webster* ruling gave the states an open invitation to pass new laws restricting abortion in defiance of *Roe*. He also expressed profound doubts about the future of abortion rights in the United States. "I fear for the future. I fear for the liberty and equality of the millions of women who have lived and come of age in the 16 years since *Roe* was decided," Blackmun wrote. "For today at least, the law of abortion stands undisturbed. For today the women of this Nation still retain the liberty to control their destinies. But the signs are evident and ominous and a chill wind blows."

Finally, Stevens wrote a separate dissent that concentrated on the preamble to the Missouri law. He argued that it was a religious statement that served no secular purpose, and therefore violated the separation of church and state guaranteed by the First Amendment. Stevens also stated his belief that Missouri should be allowed to ban public funding for abortion, in keeping with earlier Court decisions, but that all other provisions of the law should have been struck down.

Impact of the *Webster* Ruling

Activists on both sides of the abortion issue generally viewed the Supreme Court's decision in *Webster v. Reproductive Health Services* as a victory for the pro-life movement. Many people agreed with Blackmun's assessment of the ruling: although it preserved a woman's basic right to choose abortion, it also extended broad new regulatory powers to the states. "The Court has left a woman's right to privacy hanging by a thread and passed the scissors to the state legislatures," NARAL leader Kate Michelman declared in *Abortion: The Clash of Absolutes*.

> *"The [Supreme] Court has left a woman's right to privacy hanging by a thread and passed the scissors to the state legislators," declared Kate Michelman.*

Pro-choice leaders felt that the ruling provided a clear indication that the increasingly conservative Supreme Court no longer saw abortion as a fundamental right. Although the majority claimed that the *Webster* ruling left *Roe* "undisturbed," in fact it allowed states to ignore the part of *Roe* that prohibited regulation of abortion, except to protect maternal health, during the first two trimesters. "By allowing states and municipalities to deny funding and ordain extensive consent and notification procedures and one-day waiting periods for women seeking abortions before the end of the second trimester, the Court had left Blackmun's formula in tatters," Hull and Hoffer explained. "The real danger to women's rights promoters in the shift of the Court's reasoning was that, framed in the language of undue burden, choice was no longer a 'fundamental right' of privacy."

As predicted, a number of state legislatures interpreted the *Webster* ruling as a signal that the Court would allow further limits on abortion. Shortly after the decision was announced, Pennsylvania passed a bill that contained a series of tough new abortion restrictions. Signed into law by Governor Robert P. Casey, it was immediately contested in court by Planned Parenthood of Southeastern Pennsylvania. This case soon began making its way toward the Supreme Court as the next major challenge to *Roe*.

In the meantime, the makeup of the Supreme Court continued to change. President Bush soon had the opportunity to replace two more justices who had been steadfast defenders of *Roe:* Brennan and Marshall. The new justices Bush chose were David H. Souter, a relatively unknown New Hampshire judge who refused to comment on his abortion views; and Clarence Thomas, an African-American judge who was known to be a pro-life Catholic. Many observers believed that both Souter and Thomas would join forces with Rehnquist, White, Scalia, and Kennedy to overturn *Roe* at the next opportunity. "Since [the confirmation of Thomas] we have simply been waiting for the Supreme Court to observe the final formalities and sign the death certificate," Sarah Weddington wrote in her autobiography.

Chapter Six

ROE SURVIVES A MAJOR CHALLENGE

━━◈◈◈━━

I need to see you as soon as you have a few free moments. I want to tell you about some developments in *Planned Parenthood v. Casey,* and at least part of what I have to say should come as welcome news.

—Justice Anthony Kennedy, in a 1992 note informing *Roe* author Harry Blackmun that the 1973 decision would not be overturned

Pro-choice activists had long relied upon the U.S. Supreme Court to protect the right to abortion it had established in *Roe v. Wade.* But they recognized that the justices had come very close to overturning that decision in *Webster v. Reproductive Health Services.* The 1989 *Webster* ruling served as a wake-up call for the pro-choice movement. "The message that those who supported abortion rights had to act immediately or lose their rights came through loudly, clearly, and without confusion," Laurence Tribe wrote in *Abortion: The Clash of Absolutes.*

During the first year following the *Webster* decision, many abortion-rights and women's-rights groups experienced significant increases in both membership and donations. The National Abortion Rights Action League (NARAL) expanded from 150,000 to 400,000 members, while the National Organization for Women (NOW) grew from 170,000 to 250,000 members. At the same time, NARAL's annual income nearly tripled from $4.3 to $11.9 million, and Planned Parenthood's income nearly doubled from $7 to $13 million. These organizations used some of their funds to support pro-choice candidates in the 1990 congressional elections. The mobilization of pro-choice voters led to the defeat of a number of pro-life Republicans.

Rust v. Sullivan and the "Gag Rule"

Despite the election results, President George H. W. Bush continued to pursue policies and make judicial appointments to advance the pro-life cause. One of these policies—a ban on abortion counseling at publicly funded family-planning clinics across the country—generated a great deal of controversy.

Known by critics as the "gag rule," because it restricted the information that some doctors could give to patients, the policy had originally been enacted under President Ronald Reagan in 1988. It prohibited recipients of public funding under Title X—a government program operated by the Department of Health and Human Services (HHS) that offered reproductive health and family planning services—from engaging in any abortion-related activities. They were not only prohibited from performing abortions, but also from providing abortion counseling and referrals.

By 1991, Title X provided $141 million annually to nearly 4,000 family-planning clinics across the country. Under the so-called "gag rule," these facilities stood to lose their government funding if any staff member mentioned abortion to a client. A doctor was not even allowed to present abortion as an option for a patient who had a medical condition that might make continuing a pregnancy dangerous to her health. If a pregnant woman asked about abortion, clinic staff were required to tell her that the government did not consider abortion an "appropriate method" of birth control.

Irving Rust, a doctor at a publicly funded reproductive health clinic, sued HHS Secretary Louis Sullivan in an attempt to stop the government from enforcing the gag rule. His lawsuit argued that the ban on abortion-related activities violated the free-speech rights of health care providers and patients guaranteed by the First Amendment. The Bush administration defended the policy in court. Lawyers for the government pointed out that it was legal to restrict dangerous speech, and they argued that abortion-related speech was dangerous because it promoted the death of the fetus.

Rust v. Sullivan reached the U.S. Supreme Court in 1991. By this time, Bush had appointed David Souter to the Court with the goal of creating a conservative majority. Souter joined Chief Justice William Rehnquist and Justices Byron White, Antonin Scalia, and Anthony Kennedy in a 5-4 decision upholding the gag rule. The majority found the intent of Congress unclear in the enactment of Title X, so it decided that HHS had the power to make its own rules about how to allocate funding. The justices also ruled that the restriction on speech was constitutional because it only resulted in a denial of funding for clinics, rather than in criminal penalties for doctors. They also pointed out that patients who were not satisfied with the medical advice they received at publicly funded clinics were free to go somewhere else.

Justices Harry Blackmun, Thurgood Marshall, John Paul Stevens, and Sandra Day O'Connor dissented in the case. Citing precedents that denied government the right to interfere with doctor-patient relationships, the dissenters claimed that the gag rule was unconstitutional. They argued that the government could not force citizens to give up their fundamental right to free speech as a condition for receiving public funding. Finally, they expressed concern about potential health risks to pregnant women who did not receive complete and unbiased medical advice at government-funded clinics.

A Changed Court Hears a New Challenge to *Roe*

Thurgood Marshall's dissenting vote in *Rust v. Sullivan* was his last act as a Supreme Court justice. He stepped down at the conclusion of that term, and President Bush nominated Clarence Thomas to replace him. During his confirmation hearings, Thomas endured tough questions about his published criticism of the *Roe* decision and his alleged sexual harassment of a former employee, Anita Hill. In the end, though, he was confirmed by a 52-48 vote in the Senate.

Many legal scholars and political activists predicted that Thomas would give conservatives on the Court the additional vote they needed to overturn *Roe v. Wade*. By this time, five of the nine sitting justices had been appointed by Bush or Reagan, and Blackmun was the only remaining justice who had voted with the majority in the landmark 1973 case.

The next major challenge to *Roe* came in the form of another case from Pennsylvania. Following the *Webster* decision, the state legislature had passed a new abortion law that included a number of familiar requirements: a 24-hour waiting period; spousal consent for married women; parental consent for minors; reporting procedures for clinics; and a statement for doctors to read that outlined the risks associated with abortion and provided information about alternatives like adoption. The Supreme Court had struck down many of these requirements in its 1986 *Thornburgh* ruling, but the *Webster* decision convinced the Pennsylvania legislature to try again.

Planned Parenthood of Southeastern Pennsylvania sued Governor Robert Casey to prevent the state from enforcing the law. After a lower court upheld all of the requirements except for spousal notification, *Planned Parenthood v. Casey* made its way to the Supreme Court, which heard oral arguments on April 22, 1992. Attorney Kathryn Kolbert, representing Planned Parenthood, argued that the Pennsylvania law placed so many obstacles in the path of a woman seeking an abortion that it effectively forced her to continue her pregnancy. She claimed that if the Court upheld the state's restrictions, it might as well overturn *Roe*. Kolbert also emphasized the importance of legalized abortion in the lives of women. "Never before has this Court bestowed and taken back a fundamental right that has been part of the settled rights and expectations of literally millions of Americans for nearly two decades," she declared.

> *"Never before has this Court bestowed and taken back a fundamental right that has been part of the settled rights and expectations of literally millions of Americans for nearly two decades," declared a Planned Parenthood attorney.*

Pennsylvania's Attorney General, Ernie Preate, defended the state law. The Court also granted time to the Bush administration to present its views on the case. U.S. Solicitor General Kenneth Starr appeared to express the president's support for the law. Both men argued that the state had a compelling interest in protecting the life of the fetus throughout pregnancy—not only during the third trimester. In light of this interest, they claimed that the Pennsylvania restrictions were reasonable and did not pose an undue burden on women seeking abortions.

A Moderate Group Emerges on the Court

When the justices held their regular conference following the oral arguments, it appeared likely that the majority would vote to uphold the Pennsylvania abortion restrictions, and also to overturn *Roe*. Rehnquist, White, Scalia, and Thomas immediately expressed a desire to reverse the 1973 decision, and Kennedy and Souter initially seemed willing to join them. But O'Connor, who had demonstrated a growing independent streak over the previous few Court terms, expressed deep reservations. Regarding *Casey,* she objected to the spousal notification provision, which she felt could endanger women whose husbands were abusive. She also expressed great reluctance to overturn *Roe*. She agreed with Kolbert's argument that American women had come to depend on access to legal abortion in the two decades since the case was decided.

Without telling the other justices, O'Connor arranged meetings with Kennedy and Souter. They discussed the importance of honoring precedents (previous Court rulings) in maintaining people's respect for the American justice system. They also considered the immense political pressure and heated public debate that surrounded the abortion issue. The three justices eventually decided to work together to write a joint opinion in the *Casey* case. The opinion would uphold most of the Pennsylvania abortion restrictions, but it would also reaffirm the Court's basic holding in *Roe*—that American women had a legal right to abortion.

The Supreme Court announced its decision in *Planned Parenthood v. Casey* on June 29, 1992. The opinion was unusual because it was written and read into the public record by three justices, rather than one. The ruling highlighted the deep divisions that had formed in the Court over the abortion issue: the more liberal members (Blackmun and

As the first woman to serve on the Supreme Court, Justice Sandra Day O'Connor played an influential role in the debate over abortion rights.

Stevens) joined the part of the opinion that reaffirmed *Roe* and dissented on the part that upheld the Pennsylvania law, while the more conservative members (Rehnquist, White, Scalia, and Thomas) did the opposite. Between these two extremes, however, stood a newly formed group of moderates (O'Connor, Kennedy, and Souter) who seemed to be searching for a compromise.

The first part of the *Casey* ruling, written by Kennedy, expressed sympathy for women facing the difficult decision of whether to terminate a pregnancy. It also emphasized the justices' opinion that, at least during the first trimester, women had a right to make such decisions for themselves. "The liberty of the woman is at stake in a sense unique to the human condition and so unique to the law," he wrote. "The mother who carries a child to full term is subject to anxieties, to physical constraints, to pain that only she must bear.... Her suffering is too intimate and personal for the state to insist, without more, upon its own vision of the woman's role.... The destiny of the woman must be shaped to a large extent on her own conception of her spiritual imperatives and her place in society."

Kennedy also stated that "the essential holding of *Roe v. Wade* should be retained and once again reaffirmed." He went on, however, to present an interpretation of *Roe* that was much narrower than the actual text of the 1973 ruling. Although Kennedy agreed that women had a right to abortion in the first trimester of pregnancy without undue interference from the state, he also said that the state had an interest in protecting the fetus from the moment of conception. In this way, he and the concurring justices gave states the legal authority to regulate abortion throughout pregnancy. States still could not prohibit abortion, so it remained legal, but their ability to restrict abortion expanded considerably.

The second part of the *Casey* opinion, written by Souter, discussed the importance of *stare decisis*, the idea that courts should respect earlier decisions in order to promote stability in the law. Souter described the *Roe* decision as a long-settled legal precedent that millions of Americans had come to depend upon. "The ability of women to participate equally in the economic and social life of the Nation has been facilitated by their ability to control their reproductive lives," he stated. Souter argued that reversing *Roe* due to political pressure would therefore erode public respect for the Court.

Planned Parenthood v. Casey Establishes the Undue Burden Test

The third part of the *Casey* opinion, written by O'Connor, explained the Court's decision to uphold the Pennsylvania law. She discussed each provision point-by-point and explained why each was permissible under the new interpretation of *Roe*. After several attempts, O'Connor had finally succeeded in replacing Blackmun's trimester formula with her own "undue burden" test as the standard for determining whether certain restrictions on abortion were legal.

The formula that Blackmun had laid out in the *Roe* decision said that states could not restrict abortion at all during the first trimester of pregnancy. Restrictions intended to protect the life of the fetus were not allowed until the point of viability, when the fetus was mature enough to survive outside the womb. O'Connor's undue burden test, in contrast, permitted states to regulate abortion throughout pregnancy, as long as the regulations did not create a "substantial obstacle in the path of a woman seeking an abortion before the fetus attains viability." O'Connor noted that under this standard, states could

As the Supreme Court prepared to hear arguments in *Planned Parenthood v. Casey,* the National Organization for Women (NOW) and other pro-choice groups organized major demonstrations.

pass laws that were openly intended to discourage women from having abortions. "A state measure designed to persuade her to choose childbirth over abortion will be upheld if reasonably related to that goal," she wrote.

All of the provisions of the Pennsylvania law passed the undue burden test except for the requirement that married women notify their spouses before having an abortion. The Court thus upheld a number of restrictions that it had struck down in earlier cases, such as *Akron* and *Thornburgh.* Nevertheless, the majority opinion in Casey also insisted that American women still had a legal right to abortion. "Our adoption of the undue burden analysis does not disturb the central holding of *Roe v. Wade,* and we reaffirm that holding," the Court stated. "Regardless of whether exceptions are made for particular circumstances, a State may not prohibit any woman from making the ultimate decision to terminate her pregnancy before viability."

The attempt at compromise by the three moderate justices did not get the full support of their colleagues on either side of the abortion issue. Scalia joined the part of the *Casey* opinion that upheld the Pennsylvania restrictions, but he also wrote a stinging dissent attacking the part of the ruling that reaffirmed *Roe*. "The right to abort, we are told, inheres in 'liberty' because it is among 'a person's most basic decisions'... it involves a 'most intimate and personal choice,'" he wrote. "The same adjectives can be applied to many forms of conduct that this Court has held are not entitled to constitutional protection—because, like abortion, they are forms of conduct that have been long criminalized in American society. Those adjectives might be applied, for example, to homosexual sodomy, polygamy, adult incest, and suicide, all of which are equally 'intimate' and 'deeply personal' decisions involving 'personal autonomy and bodily integrity.'" He declared that the Court should "get out of this area [of law], where we have no right to be, and where we do neither ourselves nor the country any good in remaining."

Blackmun, on the other hand, praised the moderate group for preserving his basic holding in *Roe*. He called their decision to reaffirm a woman's legal right to abortion "an act of personal courage" in the face of tremendous political pressure. But Blackmun also criticized the part of the majority opinion that upheld various Pennsylvania abortion restrictions. He concluded by pointing out that the final vote had been very close. "I am 83 years old. I cannot remain on this Court forever, and when I do step down, the confirmation process for my successor may well focus on the issue before us today," he wrote. "I fear for the darkness as four Justices anxiously await the single vote necessary to extinguish the light."

Reaction to the *Casey* Decision

After the *Casey* decision was announced, both pro-choice and pro-life leaders focused on the fact that the Court had come within one vote of overturning *Roe v. Wade*. For the pro-life movement, the ruling was mostly a terrible disappointment. Many activists felt angry, frustrated, and betrayed when the conservative justices appointed by Reagan and Bush failed to reverse *Roe*. But others, like defendant Robert Casey, chose to focus on the positive things the ruling gave the pro-life cause. "The decision, while not overturning *Roe,* clearly returns to the people the power to regulate abortion in reasonable ways, so as to protect maternal health and reduce the number of abortions in our country," he declared one day after the ruling was announced.

Many pro-choice activists also viewed the *Casey* decision as a disappointment. Although they were relieved that the ruling confirmed a woman's legal right to abortion, they worried that increasing state regulation would make it nearly impossible for many women to exercise that right. "In theory, *Roe v. Wade* is still on the books, but in terms of how it impacts women's lives, it is a shadow of its former self," Sarah Weddington said in an interview for *Newsday*. "Up to now, the Court has said, 'It's a woman's decision, and you people in the legislature, leave her alone.' Now they're saying, 'It's still her decision, but you people in the legislature can erect hurdles and roadblocks so that only women who are the most determined, who have the most money, who are the most sophisticated make it through.'"

Still other observers felt that the Casey ruling represented an important change in the Court's view of abortion. *New York Times* columnist Anna Quindlen, for instance, argued that—for the first time in dozens of cases heard since 1973—the justices demonstrated a full understanding of the abortion decision and its impact on women. "Justices once thought hostile to the unique questions of liberty and privacy raised by this issue apprehend them in ways we did not imagine," she wrote. "They got it, folks. And I, for one, applaud."

> *"The [Planned Parenthood v. Casey] decision, while not overturning* Roe, *clearly returns to the people the power to regulate abortion in reasonable ways," stated Pennsylvania Governor Robert Casey.*

The Court's compromise in *Casey* also reflected the profound ambivalence with which many Americans viewed abortion. A *USA Today*/CNN/ Gallup poll conducted the day after the decision was announced found that 34 percent of respondents supported unrestricted access to abortion, while 13 percent felt that abortion should be illegal. But the largest group of respondents, 48 percent, fell somewhere between those two positions—they wanted abortion to be legal, but subject to some restrictions. When asked for an opinion on the restrictions that were upheld in *Casey,* an average of 70 percent expressed support for each one.

Close Call Mobilizes Pro-Choice Voters

The Supreme Court handed down its *Casey* decision just a few months before the 1992 presidential election. Republican President George Bush ran for reelection on a pro-life platform that included support for a constitutional

President Bill Clinton (center, flanked by Vice President Al Gore and Attorney General Janet Reno) supported abortion rights throughout his eight years in the White House.

amendment banning abortion. His Democratic opponent, Arkansas Governor Bill Clinton, ran on a pro-choice platform. Throughout his campaign, Clinton promised to appoint federal judges who would support a woman's right to choose abortion. Upset at how close the Supreme Court had come to reversing *Roe,* pro-choice voters flocked to the polls to help Clinton win the election.

Shortly after taking office, Clinton made a number of policy changes that pleased his pro-choice supporters. First, he lifted the gag rule that had prohibited doctors at government-funded health clinics from discussing abortion with their patients. Next, the new president convinced Congress to change the Hyde amendment—which prevented federal assistance programs like Medicaid from paying for abortions—to allow victims of rape or incest to receive government-funded abortions. Clinton also allowed doctors on U.S. military bases to perform abortions.

In June 1993 Clinton became the first Democratic president in 16 years to nominate a new Supreme Court justice. Byron White, one of the dissenters in *Roe,* decided to retire. As his replacement, Clinton chose Ruth Bader Ginsburg, a professor at Columbia Law School who had argued a number of sex discrimination cases as a lawyer for the American Civil Liberties Union (ACLU). Although Ginsburg had published articles questioning the Court's reasoning in *Roe,* she was a strong supporter of abortion rights. She still won confirmation in the Senate by a vote of 96-3.

A year later, upon the retirement of *Roe* author Harry Blackmun, Clinton made a second Supreme Court appointment. He selected Stephen G. Breyer, a moderate judge who did not express a strong opinion about the abortion issue. Some pro-life activists protested his nomination anyway, arguing that Breyer must hold pro-choice views or he would not have passed Clinton's judicial "litmus test." Nevertheless, Breyer easily won confirmation in the Senate.

A New Wave of Violence

Clinton's appointment of two new Supreme Court justices helped ease the fears of pro-choice activists that *Roe* would be overturned. Supporters of abortion rights also felt confident that the president would veto any anti-abortion legislation that might be passed in Congress. At the same time, though, Clinton's policy changes and judicial appointments created a great deal of anger and frustration among pro-life activists. After waging a series of successful battles in courts and legislatures throughout the 1980s, the pro-life movement found itself facing a difficult political situation in the 1990s. Some pro-life activists decided that political change was impossible with Clinton in the White House. A small number of radical activists shifted their focus toward aggressive, often violent efforts to end abortion.

Pro-life extremists targeted abortion clinics with a new wave of bombings and arson attacks in 1992. The following year, the violence escalated to include murder. The first incident took place at an abortion clinic in Pensacola, Florida, where a radical anti-abortion protester named Michael Griffin killed David Gunn, a doctor who worked there. Although mainstream pro-life organizations condemned the murder, some activists defended Griffin's actions.

One of these activists, former minister Paul Hill (see "Anti-Abortion Extremist Paul Hill," p. 104), told a national television audience that killing

Anti-Abortion Extremist Paul Hill

The violence aimed at abortion clinics throughout the 1980s eventually escalated to include murder. In one highly publicized incident, anti-abortion extremist Paul Hill shot and killed Dr. John Britton and his volunteer escort, James Barrett, outside of an abortion clinic in Pensacola, Florida, on July 29, 1994. Hill defended his actions as "justifiable homicide" because he had prevented the doctor from performing further abortions. Hill was convicted of murder and received the death penalty. In 2003 he became the first person to be executed for killing an abortion provider.

Paul Jennings Hill was born on February 6, 1954. After graduating from Belhaven College and Reformed Theological Seminary in 1984, he spent seven years serving as a minister in the Presbyterian Church in America and the Orthodox Presbyterian Church. He then left the ministry and moved to Pensacola with his wife and three children. Hill started a business preparing vehicles to be sold at car dealerships and used car lots.

In early 1993 Hill became a pro-life activist. He often marched outside a local abortion clinic, the Ladies Center, holding a large sign that said: "Execute Murderers, Abortionists, Accessories." On March 10 of that year, a fellow activist named Michael Griffin killed a physician who worked at the clinic, Dr. David Gunn, in the nation's first abortion-related murder since the *Roe* decision.

A few days later, Hill made a controversial appearance on the nationally televised talk show "Donahue." He argued that shooting an abortion provider was justified because it prevented the murder of countless unborn

an abortionist was "justifiable homicide" because it saved the lives of innocent babies. In 1994, Hill murdered Dr. John Britton and his volunteer escort, James Barrett, outside the same Pensacola clinic. Later that year, radical pro-life activist John Salvi killed two receptionists and wounded several other people during a shooting rampage at two abortion clinics in Brookline, Massachusetts. Hill was eventually executed for his crime, while Salvi committed suicide in prison.

children. Hill claimed that, according to the Bible, "it is not enough to refrain from committing murder; innocent people must also be protected." He said that the government, by legalizing abortion, forced citizens to commit the sin of standing by while murders took place. In such cases, he argued, Christians had a duty to obey the laws of God rather than those of men.

Hill's outspoken defense of Griffin brought him a great deal of media attention and led to his appearance on several other television shows. Over time, Hill decided to commit murder himself because he believed it would advance the pro-life cause. "I realized ... that using the force necessary to defend the unborn gives credibility, urgency, and direction to the pro-life movement which it has lacked and which it needs in order to prevail," he wrote in an article called "Defending the Defenseless." "I was certain that if I took my stand at this point, others would join with me, and the Lord would eventually bring about a great victory."

After Hill killed Britton and Barrett, the mainstream pro-life movement condemned his actions. "We have no right to destroy life," the Reverend Emory Hingst told the *National Catholic Reporter*. He added that the reasoning used by Hill and other extremists "remind me of how militant Muslims and others on the edge of fundamentalism rationalize their actions. They are a small minority."

Hill was quickly arrested, tried, and convicted of murder. During his trial, the judge denied his request to present "justifiable homicide" as a formal defense. After receiving a sentence of death, Hill expressed no regret for his actions and waived his right to appeal his conviction. He was executed by lethal injection on September 3, 2003.

Outraged by the violent acts of a few radical individuals and fringe groups, many Americans adopted a negative view of the entire pro-life movement. Although the leaders of mainstream pro-life groups denied any responsibility for the violence, critics accused them of framing the abortion debate in a way that inflamed the passions of extremists. They pointed to pro-life literature that described abortion as the murder of innocent children and called doctors who performed abortions "baby killers." Some prominent members of the movement compared legalized abortion to the Holocaust, when Nazi Germany orchestrated the murder of six million European Jews during World War II. Critics claimed that radical protesters might view such terminology as a justification for murder.

Congress Passes the FACE Act

Public outrage over the wave of violence helped convince Congress to take steps to protect abortion clinics. In 1994 it passed the Freedom of Access to Clinic Entrances (FACE) Act, which made it a federal crime for pro-life protesters to blockade the entrances to abortion clinics. The legislation also established new criminal and civil penalties for people convicted of threatening or violent acts against abortion clinics. The stated purpose of the FACE Act was "to protect and promote the public safety and health ... by establishing federal criminal penalties and civil remedies for certain violent, threatening, obstructive, and destructive conduct that is intended to injure, intimidate, or interfere with persons seeking to obtain or provide reproductive health services."

Pro-life leaders said that the FACE Act violated their constitutional rights to freedom of speech and freedom of assembly. They argued that all pro-life protesters should not be subject to criminal sanctions based on the violent acts of a few individuals. They also claimed that blockades and similar protest tactics had been used legally in the past by feminist and civil rights organizations. A pro-life group's lawsuit challenging the constitutionality of the FACE Act was unsuccessful, however, and the Supreme Court refused to hear an appeal.

A number of abortion providers sued pro-life protesters under the FACE Act, and a few clinics were awarded large amounts in civil damages. For example, an abortion doctor in Dallas, Texas, won an $8.5 million court judgment against several pro-life groups. He successfully argued that the groups had used intimidation, harassment, and blockades to force his clinic to go out of business. Many abortion providers had trouble collecting the damages they won in court, however, because the more aggressive pro-life activists learned to hide their money and other assets. The FACE Act proved to be a disappointment to others in the pro-choice movement, as well, because it resulted in very few criminal prosecutions.

The Supreme Court Restricts Anti-Abortion Protests

A 1994 Supreme Court decision gave pro-choice groups another weapon to use in their legal battles against pro-life protesters. In *National Organiza-*

Responding to a wave of violent incidents at abortion clinics, the federal government cracked down on pro-life protests during the 1990s. In this photo, an Operation Rescue member is arrested for blockading the entrance to a clinic in Washington, D.C.

tion for Women (NOW) v. Joseph Scheidler, the justices ruled that pro-choice groups had a right to sue pro-life protesters under the federal Racketeering Influenced Corrupt Organization (RICO) laws. RICO laws were originally enacted to help victims of organized crime collect monetary damages from mobsters. In ruling that RICO statutes applied to anti-abortion protests, the Court essentially found that such tactics as harassment, threats, blockades, and destruction of property constituted a criminal conspiracy against abortion clinics.

The Supreme Court continued to limit anti-abortion protests through the remainder of the 1990s. In such cases as *Madsen v. Women's Health Center* (1994), *Schenck v. Pro-Choice Network* (1997), and *Hill v. Colorado* (2000), the Court repeatedly upheld laws that allowed abortion clinics to create a fixed "buffer zone" that was off-limits to pro-life protesters. Abortion providers argued that the buffer zones were needed to enable staff members and patients to enter the clinics safely, without being subjected to threats and harassment from protesters. Pro-life activists, on the other hand, argued that the buffer zones prevented them from exercising their right to free speech. Although the Court allowed fixed buffer zones around clinic entrances, it struck down laws that attempted to establish moving buffer zones to keep protesters away from people entering and leaving clinics.

By 1999, more than 40,000 people had been arrested for violating the various laws aimed at protecting abortion clinics. But the crackdown on clinic protests led several extremists to attack abortion providers in other locations. In October 1998, for instance, a sniper killed Dr. Barnett Slepian as he stood in the kitchen of his home in Amherst, New York. A number of radical pro-life groups put the names and addresses of doctors who performed abortions on their Web sites.

In the meantime, law-abiding pro-life groups and their many supporters continued their efforts to end abortion through the political process. They succeeded in restoring a pro-life Republican majority to the U.S. House of Representatives during the 1994 elections. Between 1995 and 2003, they also successfully lobbied state legislatures to pass more than 300 new laws restricting abortion. The pro-life movement thus made quiet gains during Clinton's presidency. As Clinton's second term drew to a close in the late 1990s, opponents of abortion appeared poised to move the abortion debate back to the forefront of American politics.

Chapter Seven

ROE'S LEGACY: THE BATTLE CONTINUES

◄───⋘∿⋙───►

A generation later there is no more unsettled and unsettling question in American public life, and a settlement is nowhere in sight. For the next generation as well, it seems possible that abortion will be the ... crossroads where conflicting visions of the kind of people we are and should be will do battle.

—"*Roe: 25 Years Later," First Things,* January 1998.

Eight years with a Democrat in the White House encouraged many Americans with pro-choice leanings. President Bill Clinton's Supreme Court appointments reduced the threat that *Roe v. Wade* would be overturned, and the president seemed likely to veto any new federal restrictions on abortion. This situation caused some pro-choice voters to relax and become complacent. "As women got used to possessing some reproductive rights—and to making what felt like private, individual decisions about when and if to call on these rights— many Americans seemed to forget about the past," Rickie Solinger charged in *Pregnancy and Power.* "The vulnerability and danger that women had faced in all areas of their lives before the laws changed seemed to slip away."

In the meantime, the number of abortions performed each year in the United States declined steadily during the 1990s. Many people on both sides of the issue applauded this trend. Some attributed the changes to such factors as improved methods of birth control, more effective sex education, and a gradual change in attitudes toward abortion. Others credited the changes to efforts to promote strong moral values, abstinence programs, and alternatives like adoption.

Some pro-choice leaders, however, argued that the number of abortions had declined mainly because women's access to the procedure had become more limited. The Supreme Court ruling in *Planned Parenthood v. Casey* had narrowed the scope of *Roe* and allowed states to pass new laws restricting abortion. These laws made it more complicated, time-consuming, and expensive for women to terminate pregnancies. In addition, news reports about incidents of harassment and violence made some women afraid to go to abortion clinics. Finally, fewer clinics offered abortion services, and fewer doctors were willing to perform the procedure.

RU 486: The Abortion Pill

Although the availability of surgical abortion generally declined during the 1990s, the pro-choice movement gained a new non-surgical abortion method toward the end of Clinton's time in office. A French pharmaceutical company, Roussel Uclaf, developed a drug that caused a miscarriage to occur when a woman took it in early pregnancy. The company had sold this drug, RU 486 or mifepristone, in Europe for several years. Roussel Uclaf did not attempt to market it in the United States, however, because pro-life groups threatened to organize a boycott of the company's other pharmaceutical products. Since the company did not seek U.S. government approval, the drug remained illegal in America.

Pro-choice activists wanted to make RU 486 available to American women. They felt that the drug had the potential to change the nature of the debate by reducing the role of abortion clinics in ending unwanted pregnancies. Instead of having to make one or more trips to an abortion clinic—where she might be harassed by protesters—a woman could get a prescription for RU 486 from her doctor, pick it up at a neighborhood pharmacy, and take the pills in the privacy of her home. Pro-life activists opposed the drug, arguing that chemical abortions still resulted in the death of a fetus. They also claimed that RU 486 made abortion too easy, and thus allowed women to avoid taking responsibility for terminating their pregnancies.

In 1992, longtime pro-choice activist Lawrence Lader arranged for a pregnant woman to bring RU 486 into the country illegally from France. He wanted her to be charged with a crime so that he could file a lawsuit, with the ultimate goal of legalizing the drug through a court order. In the meantime, pro-choice groups asked the Food and Drug Administration (FDA) to approve RU 486 for use in the United States. Under pressure from pro-life members of Congress, the agency refused to consider the drug for approval

Abortion became a central issue in American politics, including the 2004 presidential race between Democratic candidate John Kerry (left) and Republican President George W. Bush.

for many years. Finally, citing the history of safe use of the drug overseas and the need to keep politics out of medical decisions, the FDA approved the manufacture and sale of RU 486 on September 28, 2000. The FDA decision effectively ended Lader's legal case.

Although proponents claim that RU 486 is easy to use and is 95 percent effective in ending pregnancies, they acknowledge that it does have limitations. It can only be used in the first nine weeks of pregnancy, for instance, and it is not recommended for older women or for women who smoke. It can also cause side effects like abdominal pain and heavy bleeding.

Another method of chemical abortion is the Plan B emergency contraceptive, also known as the "morning-after pill." This drug consists of a high dose of the hormones typically found in birth-control pills. Taken within three days of unprotected sex, Plan B can prevent a fertilized egg from being implanted in a woman's uterus. In 2006 the FDA approved it as an over-the-counter (non-prescription) drug for use by women 18 and older. Some people consider Plan B a form of birth control rather than an abortion pill, since it causes the egg to be expelled before the embryo begins to develop. But others disagree, arguing that human life begins at the moment of conception. Critics also claim that the drug poses dangers to women's health and may also increase their risks of getting sexually transmitted diseases.

Bush Appoints New Justices

The 2000 presidential election took place just a few months after the FDA approved RU 486. Pro-life Republican candidate George W. Bush, the former governor of Texas and eldest son of President George H.W. Bush, ran against pro-choice Democratic candidate Al Gore, who had served as vice president under Clinton. The results of the election were so close that the winner could not be determined for several weeks. After several controversial recounts in the battleground state of Florida, the Supreme Court finally stepped in to halt the process. By a 5-4 vote that broke down along conservative-liberal lines, the Court ended a recount that was Gore's main hope for claiming victory. Bush was declared the winner of the election and became the next president of the United States.

Members of the pro-life movement celebrated Bush's victory. Shortly after taking office, the new president pleased his supporters by reversing some of Clinton's policies on abortion. For instance, he reinstated the gag rule, which prohibited doctors at federally funded family-planning clinics from discussing abortion with their patients. He also restored the ban on federal funding for abortion and appointed John Ashcroft—a longtime opponent of abortion—as attorney general. Many pro-choice activists were alarmed by what they viewed as the administration's assault on abortion rights. According to *Newsweek,* membership in the National Abortion Rights Action League (NARAL) increased by 70 percent following Bush's election.

As Bush's first term in office neared an end, many observers predicted that the winner of the 2004 presidential election would have the opportunity to make significant changes to the Supreme Court. After all, Clinton had made the last new appointment a decade earlier, and several of the justices had experienced health problems since then. In the election, Bush defeated his Democratic rival, Senator John Kerry of Massachusetts, to win a second term.

Pro-choice activists protest against the 2005 nomination of John Roberts as Chief Justice of the Supreme Court.

The predictions of Supreme Court changes came true in July 2005, when Justice Sandra Day O'Connor announced her retirement. Bush nominated John Roberts, a conservative federal judge, to replace her. Before Roberts could be confirmed, however, Chief Justice William Rehnquist died of cancer. Bush then decided to nominate Roberts to replace Rehnquist instead. Roberts was confirmed as chief justice in late 2005, and another conservative federal judge, Samuel Alito, took over O'Connor's seat in early 2006.

During its first term, the Roberts Court showed signs of shifting toward a more conservative judicial philosophy, especially in its rulings on cases dealing with abortion, racial diversity, and religion. Roberts and Alito generally voted with the Court's most reliable conservatives, Antonin Scalia and Clarence Thomas. Meanwhile, Justices Ruth Bader Ginsburg, John Paul Stevens, David Souter, and Stephen Breyer continued to take a more liberal position on most of the cases they heard. Anthony Kennedy, who had worked with O'Connor to craft the opinion in *Casey*, became a swing voter who usually sided with the conservatives. The Court handed down a number of 5-4 rulings that were decided along these lines.

Many pro-life leaders were pleased with the changes Bush made to the Supreme Court. They hoped that the new justices would eventually vote to end legal abortion in the United States. In the meantime, pro-life legislators in several states passed new laws restricting abortion. Some of these laws went beyond the limits that the Court had established in *Casey*, in part because pro-life lawmakers wanted to test the new justices' commitment to preserving *Roe*. South Dakota, for instance, passed a law banning nearly all abortions, except when a doctor deemed it necessary to save a woman's life. The state legislature also established criminal penalties of up to five years in prison for doctors who performed abortions in violation of the law.

Partial-Birth Abortion

The first major abortion decision made by the Roberts Court concerned a controversial late-term abortion procedure. Called intact dilation and extraction in medical terminology, it was known to critics as partial-birth abortion. Although it was used very rarely—and usually in cases where the mother's health was at risk—this abortion method disgusted and horrified many people. It involved pulling the fetus into the birth canal, then crushing its skull before removing it from the mother's body. Pro-life activists considered this procedure barbaric and morally indefensible, and even some supporters of abortion rights expressed reservations about the practice.

The first partial-birth abortion case had reached the Court in April 2000. It concerned a Nebraska law that banned the procedure and established severe criminal penalties for doctors who used it. Dr. Leroy Carhart, a Nebraska abortion provider, sued the state attorney general, Donald Stenberg. Carhart argued that for some women, under certain circumstances, intact dilation and extraction was the safest abortion method. He also claimed that the law was so vaguely worded that it could apply to other, more commonly used abortion methods, like dilation and evacuation. In a bitter 5-4 decision in *Carhart v. Stenberg*, the Supreme Court agreed with the doctor and struck down the Nebraska law. The majority found that the law created an undue burden for women seeking abortions and prevented doctors from using their best medical judgment to protect their patients' health.

President George W. Bush stands with the U.S. Supreme Court after the 2005 confirmation of Chief Justice John Roberts. Standing from left to right are Ruth Bader Ginsberg, David H. Souter, Antonin Scalia, John Paul Stevens, Roberts, Bush, Sandra Day O'Connor, Anthony Kennedy, Clarence Thomas, and Stephen Breyer.

Pro-life activists were appalled by the ruling and continued fighting to outlaw partial-birth abortion. Thirty more states passed their own bans on the procedure over the next few years, but many of the laws were struck down by federal courts. In 2003 the U.S. Congress took action on the issue by passing the Partial-Birth Abortion Ban Act, which Bush signed into law. It prohibited the use of any abortion method that was performed with part of the fetus extending outside of the mother's body.

Carhart and a group of other doctors filed a lawsuit against the federal government and Bush's new attorney general, Alberto Gonzales, to prevent the law from taking effect. As before, the doctors argued that the law was vaguely worded, posed an undue burden under *Casey,* and violated the 2000 *Stenberg* ruling because it did not include an exception to protect the mother's health. Gonzales defended the law, claiming that it clearly applied only to one specific method of abortion, and therefore did not create an undue burden. He also argued that a health exception was not required because, in writing the law, Congress had determined that partial-birth abortion was never necessary to protect a woman's health.

On April 18, 2007, the Roberts Court voted 5-4 to uphold the federal Partial-Birth Abortion Ban Act. The majority opinion, written by Kennedy, found that the law was not vague, applied only to the intact dilation and extraction method, and therefore did not create an undue burden for women seeking abortions. The Court also decided that the law did not have to include an exception to protect the mother's health. The ruling said Congress could make its own determination about whether the procedure was ever medically necessary, even if that was a subject of disagreement among doctors. In a dissenting opinion, Ginsburg claimed that the majority had demonstrated its feelings of "hostility to the right *Roe* and *Casey* secured."

Pro-life leaders applauded the Court's ruling in *Carhart v. Gonzales*. Calling it "an important step forward," the *National Right to Life News* declared that "abortionists can no longer get away with bringing a child to within inches of live-birth status before killing her." Pro-choice activists, on the other hand, worried that the ruling would encourage state legislatures to move further toward passing outright bans on abortion. Writing in *Women's Health Activist*, Sarah Nelson described the ruling as "the judicial equivalent of declaring open hunting season on access to safe and legal abortion services."

Many doctors also opposed the ruling, which they felt intruded on their ability to make sound medical decisions for their patients. Dr. Wendy Chavkin, the head of Physicians for Reproductive Choice and Health, issued a statement denouncing the Supreme Court decision. "This ruling is a clarion call to all Americans who believe politics has no place in the doctor's office," she wrote. "If a federal law can ban an abortion method—even in cases when a woman's health is at risk—what will be next? Will politicians be allowed to outlaw every medical procedure they personally oppose?"

The Debate Continues

The 2007 Supreme Court ruling in *Carhart v. Gonzales* was yet another battle in the long war over abortion rights in America. On January 22, 2008, the thirty-fifth anniversary of *Roe v. Wade*, the nation remained as deeply

Statistics on Abortion in the United States

The Alan Guttmacher Institute conducts research and compiles statistics on abortion worldwide. A variety of information is available on the organization's Web site, http://www.guttmacher.org. The list below includes data from a 2002 AGI study of abortion in the United States:

—Over the 30-year period following the 1973 *Roe* decision, more than 42 million legal abortions were performed.

—The number of abortions per 1,000 women aged 15-44 increased from 16.3 in 1973 to peak at 29.3 in 1981, then declined steadily to reach a level of 21.1 by 2001.

—Abortion ended an estimated 40 percent of unplanned pregnancies, and 24 percent of all pregnancies.

—60 percent of the women who had abortions in a certain year had previously given birth to a child, while 48 percent had previously had an abortion.

—54 percent of the women undergoing abortions reported using contraceptives during the month they became pregnant, while 46 percent did not.

—88 percent of all abortions took place during the first 12 weeks of pregnancy.

—Less than 0.3 percent of women undergoing abortions experienced complications that required a hospital visit.

—As of 2001, the total number of abortion providers in the country was 1,819, a decline of 11 percent from five years earlier. Only 13 percent of U.S. counties had an abortion provider.

—The average cost of a routine surgical abortion in early pregnancy was $372, and the average cost of a chemical (RU-486) abortion was $490.

divided as ever on the issue of legal abortion (see "The War That Never Ends: Abortion in America," p. 208). These divisions have caused fundamental changes in American society, culture, and politics during the three-and-a-half decades since the landmark decision.

Many people believe that the intense debate over abortion has led to significant changes in the American political system. Beginning with the election of Ronald Reagan in 1980, the Republican Party defined itself as pro-life, and the Democratic Party adopted the pro-choice position (see "The Democratic Party Platform Supports Reproductive Choice," p. 206, and "The Republican Party Platform Opposes Abortion," p. 207). Party affiliations, which had long been determined by factors like social class and education levels, were increasingly determined by people's views on abortion. Religious conservatives flocked to the Republican Party, for example, whether they were wealthy New England Catholics or working-class Southern Baptists. As the two parties became more polarized in their positions on abortion, many people noticed an overall decline in the tone of political discourse in the United States. Productive, civilized debate on the substance of issues increasingly gave way to name-calling, posturing, and obstruction.

The abortion issue also had a profound impact on the American legal system. The U.S. Constitution created three branches of government—executive, legislative, and judicial—that were supposed to remain separate and balance the power of each other. To ensure that the Supreme Court would not be subject to political pressure, justices were nominated by the president, and confirmed by the Senate, to serve lifelong terms. In the years following the *Roe* decision, however, every potential Supreme Court justice has been evaluated primarily on the basis of his or her views on legal abortion, rather than on the basis of experience, constitutional knowledge, or overall judicial philosophy. Some critics claim that this practice has led to a decline in both the quality of justices and in people's respect for the law.

Some feminists believe that the legalization of abortion was a key factor in improving the status of women in American society. They argue that abortion rights allowed women to take greater control over their lives and destinies. Making their own decisions about whether and when to have children, they contend, helped women achieve greater equality with men in the areas of education, employment, and family life. After feminists gained abortion rights, they went on to win passage of many laws protecting women's rights in the home and workplace, including laws against spousal abuse, sexual harassment, and discrimination on the basis of pregnancy. Supporters of legal abortion also claim that *Roe v. Wade* protected women's health by putting an end to dangerous "back alley" and self-induced abortions. The number of women who died or suffered serious infections from abortion procedures dropped dramatically after 1973, until abortion became statistically safer than childbirth.

On the other hand, some feminists oppose abortion because they believe that it allows men to take advantage of women and avoid responsibility for fathering children. Faced with a sexual partner's unplanned pregnancy, some men pressure the woman to have an abortion by threatening to withhold financial and emotional support if she decides to continue the pregnancy. These feminists point out that women who feel coerced to have an abortion are more likely to suffer feelings of guilt and depression afterward. Other women's rights advocates oppose abortion because they feel it contributes to social and racial injustice. They argue that poor, minority, and immigrant women are often encouraged to end unplanned pregnancies, rather than bear children that will require welfare and other forms of public assistance to support.

Finally, many people believe that the legalization of abortion has contributed to an overall decline in moral values in American society. Opponents of abortion claim that the *Roe v. Wade* decision helped create a "culture of death" in the United States. They argue that the Supreme Court ruling made people think it was acceptable to end a human being's life for the sake of convenience. As evidence of this trend, they point to movements toward legalizing euthanasia for extremely ill, disabled, or elderly people. Many people also believe that the availability of abortion has led to an increase in immoral and irresponsible sexual behavior in the United States. The ability to terminate an unwanted pregnancy, they argue, encourages women to be promiscuous and to reject traditional female roles. They feel that this behavior is reinforced by American popular culture, which bombards people with sexually suggestive messages.

Roe's Place in the Debate

The *Roe v. Wade* decision has long served as the focal point in the national debate over abortion. The pro-life side has spent more than three decades fighting to overturn the ruling, which it often portrays as the main source of the bitter controversy over abortion. The pro-choice side has fought equally hard to preserve the ruling, which it often portrays as the only thing protecting women's rights in America. Both sides agree that overturning *Roe* will create a whole new world, but they strongly disagree about the desirability of that world.

In reality, however, some people question whether overturning *Roe* would have a major impact on the lives of most Americans. Even if the Supreme Court reversed the 1973 decision, abortion would not suddenly become illegal in the United States. Instead, the legal status of abortion would once again become a matter for state governments to decide. In some cases, state laws that applied before *Roe* would come back into effect. Only four states made abortion legal under all circumstances in 1973, but most others allowed abortion under certain circumstances. In other cases, state abortion laws that had been revised since *Roe* would continue to apply. A few state legislatures might decide to ban abortion, while other states might decide to present the question to voters. In short, no one is certain what would happen, but many experts predict that abortion would mostly remain legal but be subject to restrictions. In other words, its status would likely remain similar to what it has become under the Supreme Court's narrowing interpretation of *Roe*.

If *Roe* were overturned, making abortion illegal throughout the United States would still require either a constitutional amendment or a federal ban. If this were to occur, statistics from other countries suggest that abortions would still be performed, but the procedure would become significantly more dangerous for women. A 2007 study by the pro-choice Alan Guttmacher Institute and the World Health Organization found that abortion is no less prevalent in countries where it is prohibited, but it is less safe.

Even if *Roe* was overturned, therefore, the abortion issue would continue to generate intense debate. Some observers point out that, for both pro-life and pro-choice groups, the real subject of the debate extends beyond abortion. "The storm that formed during and after *Roe* was so bitter because both sides saw abortion not as a simple, limited legal issue, but as one that represented two opposing moral worlds," N.E.H. Hull and Peter Charles Hoffer noted in *Roe v. Wade: The Abortion Rights Controversy in American History.* "For pro-abortion rights forces, choice was a moral principle that went far beyond abortion rights; for anti-abortion rights groups, fetal life was a moral principle that reached out to the sacred memory of traditional families and motherhood."

Some people claim that overturning *Roe* would at least remove the debate from the American legal system, which is not well-equipped to deal with it. "We're in a real mess here, trying to fit a profound and intimate mat-

The bitter debate over abortion continued in 2006, when pro-life activists marched in Washington, D.C., to mark the 33rd anniversary of the *Roe v. Wade* decision.

ter into a system more suited to tax codes and property issues," columnist Anna Quindlen wrote in *Newsweek*. "That's because abortion is unlike any other matter and pregnancy is different from any other state of being."

Seeking Common Ground

The long, bitter national debate over abortion has led most Americans to choose a side. Membership in American society practically demands it: political parties, candidates for office, religious groups, and many other organizations have come to define themselves by their positions on abortion. Yet many polls show that, on a personal level, most Americans have conflicting, even ambivalent feelings about abortion (see "Anna Quindlen Describes Her Conflicting Feelings about Abortion," p. 192). "Most of us are torn by the abortion question. There is something deeply misleading about discussing the abortion debate solely in terms of a clash between pro-life 'groups' and pro-choice 'groups,' as though each of us could properly be labeled as belonging to one camp or the other," Laurence Tribe wrote in *Abortion: The Clash of Absolutes*. "Whatever someone's 'bottom line'—whether it is that the choice must belong to the woman or that she must be prevented from killing the fetus—it is hard not to feel deeply the tug of the opposing view."

Most people who consider themselves pro-choice recognize that abortion is a very difficult choice for many women to make. They hope that no woman they love—whether wife, girlfriend, daughter, sister, aunt, niece, or friend—will ever face that decision. They may even support a variety of restrictions on access to abortion services, such as 24-hour waiting periods or parental consent laws. In the end, though, they believe that the law should not be able to force a woman to bear a child against her will, any more than the law should be able to force a woman to have an abortion against her will. They feel that women must have a fundamental right to make their own reproductive decisions, based on their own life situations and moral codes.

At the same time, most people who consider themselves pro-life are not anti-women's rights. They have a profound concern for the health and welfare of women facing unplanned pregnancies. They recognize that many women choose abortion because continuing the pregnancy will put them in a very difficult situation. They know that an unplanned pregnancy can force a woman to discontinue her education, interrupt her career, or endure financial hardship. In the end, though, they believe that a woman who chooses abortion only compounds her problems by taking an innocent life. They feel that unborn children have a fundamental right to life that must be respected, and they are committed to helping women find workable alternatives to abortion.

Although many people express sympathy for the positions of both sides in the abortion debate, perhaps it will prove impossible to reach a compromise in the fundamental conflict between a woman's liberty and her fetus's life. But some people suggest it may be possible to achieve a common goal of making abortion rare by finding ways to reduce the number of unplanned pregnancies in the United States. "If advocates on both sides of the abortion debate would just pause, they would recognize at least one broadly shared interest, that of working toward a world of only wanted pregnancies," Tribe stated. "Better education, the provision of contraception, indeed the creation of a society in which the burden of raising a child is lighter, are all achievable goals that are lost in the shouting about abortion."

BIOGRAPHIES

Harry A. Blackmun (1908-1999)
U.S. Supreme Court Justice
Author of the Majority Opinion in the Roe v.
Wade *Case*

Harry Andrew Blackmun was born on November 12, 1908, in Nashville, Illinois. He grew up in Minneapolis-St. Paul, Minnesota. His father, Corwin Manning Blackmun, owned a grocery store and then a hardware store during Harry's childhood years. His mother was Theo Huegely Ruetner Blackmun. Harry attended kindergarten with Warren E. Burger, and the two boys struck up a close friendship that lasted into the 1970s, when they served together on the U.S. Supreme Court.

A Distinguished Legal Career

After graduating from public high school in St. Paul, Blackmun enrolled at Harvard University in Cambridge, Massachusetts, and majored in mathematics. He earned a bachelor's degree with honors in 1929 and promptly entered Harvard Law School, from which he graduated in 1932. After a brief stint as a law clerk to a federal appeals court judge, Blackmun took a teaching position at the St. Paul College of Law. He also became an attorney with Dorsey, Colman, Barker, Scott and Barber, a top Minneapolis firm, where he specialized in estate and tax law. On June 21, 1941, he married Dorothy E. Clark, with whom he eventually had three daughters.

In 1943 Blackmun was made a full partner in his law firm, and two years later he began teaching at the University of Minnesota Law School. In 1950 he became general legal counsel, or lead attorney, to the world-famous Mayo Clinic, a medical facility based in Rochester, Minnesota. The next several years were among the most enjoyable and satisfying of Blackmun's life, both personally and professionally.

In 1959 President Dwight Eisenhower appointed Blackmun to the U.S. Court of Appeals for the Eighth Circuit Court. During the next decade, Blackmun gained a reputation as a conservative, "law-and-order" judge—although he also proved sympathetic to civil rights causes in several cases.

A "Safe" Choice

In 1969 Blackmun's life was forever changed by the abrupt resignation of U.S. Supreme Court Justice Abe Fortas, who had been accused of breaking various rules of ethics. Republican President Richard M. Nixon first nominated federal judge Clement F. Haynesworth, Jr., to replace Fortas. But the U.S. Senate, which was controlled by the Democratic Party, refused to confirm Haynesworth because of concerns that he was hostile to civil rights. Nixon's second nominee, federal judge G. Harrold Carswell, was rejected for the same reason.

Angered and frustrated by the Senate opposition, Nixon decided to nominate Blackmun, whom he viewed as a reliably conservative judge whose record on civil rights cases would satisfy the Democrats. Blackmun's lifelong friend Warren Burger, who had become Chief Justice of the Supreme Court in June 1969, applauded Nixon's choice. Senate Democrats approved of Blackmun as well. He was confirmed in the Senate by a 94-0 vote on May 12, 1970, less than a month after Nixon had announced his nomination.

During the first few years that Blackmun sat on the Supreme Court bench, he was widely viewed as a faithful follower of Burger. At that time, Burger was seeking to steer the Court toward a more conservative legal philosophy than it had shown in the 1950s and 1960s under Chief Justice Earl Warren. Blackmun voted so often with Burger during his first years on the court that the boyhood chums were sometimes jointly referred to by court watchers as the "Minnesota Twins."

As time passed and Blackmun's confidence increased, however, he emerged as an independent-minded judge who did not always vote in line with mainstream conservative thought. These votes, combined with Blackmun's disapproval of Burger's unpredictable leadership style, led to a rupture in their friendship that was never repaired. By the late 1970s the two men were barely speaking to one another.

Blackmun and *Roe v. Wade*

Blackmun's most famous and controversial moment as a Supreme Court justice came in 1973, when he wrote the majority opinion in *Roe v. Wade,* which made abortion legal across the United States. Writing for the 7-2 majority, Blackmun declared that the legal right to privacy included a woman's right to abortion. Specifically, Blackmun wrote that the First, Fourth, Ninth, and Fourteenth Amendments of the U.S. Constitution protected an individual's "zone of privacy" against intrusive state laws in such areas as marriage, parenting, and contraception, including "a woman's decision whether or not to terminate her pregnancy."

Blackmun's leading role in the *Roe v. Wade* decision made him a hero to millions of people who supported legal abortion. But Americans who opposed legal abortion bitterly criticized his vote and his opinion, and Blackmun received huge volumes of hate mail for the rest of his life because of his stand on *Roe v. Wade.*

Blackmun was unfazed by the controversy. He remained a reliable supporter of abortion rights for the remainder of his time on the Court. In 1977, for example, he was incensed when the Supreme Court upheld a law making it illegal for poor women to receive federal assistance in paying for abortions. "There is another world 'out there,' the existence of which the Court, I suspect, either chooses to ignore or fears to recognize," Blackmun wrote in his dissent.

As time passed, Blackmun publicly wondered about the future of abortion rights in America. In his dissent in the 1989 abortion case *Webster v. Reproductive Health Services,* Blackmun warned that his colleagues were chipping away at *Roe v. Wade* by allowing too many restrictions on abortion rights. He also charged that the Court was giving the federal government too much power to intrude into women's lives. "I fear for the future," he wrote. "The signs are evident and ominous, and a chill wind blows."

Blackmun retired from the Supreme Court in early 1994. Speaking at a farewell press conference, the judge offered a spirited defense of his most famous opinion. "Roe against Wade hit me early in my tenure on the Supreme Court," he said. "And people forget that it was a 7-to-2 decision. They always typify it as a Blackmun opinion. But I'll say what I've said many times publicly—I think it was right in 1973, and I think it was right today. It's a step that had to be taken as we go down the road toward the full emancipation of women."

Abortion was not the only issue for which Blackmun became known, however. During his 24 years on the Court, he emerged as a fierce defender of First Amendment rights and especially of free speech. He also evolved into a strong critic of capital punishment, which he had supported earlier in his career. Blackmun became convinced that death sentences were disproportionately given to minorities and poor people, and that innocent people had been put to death. He also believed that capital punishment had no deterrent effect, and was simply a tool of revenge. "The death-penalty experiment has failed," he said. "I no longer shall tinker with the machinery of death."

Blackmun died at Arlington Hospital in Arlington, Virginia, on March 4, 1999, following complications from hip-replacement surgery. In accordance with his wishes, his private papers were released to the public in March 2004, five years after his death. According to Supreme Court scholars, these papers provided a treasure chest of information about the inner workings of the Supreme Court during his tenure.

Sources:

Greenhouse, Linda. *Becoming Justice Blackmun: Harry Blackmun's Supreme Court Journey.* New York: Times Books, 2006.

Greenhouse, Linda. "Documents Reveal the Evolution of a Justice," *New York Times,* March 4, 2004.

National Public Radio (NPR) Online. "Justice Harry Blackmun's Papers," March 2004, www.npr.org/news/specials/blackmun.

Schwartz, Bernard. *A History of the Supreme Court.* New York: Oxford University Press, 1993.

Woodward, Bob, and Scott Armstrong. *The Brethren: Inside the Supreme Court.* New York: Simon and Schuster, 1979.

Robert H. Bork (1927-)
Conservative Legal Scholar and Judge
Leading Critic of the Roe v. Wade *Decision*

Robert Heron Bork was born on March 1, 1927, in Pittsburgh, Pennsylvania. His parents were Harry Philip Bork, a purchasing agent for a steel company, and Elizabeth Kunkle Bork, a schoolteacher. Smart and curious, Bork became interested in politics at a young age. He embraced socialism in his mid-teens and spent hours discussing politics and current events with his mother. "My mother and I used to sit up and argue late into the night about anything and everything," he recalled in an interview with the *Bar Report*. "Long about midnight my father would come to the top of the stairs and shout down, 'It's time to come to bed. This is not a debating society.' But that's exactly what it was—my mother and I had our own debating society."

A Marine and a Legal Scholar

After graduating from high school, Bork attended the University of Pittsburgh for two semesters before enlisting in the Marine Corps in early 1945. World War II ended before he saw any action, however, so then he enrolled at the University of Chicago. After earning a bachelor's degree in 1948, Bork enlisted for a second tour with the Marines and was stationed in Korea from 1950 to 1952.

Once he completed his military service, Bork began working toward a law degree at the University of Chicago Law School. During this time he discarded his earlier socialist beliefs and developed a conservative outlook on issues and events in America and around the world. In June 1952 he married Claire Davidson, with whom he eventually had three children. One year later he graduated from law school and took a job as an antitrust law specialist with a top Chicago firm. He enjoyed the work but became restless after several years. Eager for a new challenge, he accepted a teaching position at Yale University Law School in 1962.

Bork spent the next nineteen years affiliated with Yale. During that time he became a nationally recognized conservative scholar on constitutional law. According to Bork's legal philosophy, which he described in numerous essays and lectures in the 1960s and 1970s, judges should consider all cases based on a literal interpretation of the Constitution's wording. Bork believed that the courts' job was to uphold the Constitution—not to make judgments in an attempt to correct perceived social problems. In 1963, for example, he criticized a proposed Public Accommodations Act that would force hotel, bar, and restaurant owners to end discrimination against minorities. In Bork's view, this proposed law—which became part of the 1964 Voting Rights Act—amounted to a violation of the owners' constitutional right to choose with whom they associated.

Bork also believed that court decisions should be guided by the "original intent" of the makers of the Constitution. In accordance with this view, Bork argued that the Fourteenth Amendment could not be used as the basis for affirmative action for women because the creators of that amendment had written it specifically to apply to black citizens. "The truth is that the judge who looks outside the historic Constitution always looks inside himself and nowhere else," Bork later wrote in his book *The Tempting of America: The Political Seduction of the Law.*

Bork and *Roe v. Wade*

One of the U.S. Supreme Court decisions that most angered Bork was the 1973 *Roe v. Wade* decision, which struck down state laws against abortion and legalized the procedure across the United States. In Bork's view, the seven Supreme Court justices who voted to make abortion legal in the United States ignored the contents of the Constitution. "I objected to *Roe v. Wade* the moment it was decided," he later wrote in *Slouching Towards Gomorrah,* "not because of any doubts about abortion, but because the decision was a radical deformation of the Constitution. The Constitution has nothing to say about abortion, leaving it, like most subjects, to the judgment and moral sense of the American people and their elected representatives. . . . *Roe* is nothing more than the Supreme Court's imposition on us of the morality of our cultural elites."

But Bork also objected to abortion on moral grounds. "In thinking about abortion, it is necessary to address two questions," he stated in *Slouching*

Towards Gomorrah. "Is abortion always the killing of a human being? If it is, is that killing done simply for convenience? I think there can be no doubt that the answer to the first question is yes; and the answer to the second is almost always. . . . It is undeniable that bearing and rearing a child sometimes places a great burden on a woman or a family. That fact does not, however, answer the question whether the burden justifies destroying a human life."

From Nixon Official to Reagan Judge

In 1973 Bork accepted an appointment from President Richard M. Nixon to serve as solicitor general, the third-ranking official at the U.S. Justice Department. Within a matter of months, the Watergate political crisis that was then swirling around the Nixon White House touched Bork as well. On October 20, 1973, Nixon ordered Attorney General Elliot Richardson and Deputy Attorney General William Ruckelshaus to fire Archibald Cox, a special prosecutor investigating possible criminal activity by Nixon and other top administration officials. Richardson resigned rather than carry out Nixon's order, and Ruckelshaus was fired when he refused to dismiss Cox. Bork agreed to carry out the orders, firing Cox and his entire staff later that same evening. This "Saturday Night Massacre," as it came to be called, outraged millions of Americans and accelerated Nixon's fall from power.

Bork remained as solicitor general after Nixon resigned from office in August 1974. He kept the position until early 1977, when he returned to Yale. Over the next four years, he taught law classes and published a book on antitrust law called *The Antitrust Paradox: A Policy at War with Itself* (1978). His wife Claire died in 1980, and two years later he married Mary Ellen Pohl.

In 1982 Bork accepted an appointment from President Ronald Reagan to the Federal Court of Appeals for the District of Columbia Circuit. Over the next five years he became known for his conservative record as a judge. When Supreme Court Justice Lewis Powell retired in the summer of 1987, Reagan nominated Bork to replace him. Supporters hailed him as a brilliant legal scholar and thoughtful judge without any hint of controversial personal behavior. But everyone knew that if the conservative Bork replaced the moderate Powell, the Supreme Court—which was closely divided between liberal and conservative members—might well take on a more conservative cast on a whole range of issues, including abortion rights, school prayer, environmental regulation of businesses, personal privacy, and affirmative action.

A wide range of organizations mobilized against Bork's nomination, and Democratic lawmakers who represented liberal constituencies condemned Bork's views. Democratic Senator Ted Kennedy declared in a speech that "Robert Bork's America is a land in which women would be forced into back-alley abortions, blacks would have to sit at segregated lunch counters, rogue police could break down citizens' doors in midnight raids, schoolchildren could not be taught about evolution, writers and artists would be censored at the whim of government, and the doors of the federal courts would be shut on the fingers of millions of citizens for whom the judiciary is often the only protector of the individual rights that are the heart of our democracy."

Bork and his many supporters viewed these sorts of comments as outrageous distortions of his record and views. But they proved unable to turn the tide of Senate opinion in his favor. After enduring five days of grueling questioning before the Senate Judiciary Committee, Bork watched as his nomination was defeated by a 58-42 vote in the Senate. Several weeks later, Anthony M. Kennedy received Senate confirmation by a 97-0 vote to take Powell's place.

Years later, Bork insisted that his Supreme Court nomination failed because "I was perceived as the swing vote on abortion. I think *Roe v. Wade* was probably the litmus issue," he said in a 1998 interview with *Bar Report*. "The opposition didn't want a narrow focus on a matter that would be pending before the Court, and a matter on which many people agreed with me, so they got people all worked up about false and extraneous issues. They used anything they could dream up, without regard to truth."

A Steadfast Conservative Voice

In 1989 Bork published *The Tempting of America: The Political Seduction of the Law,* a spirited defense of his philosophy of judicial restraint over judicial activism. In 1996 Bork published his best-known book, *Slouching Towards Gomorrah: Modern Liberalism and American Decline.* In this work Bork expressed his belief that America's moral and cultural foundations had fallen apart since World War II. He argued that liberals were responsible for much of this deterioration.

Bork's public profile has waned somewhat since *Slouching Towards Gomorrah* was published, but he is still popular with conservative readers and political activists. In 2003 he published *Coercing Virtue: The Worldwide Rule of Judges,* and he served as editor of 2005's *A Country I Do Not Recognize: The*

Legal Assault on American Values. He is associated with a variety of conservative think tanks and organizations, including the Hudson Institute and the Federalist Society. He also serves as a professor at the Ave Maria School of Law in Ann Arbor, Michigan.

Sources:

Bork, Robert H. *Slouching Towards Gomorrah: Modern Liberalism and American Decline.* New York: Regan, 1996.

Bronner, Ethan. *Battle for Justice: How the Bork Nomination Shook America.* New York: Anchor, 1990.

"Legends in the Law: A Conversation with Robert H. Bork," *Bar Report,* December/January, 1998.

Pertschuck, Michael, and Wendy Schaetzel. *The People Rising: The Campaign against the Bork Nomination.* New York: Thunder's Mouth Press, 1989.

Frances Kissling (1943-)
Pro-Choice Activist
President of Catholics for a Free Choice from
1973 to 2007

Frances Kissling was born Frances Romanski on June 15, 1943, in New York City, New York. Her parents were Florence Rynkiewicz, a medical administrator, and Thomas Romanski. She was the oldest of four children. Her birth parents divorced when she was young. Frances became the adopted daughter of Charles Kissling, a building contractor, when Kissling married her mother.

Frances Kissling grew up in a working-class neighborhood in Flushing, New York. She attended Catholic school throughout her youth and developed a deep admiration for the nuns who educated her. After graduating from high school she joined a convent with the intention of becoming a nun herself. Within a few months, however, she decided to leave the convent because of strong disagreements with Catholic Church teachings on such issues as sexuality, divorce, and birth control. Kissling was particularly angered by the Church's insistence that people who divorce and later remarry are living in sin. She felt that this theological position, which made her mother an adulteress in the eyes of the Church, was deeply unfair.

Joining the Pro-Choice Movement

Kissling enrolled at New York's New School for Social Research, earning a bachelor's degree in 1966. During the next few years she became a dedicated social activist, participating in demonstrations against the Vietnam War and speaking out for women's rights. Her connections to the Catholic Church became nearly nonexistent during this period in her life.

In 1970 Kissling became the director of an abortion clinic in Pelham, New York. At that time, New York was one of only a handful of states where pregnant women could obtain legal abortions. In January 1973 the U.S. Supreme Court decision in *Roe v. Wade* legalized abortion across the country.

A short time later Kissling left the clinic in Pelham and spent the next few years working to establish safe abortion clinics in Italy, Austria, and Mexico.

In 1976 Kissling helped found the National Abortion Federation (NAF), a trade association of professionals who provided abortion services. She was working for the NAF in 1977 when the U.S. government passed the Hyde Amendment, which cut off all federal funding for abortion. Kissling and other activists who supported legal abortion were outraged by this development, which they believed would make it harder for poor women to afford safe, legal abortions at clinics. In 1979 Kissling and co-author Ellen Frankfort published *Rosie: The Investigation of a Wrongful Death,* a nonfiction book about a poor young woman who died from a botched, illegal abortion following the ban on federal funding for abortions.

Around this same time, Kissling returned to the Catholic Church after a long absence. Her goal in returning, however, was to change conservative church perspectives on sexuality, contraception, and abortion. "When I say I came back to the church, I never came back on the old terms," she explained to Annie Lally Milhaven in an interview for *The Inside Stories.* "I came back to the church as a social change agent. . . . When I talk about coming back into the church, I'm not talking about coming back to Sunday mass, confession and all those things that are the memories of my childhood. I'm talking about coming back to a new vision of the church established in the late 1970s by women within the church."

Leading Catholics for a Free Choice

In 1982 Kissling was named president of Catholics for a Free Choice (CFFC), an organization that had been founded in 1973 to promote safe, legal abortion and contraceptive rights for all women. Throughout the 1980s and 1990s Kissling became known for her strong support for reproductive rights, as well as her fierce criticism of the Catholic Church for its opposition to abortion, contraception, women priests, sex education, and homosexuality. Kissling voiced many of these opinions in the pages of *Conscience,* a bimonthly magazine produced by CFFC. But she has also offered her perspective through interviews with numerous national magazines and television news programs over the years.

Kissling's outspoken nature and CFFC's advocacy work have drawn strong condemnation from some quarters. Catholic Church officials, for example, have flatly challenged whether Kissling and the organization can legitimately describe themselves as Catholic. In May 2000 the U.S. Conference of Catholic Bishops issued a formal statement in which it rejected CFFC claims that it speaks as an "authentic Catholic voice. . . . In fact, the group's activity is directed to rejection and distortion of Catholic teaching about the respect and protection due to defenseless unborn human life."

Other pro-life critics charge that Kissling and the group are simply a front used by pro-abortion activists to advance their cause. "The Catholic Church has always been the single most consistent proponent of life and opponent of abortion in American culture," said one Catholic official to *Crisis Magazine,* a conservative Catholic monthly. "So if you're 'pro-choice,' breaking its credibility becomes a serious priority. That's the value of Catholics for a Free Choice. It's a tool to use against the Catholic Church. Nothing more."

Kissling strongly objects to these charges. "I know with every ounce of my being that you don't have to agree with the positions of the church on issues of abortion and contraception to be Catholic," she told the *New York Times* in 2007. She also asserts that in many ways, the battles that she and CFFC wage over reproductive rights are part of a larger campaign to raise women to equal status with men in the Catholic Church and all parts of American society.

A Quest for Common Ground

Kissling remained a strong defender of abortion rights in the 2000s. During this period, though, she also wrote a number of essays in which she challenged the pro-choice movement to acknowledge that the fetus "is not nothing" and to make greater efforts to find common ground with pro-life activists. In a 2004 article in *Conscience* called "How to Think about the Fetus," for example, Kissling issued a call for a "new era in pro-choice advocacy—one that combines a commitment to laws that affirm and enhance the right of each woman to decide whether to have an abortion or bear and raise a child with an expressed commitment to human values that include respect for life, recognition of fetal life as valuable, and a concern for fostering a society in which all life is valued."

Two years later Kissling expressed similar sentiments in an opinion piece for *Salon.com:*

> It is important that we express our belief that the ability to create and nurture and bring into the world new people should be

exercised carefully, consciously, responsibly, and with awe for our capacity to create life," she wrote. "That is one reason why we must commit ourselves to working to make abortion unnecessary, and be willing to use those words.

In Kissling's view, the best way to make abortion "unnecessary" is to increase funding for family planning, stop supporting abstinence-only sex education, and educate all girls and women about the importance of contraception. "If you can't afford financially or emotionally to bring a child into the world, if you simply do not want children or a child, you have a responsibility to use contraception," she said. "Straight talk means accepting that however justifiable and whatever good comes from the decision to end a pregnancy, the act of abortion involves a departure from our common desire to live in a world where all positive forms of life can be nourished."

Kissling voluntarily stepped down as president of the CFFC in February 2007. She explained that she made the decision because she did not want to risk becoming "boring or predictable." She was succeeded as president by Jon O'Brien.

Sources:

Banerjee, Neela. "Backing Abortion Rights While Keeping the Faith," *New York Times,* Feb. 26, 2007.

Kissling, Frances. *How to Talk About Abortion.* Washington, DC: Catholics for a Free Choice, 2000.

Kissling, Frances. "I Love *Roe,*" *RHRealityCheck.org,* http://www.rhrealitycheck.org.

Kissling, Frances. "Is There Life after *Roe?*" *Conscience,* Winter 2004-05.

Kissling, Frances. "Should Abortion Be Prevented?" *Salon.com,* Oct. 3, 2006, http://www.salon.com/opinion/feature/2006/10/03/abortion.

Lopez, Kathryn Jean. "Aborting the Church: Frances Kissling & Catholics for a Free Choice," *Crisis Magazine,* April 2002.

Milhaven, Annie Lally, ed. *The Inside Stories: Thirteen Valiant Women Challenging the Church.* New London, CT: Twenty-third Publications, 1987.

Norma McCorvey (1947-)
Plaintiff in the 1973 Roe v. Wade *Case*
Known in Court Documents by the Fictitious
Name Jane Roe

Norma McCorvey was born Norma Leah Nelson on September 22, 1947, in Lettesworth, Louisiana, a small town about sixty miles north of Baton Rouge. Her father was Olin "Jimmy" Nelson, a radio and television repairman. Her mother was Mary Mildred Gautreaux. She had one older brother, Jimmy.

Norma's father was a leader in Lettesworth's Jehovah's Witness religious community. According to her autobiography *I Am Roe*, however, the home life that he and her mother created for their two children was a terrible one. Her parents fought and drank constantly, and her mother in particular routinely subjected Norma to physical and verbal abuse. Norma responded with disobedient and angry behavior, which further fueled the cycle of abuse.

A Troubled Childhood

When Norma was nine the family moved to Texas, but her home environment did not improve. Relations between mother and daughter became so bad that Norma was sent to a Catholic boarding school at age ten. When she was kicked out of that institution for her rebellious behavior, she was sent to a reform school in Gainesville, Texas. Norma spent four years at the all-girls reform school, and she later described these years as the happiest ones of her childhood. She developed close friendships with several other girls, and she had her first lesbian experiences. School authorities periodically tried to release Norma back to her family, but as soon as she was deposited at her mother's doorstep in Dallas, she ran away so that she could be sent back to her friends in Gainesville.

Authorities finally told Norma that if she ran away again, they would send her to jail instead of the reform school. Norma reluctantly agreed to return to Dallas, where her mother arranged for her to stay at the home of a male relative. But Norma was raped by the relative on a nightly basis for three weeks, until her mother realized what was happening and brought her home.

Norma found work as a waitress in a Dallas restaurant, where she met an older man named Woody McCorvey. Their relationship quickly became a romantic one, and on June 17, 1964, the sixteen-year-old girl married McCorvey. The marriage was a disaster from the outset. She became pregnant shortly after they relocated to California, and her husband responded to this news by beating her. His violent outbursts became so frequent that Norma McCorvey moved back to Dallas and filed for divorce. She gave birth to a daughter, Melissa, but signed her parental rights over to her mother. Years later, McCorvey claimed in her autobiography that her mother deceived her into signing away these rights. She also described the loss of Melissa as one of the greatest regrets of her life.

Drifting without Direction

McCorvey floundered for the next several years. She barely managed to support herself in a variety of jobs, working as a waitress, apartment cleaner, bartender, carnival worker, and hospital staffer. But she became heavily dependent on both alcohol and illegal drugs, and she went through a series of lesbian and heterosexual relationships that ended badly.

McCorvey's relationship with her mother also remained troubled, partly because of Melissa and partly because of her mother's deep anger about McCorvey's lesbianism. McCorvey occasionally got permission from her mother to visit Melissa, but she was kept from her daughter for long periods of time.

McCorvey also became pregnant two more times from brief relationships with men. She carried the second pregnancy to term and quietly gave the baby up for adoption. But when she became pregnant a third time in the fall of 1969, she desperately searched for someone who would perform an abortion. "This wasn't like the other times," she recalled in *I Am Roe*. "I didn't want to give birth to another unwanted child. I didn't want to have to give up another child. I didn't want a child to be born with me as its mother. There was no good reason to bring this poor thing into the world. I simply didn't want to be pregnant. *I didn't want to be pregnant.*"

Texas state law, however, only permitted abortions if the life of the mother was endangered. Unable to find anyone who would perform the illegal procedure, McCorvey "nearly went out of [her] mind with anger and panic," according to her account in *I Am Roe*. Finally, she met an attorney who urged her to contact Sarah Weddington and Linda Coffee, two young lawyers who were looking for a pregnant woman who wanted an abortion. They needed such a woman to serve as the plaintiff in a lawsuit designed to overturn the Texas law against abortion.

Becoming Jane Roe

McCorvey met Coffee and Weddington in January 1970 and agreed to be the plaintiff in their lawsuit—despite their warning that the case might not be resolved in time for her to obtain an abortion. To protect McCorvey's identity, the lawyers gave her the alias "Jane Roe." Over the next few months McCorvey watched from the sidelines as the *Roe v. Wade* court case moved forward (the *Wade* in the title was Henry Wade, the district attorney responsible for enforcing the Texas anti-abortion law in the Dallas area). "I stayed invisible, burying myself in drugs [and] alcohol, as Linda and Sarah made history in my name," McCorvey recalled.

On June 17, 1970, the Texas Fifth Circuit Court ruled in favor of McCorvey/Roe, declaring that Texas's abortion law violated the Ninth Amendment to the Constitution. Wade promptly announced that he would appeal the ruling—and that until that appeal was decided, he would prosecute any doctor who performed an abortion. By this time, McCorvey realized that she would be continuing her pregnancy to term. "This lawsuit was not really for me," she wrote in *I Am Roe*. "It was about me, and maybe all the women who'd come before me, but it was really for all the women who were coming after me."

McCorvey gave birth in June 1970 and gave the baby up for adoption. Meanwhile, the *Roe v. Wade* case progressed until it reached the U.S. Supreme Court in May 1971. The legal battle continued for another nineteen months until January 1973, when the Court declared the Texas abortion law unconstitutional. The justices ruled 7-2 that the Texas statute violated Jane Roe's constitutional right to privacy. The Court argued that the Constitution's First, Fourth, Ninth, and Fourteenth Amendments protect an individual's "zone of privacy" against intrusive state laws in such areas as marriage, contraception, child rearing, and "a woman's decision whether or not to terminate her pregnancy."

This decision paved the way for the legalization of abortion across America. McCorvey, though, had virtually no involvement in the case once it reached the Supreme Court. In fact, she learned about the Supreme Court's *Roe v. Wade* decision by reading the newspaper, just like millions of other Americans.

A Change of Heart

For much of the 1970s and 1980s, McCorvey lived a quiet existence. She established a long-term lesbian relationship with Connie Gonzales, and the couple established a successful apartment cleaning and rehabilitation business. In 1984 McCorvey revealed that she had been "Jane Roe" in the landmark case that had invalidated America's abortion laws. But it was not until 1989, when she took part in a huge pro-choice rally in Washington, D.C., that her identity became widely known.

During the early 1990s McCorvey maintained a low public profile. She knew that many people hated her for her role in making abortion legal, and she felt that many pro-choice organizations were ambivalent about having a woman with such a checkered past as a spokesperson. According to McCorvey, she was not even invited to attend a massive twentieth-anniversary celebration of the *Roe v. Wade* decision in 1993.

In the mid-1990s, though, McCorvey once again found herself in the public spotlight. In 1994 she published her autobiography, *I Am Roe*. One year later, she publicly announced that she had become a born-again Christian and no longer believed in abortion. McCorvey explained that this dramatic change came about after the pro-life group Operation Rescue (OR) opened offices next door to a Dallas family services clinic where she volunteered. She became friends with several OR members, including Ronda Mackey. Over time, she also developed a close relationship with Mackey's seven-year-old daughter.

McCorvey's growing ambivalence about abortion became outright opposition after she attended a church service with Ronda and Emily. "I no longer felt the pressure of my sin pushing down on my shoulders," she remembered. "The release was so quick that I felt like I could almost float outside." Her transformation into a pro-life activist was completed a few months later when she examined a fetal development poster in the OR offices. "I had worked with pregnant women for years," she recalled. "I had been through three pregnancies and deliveries myself. I should have known. Yet something in that poster made me lose my breath. I kept seeing the picture of that tiny, ten-week-old embryo, and I said to myself, 'That's a baby!' It's as if blinders just fell off my eyes and I suddenly understood the truth—'That's a baby!'"

McCorvey spent the next two years as an activist for Operation Rescue, but she left the organization in 1997 because of conflicts with movement leaders and discomfort with the group's confrontational tactics. She remained strongly pro-life, however, and proclaimed her continued dedication to conservative Christian beliefs. McCorvey even asserted that she ended her sexual relationship with Gonzales, though the two women continued to live together. McCorvey went on to serve as national director of the Crossing Over Ministry (formerly Roe No More Ministry), which is dedicated to overturning the *Roe v. Wade* decision.

Sources:

Garrow, David J. *Liberty and Sexuality: The Right to Privacy and the Making of* Roe v. Wade. Berkeley: University of California Press, 1998.

McCorvey, Norma, with Andy Meisler. *I Am Roe: My Life,* Roe v. Wade, and *Freedom of Choice.* New York: HarperCollins, 1994.

McCorvey, Norma, with Gary Thomas. *Won by Love.* Nashville: Thomas Nelson, 1998.

Thomas, Gary. "Roe v. McCorvey." *Christianity Today,* January 12, 1998.

Kate Michelman (1942-)
Pro-Choice Leader
President of the National Abortion Rights Action
League from 1985 to 2004

Kate Michelman was born on August 4, 1942, and raised in a working-class neighborhood in Camden, New Jersey. Her father was a plant supervisor, and her mother was a housewife. Michelman's family moved to Ohio when she was a teenager. Michelman has described herself as a "serious" teen who spent her free time listening to radio news broadcasts and organizing fundraising events for less fortunate members of the community.

After graduating from high school, Michelman enrolled at the University of Michigan in Ann Arbor. She married her childhood sweetheart at age 20 and graduated with a bachelor's degree in psychology and art history in 1966. Rather than pursue her interest in a career in childhood development, though, Michelman stayed at home to raise a fast-growing family. "I was a practicing Catholic who accepted the Church's teaching that birth control was a sin," she recalled in her 2005 autobiography, *With Liberty and Justice for All.* "Like many other Catholic wives, I practiced the 'natural' means of contraception—the rhythm method—and believed the claim that breast-feeding prevented pregnancy. I exploded every myth. We had three daughters in three years."

Deciding to Have an Abortion

In 1969 Michelman's world was turned upside down when her husband announced that he was leaving her for another woman. A couple of weeks later, Michelman learned that she was pregnant with a fourth child. After agonizing over her situation, she decided that she would not be able to raise her three daughters on her own if she had another child.

At that time, abortion was illegal in every state, although many states made exceptions in cases where the pregnancy posed a threat to the mother's health. Rather than have a potentially dangerous illegal abortion, Michelman decided to seek approval for a legal abortion on the grounds that she was mentally ill-equipped to have another child. To obtain approval for an abortion on "therapeutic" grounds, Michelman met with a board of male physicians who subjected her to an intense period of questioning. Although the doctors approved her request, Michelman then learned that she could not obtain the abortion until she had the written permission of her husband—even though he had abandoned her a few months earlier. Only after securing his permission was Michelman able to have the procedure done in 1970.

Michelman's experience convinced her to leave the Catholic Church and become a Quaker. In 1972 she married Fred Michelman. Around this same time she tapped into her training in children's services to find work as an administrator for local nonprofit organizations. She also served as an assistant professor in the Department of Psychiatry at Pennsylvania State University School of Medicine.

Influential Pro-Choice Activist

The end of Michelman's first marriage and her traumatic abortion experience changed her life in other important ways as well. She became politically active in efforts to legalize abortion across the United States, and she rejoiced in 1973 when the U.S. Supreme Court's *Roe v. Wade* decision legalized the procedure.

Michelman's activism eventually led to a change in career direction. In 1980 she became executive director of a Planned Parenthood branch in Harrisburg, Pennsylvania. Her sure-handed and dedicated direction of the Harrisburg branch was widely recognized within the pro-choice community. In 1985 she accepted a position as president of the National Abortion Rights Action League (NARAL), a pro-choice group founded in 1969 that was dedicated to keeping abortion legal in the United States.

Over the next nineteen years at the helm of NARAL, Michelman became one of the most influential and recognized leaders of the pro-choice movement in America. She appeared on numerous national television and radio programs, gave countless interviews to national and local magazines and newspapers, and organized many campaigns and demonstrations in support of NARAL's mission.

Michelman also helped chart a new course for the organization in the 1990s. In 1993 NARAL declared that its primary mission remained to ensure that abortion remained safe and legal. But the organization also proclaimed its intention to work to reduce the need for abortion by actively promoting birth control and abstinence programs. This expansion of the organization's goals prompted it to change its name to the National Abortion and Reproductive Rights Action League (the group, however, kept the NARAL acronym).

Still Dedicated to the Pro-Choice Cause

In 2004 Michelman stepped down as head of NARAL (now known as NARAL Pro-Choice America) and was replaced by Nancy Keenan. But Michelman remained actively involved in the ongoing battle to keep abortion legal in the United States. In 2005 she published her autobiography, *With Liberty and Justice for All,* which details the various reasons why she devoted her life to the pro-choice cause. Two years later she published *Protecting the Right to Choose,* another call for defending abortion rights.

One of the arguments that Michelman makes in these two books—and in many speeches and interviews—is that abortion rights and women's rights are inseparable. "On the larger question of choice as a value, I believe that more today than I did 25 years ago," she told *Conscience* in 2004. "But do I believe that we've got to do a better job in helping people to understand what we mean by pro-choice, or freedom to choose, or the right to choose? You bet. I think we will fail in the long term if we do not attend to that mission—especially among young people. I know the civil rights movement is going through the same struggle, and civil rights leaders need to remind younger African Americans what it was like not to have rights. We women have to do the same. We have to remind people what it was like not to have the right to choose."

Sources:

Michelman, Kate. "Leading from the Front" (Interview with Frances Kissling). *Conscience,* March 22, 2004.

Michelman, Kate. *With Liberty and Justice for All: A Life Spent Protecting the Right to Choose.* New York: Hudson Street Press, 2005.

Saletan, William. *Bearing Right: How Conservatives Won the Abortion War.* Berkeley: University of California Press, 2003.

Margaret Sanger (1879-1966)
Feminist and Birth Control Advocate
Founder of the Organization That Became
Planned Parenthood

Margaret Louise Higgins Sanger was born on September 14, 1879, in Corning, New York. Her father was Michael Hennessey Higgins, a stonemason and outspoken atheist who had immigrated to the United States from Ireland in the 1860s. Her mother was Anne Purcell Higgins, a devout Catholic Irish-American. Margaret was the sixth of eleven children who resulted from Ann Higgins's eighteen pregnancies during her lifetime. Years later, Margaret would blame her mother's many pregnancies as a major factor in her death from tuberculosis at age fifty.

Margaret was raised in a crowded, impoverished household that suffered greatly from her father's heavy drinking and radical political beliefs, which made him unpopular in the community. With the help of generous older siblings, however, she was able to escape from these grim circumstances. She enrolled at Claverack College and Hudson River Institute in 1896, and four years later she entered the nursing program at White Plains Hospital in New York. In 1902 she married architect William Sanger, then graduated from the hospital program a few months later.

Embraces Radical Politics

The Sanger marriage produced three children who spent their first years in the quiet town of Hastings, a suburb of New York City. In 1910, though, the Sangers decided to move into the city itself, and this decision had an enormous impact on their marriage and on Margaret Sanger's path in life.

Sanger took a job as a nurse when they moved into the city. Her experiences treating poor families on New York's Lower East Side awakened long-simmering radical political beliefs. Many of the pregnant women she treated came from families that were already struggling to provide for existing children, both emotionally and financially. But the nation's various federal and state "Comstock Laws" made it illegal for medical professionals to give these women information about birth control options.

Sanger was outraged by these circumstances. She argued that the Comstock Laws trapped working-class women in lives of perpetual pregnancy that pushed them into despair and exhaustion—or endangered their lives by forcing them to seek out untrained abortionists. Sanger further argued that her patients' limited access to birth control resources and information was directly due to the fact that they were poor, pointing out that wealthy women often used their resources to get around the Comstock Laws. During this time, Sanger also came to feel that the institution of marriage was a tool used by men to keep women in a subordinate and dependent position in American society.

These convictions were deepened by Sanger's association with radical left-wing intellectuals, artists, and activists who lived and worked in New York City, including such diverse figures as author Max Eastman and anarchist Emma Goldman. Sanger became a committed socialist and a fierce critic of American-style capitalism. She even took part in labor strikes organized by the Industrial Workers of the World (IWW), a socialist labor movement that described itself as dedicated to delivering the working class from the bondage of capitalism.

Advocate for Birth Control

In 1912 Sanger's certainty that birth control and sex education were essential in securing economic and personal freedom for America's working women led her to launch a regular column on sex education for the *New York Call*, one of the nation's leading socialist newspapers. In March 1914 Sanger published the first issue of *The Woman Rebel*, a radical feminist monthly that described birth control as a fundamental right of women.

The Woman Rebel quickly caught the attention of legal authorities. Three issues of the monthly publication were confiscated for including content that promoted the use of contraception. In August 1914 federal authorities indicted Sanger for violating laws against sending obscene materials through the mail. A few weeks later Sanger fled for England under the alias "Bertha Watson," leaving her husband and children behind. Even as she was sailing across the Atlantic, however, she defied the law by ordering supporters back in the United States to distribute 100,000 copies of *Family Limitation*, a pamphlet that provided explicit instructions on the use of a variety of contraceptive methods.

Sanger was welcomed in England by a wide assortment of British radicals and feminists. These people hailed her work in America but also urged her to expand her arguments for birth control. Most notably, they convinced her that access to birth control was essential to healthy female sexuality. From this point forward, Sanger's written works repeatedly claimed that birth control would enable married and unmarried women alike to enjoy sexual relations more than ever before, because they would be able to engage in sexual activity without worrying about becoming pregnant. Sanger's stay in England also brought about the end of her marriage, although her formal divorce did not occur until several years later. Separated from her husband, she carried on affairs with a number of men, including H.G. Wells and Havelock Ellis.

Opens Nation's First Birth Control Clinic

In October 1915 Sanger returned to New York to face the postal obscenity charges. One month later, her five-year-old daughter Peggy died after a long bout with pneumonia. Public sympathy for Sanger led prosecutors to drop the charges against her, but Sanger was haunted by guilt over her absence for much of the last year of her daughter's life.

The loss did not slow Sanger's crusade for birth control, however. She traveled across the country promoting her cause, and her uncompromising defiance resulted in her arrest on several occasions. In October 1916 she opened the nation's first birth control clinic in Brownsville, Brooklyn. This event galvanized the opposition of Comstock himself, as well as Roman Catholic Church leaders and many other Americans who believed that birth control promoted immoral and promiscuous behavior.

On October 24, 1916—after only nine days in operation—the clinic was raided and Sanger and her staff were arrested. Sanger was convicted on charges of illegally distributing birth control and spent thirty days in jail. But the episode brought her a new wave of support from wealthy sympathizers and liberal activists and writers. It also failed to convince her to end her birth control activism. In January 1917 she launched a new monthly magazine, *The Birth Control Review*. This periodical was explicitly dedicated to advancing the feminist case for birth control, sexual education, and reproductive freedom. "Throughout the ages, every attempt woman has made to strike off the shackles of slavery has been met with the argument that such an act would result in the downfall of her morality," she wrote in "Morality and Birth Control," an essay that appeared in the February 1918 issue of the magazine:

> Suffrage was going to 'break up the home.' Higher education would unfit her for motherhood, and co-education would surely result in making her immoral. Even today, in some of the more backward countries reading and writing is stoutly discouraged by the clerical powers because 'women may read about things they should not know.' We now know that there never can be a free humanity until woman is freed from ignorance, and we know, too, that woman can never call herself free until she is mistress of her own body. . . . Birth control is the first important step woman must take toward the goal of her freedom.

Sanger's decision to appeal her conviction in Brownsville also gave the growing birth control movement a significant legal victory. In January 1918 the New York Court of Appeals upheld her conviction—but also greatly expanded the circumstances under which doctors could legally prescribe contraceptives to patients.

Controversial Involvement in Eugenics Movement

In 1921 Sanger launched the American Birth Control League, an organization formed with the goal of winning mainstream support for birth control. But Sanger's efforts to enlist the support of doctors, nurses, and social workers were largely neutralized by the Catholic Church and other opponents of birth control, and she became increasingly frustrated by the lack of progress in her mission.

During this period, Sanger's arguments about the benefits of birth control underwent significant changes. For much of the 1910s, she had framed the birth control issue as one of economic justice and class warfare. She argued that birth control and sex education were being denied to working-class women so that America's wealthy elite would always have an abundance of cheap labor for its factories and businesses. In the 1920s, though, Sanger became allied with some segments of America's controversial eugenics movement. Eugenics was a social philosophy that claimed that the human race could be improved over time by encouraging "breeding" between people who possessed high intelligence, good health, and other desirable traits—and by discouraging reproduction by people who were believed not to possess these characteristics.

The eugenics movement was not a fringe movement. Respected men ranging from Oliver Wendell Holmes to Alexander Graham Bell supported the philosophy. Over time, however, some extreme wings of the eugenics movement called for government intervention to prevent "inferior" people from having children. Others used the philosophy as the basis for defending blatantly racist views of other ethnic groups. These beliefs eventually took their most nightmarish form in Nazi Germany, which used the pseudo-science of eugenics to justify the murder of six million European Jews in the Holocaust.

Sanger did not support the idea of limiting population growth solely on the basis of class, race, or ethnicity, but she did at times express a belief that birth control could be used to better the overall "stock" of the American people. Her affiliation with the eugenics movement cast a dark shadow over her record in the 1930s, when the scientific and moral shortcomings of eugenics were widely exposed.

In 1922 Sanger married the wealthy oilman James Noah H. Slee, who became a major funder of his wife's campaign to provide American women with greater access to sex education and birth control. In 1923 she recruited supportive doctors and opened the Birth Control Clinical Research Bureau in New York City. Over the next several years the clinic became a model for other birth control clinics and an important research center on contraceptives and sexual health.

Fading Power and Influence

In the late 1920s Sanger and her allies tried to broaden support for birth control among mainstream middle-class Americans. Sanger consciously abandoned much of the radical feminist rhetoric she had used in the past. But this shift in strategy failed to soften her reputation among many ordinary Americans as a political radical who flouted "traditional" standards of sexual behavior and beliefs. In 1928 she was forced to resign from the presidency of the American Birth Control League under pressure from colleagues who viewed her reputation as an obstacle to the movement to legalize birth control.

In 1929 Sanger formed the National Committee on Federal Legislation for Birth Control to lobby for laws that would grant doctors the legal right to import contraceptives from overseas. This legislative campaign failed, but in its 1936 *One Package* decision the U.S. Court of Appeals ruled that physicians were exempt from the Comstock Law's ban on the importation of birth control materials. This decision gave doctors right to prescribe or distribute contraceptives—although the ban on the importation of contraceptives for personal use was not lifted for another thirty-five years.

Sanger published autobiographies in 1931 and 1938. Both works contained passionate defenses of birth control and feminism, but the books have been dismissed by scholars as unreliable sources of information about her life. In 1939 the American Birth Control League and the Birth Control Clinical Research Bureau merged into the Birth Control Federation of America (later renamed the Planned Parenthood Federation of America). This merger of organizations that Sanger had founded cemented her reputation as the leading figure in the American birth control movement.

By the early 1940s Sanger had retired from active participation in the birth control movement. In the late 1940s, though, she resumed her advocacy, this time on the world stage. Working with family planning experts and birth control activists in Europe and Asia, she helped found the International Planned Parenthood Federation in 1952 and served as its first president until 1959. She then retired to Arizona, where she died in a Tucson nursing home on September 6, 1966. She lived long enough to see a new generation of activists achieve her lifelong goal of legalizing birth control with the 1965 U.S. Supreme Court decision *Griswold v. Connecticut*.

Half a century after her death, Sanger remains one of the most controversial and complex women in American history. Many people who oppose abortion view her as an immoral and destructive figure in the nation's history. Supporters acknowledge that she had flaws, but they generally stand behind biographer Ellen Chesler's proclamation that "every woman in the world today who takes her sexual and reproductive autonomy for granted should venerate Margaret Sanger."

Sources:

Chesler, Ellen. *Woman of Valor: Margaret Sanger and the Birth Control Movement in America.* New York: Simon and Schuster, 1992.

Kennedy, David M. *Birth Control in America: The Career of Margaret Sanger.* New Haven, CT: Yale University Press, 1991.

Margaret Sanger Papers Project. http://www.nyu.edu/projects/sanger.

Sanger, Margaret. *My Fight for Birth Control.* New York: Farrar and Rinehart, 1931.

Randall Terry (1959-)
Conservative Political and Religious Activist
Founder of the Confrontational Pro-Life Group
Operation Rescue

Randall Terry was born in 1959 and raised in upstate New York. The son of two public school teachers, he went through an extended period of adolescent rebellion that was capped by his decision to drop out of high school at age 16. After several months, though, he returned home and earned his general equivalency diploma (GED). Around this same time he experienced a religious conversion and joined the Pentecostal Church. In 1978 he enrolled at the Elm Bible Institute in Lima, New York, where he met his first wife, Cindy Dean.

After putting aside plans to serve as a religious missionary in South America with his new wife, Terry became a used car salesman in Binghamton, New York. Terry's conservative religious convictions deepened during this time, and he came to view abortion as a moral evil. In 1983 he began conducting one-man protests outside a local family services clinic that provided abortions to women with unwanted pregnancies. He was eventually joined in these protests by his wife and several other members of his church. According to Terry, their ongoing efforts convinced a few pregnant women to turn away from the clinic and carry their pregnancies to term. These successes convinced Terry that his cause was righteous and his methods effective.

In May 1984 Terry founded Project Life, a pro-life religious group that maintained a modest "pregnancy center" that provided free medical services and encouragement to pregnant women. As the months passed, though, Terry decided to adopt more confrontational tactics to stop the abortions being performed in area clinics. "We were all clamoring about abortion being murder, but we had not even peacefully tried to blockade abortion mills," he wrote in his 1988 book *Operation Rescue*. "As these ideas took shape in my mind and the truths of God's Word grabbed my heart, the foundation for Operation Rescue was laid."

Operation Rescue

Terry founded the militant anti-abortion organization Operation Rescue in October 1986. Over the next several months, Terry and the group attracted national attention for their confrontational protest strategies. Their standard tactic involved surrounding a targeted abortion clinic without warning and trying to prevent any women from entering. The protesters' strategies ranged from screaming and shouting at women to pressing their bodies against car doors to prevent women from getting into the clinic. When police officers showed up to stop their activities, the demonstrators offered passive resistance by "going limp" and forcing police to physically carry them from the scene.

Terry described these activities as a form of civil disobedience that could awaken the American people to the evils of abortion. "From the platform of repentance, we must take our bodies down to the abortion mills and peacefully and prayerfully place ourselves between the killer and his intended victims," he wrote in *Operation Rescue*. "This is the only way we can produce the social tension necessary to bring about political change."

Some longtime pro-life activists and groups expressed serious doubts about the wisdom of this course of action. They argued that most Americans disapproved of the Operation Rescue tactics and worried that Terry's actions might actually hurt the pro-life movement. But Terry dismissed these concerns. "Look at the arrests in the civil rights movement," he said in an interview with *Time*. "The majority of Americans were against the tactics of the civil rights workers, the lunch-counter sit ins, etc. And yet those street-level protests produced political change."

The methods employed by Operation Rescue, though, brought Terry a host of legal problems. In 1989 he was sentenced to 24 months in prison for criminal assembly and unlawful trespassing at a clinic in Atlanta, Georgia. The judge offered Terry a suspended sentence if he agreed to pay a $1,000 fine and stay away from Atlanta for two years, but he refused. He declared that in his view, preventing the murder of innocent children was not a crime.

The sit-ins, blockades, and other activities of Operation Rescue also brought financial difficulties. In 1990 Terry closed the doors of the Binghamton headquarters of Operation Rescue because of lawsuits filed by various pro-choice organizations. But this setback did not cripple the organization. Instead, Operation Rescue's 110 local chapters continued carrying out his work all around the country. The closure also did not change Terry's confrontational ways. In 1992, for example, he arranged to have a dead fetus presented to presidential candidate Bill Clinton at the Democratic National Convention. Terry also claims that between 1987 and 1994, Operation Rescue demonstrators were arrested more than 70,000 times.

Bankruptcy and Condemnation from the Right

In 1994 Terry left Operation Rescue and Flip Benham became national director of the organization (which later changed its name to Operation Save America). Terry remained an outspoken critic of abortion, though, and he also became known for his opposition to gay rights and his support for prayer in public schools. In 1998 he ran for a New York seat in the U.S. Congress but was badly defeated.

In the late 1990s Terry lost long legal battles with the National Organization for Women (NOW) and Planned Parenthood over damages caused in clinic attacks. In order to pay a total of $1.6 million in damages to the groups, Terry declared bankruptcy. At that point he began soliciting money from supporters via his personal Web site, claiming that he needed the funds to provide for his family.

Terry had long been viewed as a dangerous and publicity-hungry extremist by Americans who did not share his views, but people of the religious right had historically been reluctant to criticize him. This situation changed in 2000, when Terry left his wife of 19 years, with whom he had raised four children (including three adopted children). He then married Andrea Kollmorgen, a former assistant with whom he eventually had three sons. This series of events—along with charges of fraud and adultery and other sins—brought Terry heavy criticism from many fundamentalist Christian and anti-abortion leaders. Benham, for instance, declared that Terry had "completely disqualified himself from any leadership position in the Christian community" through his actions. Terry was also pushed out of his church of fifteen years, the Landmark Church of Binghamton. The activist has denied all accusations of adultery, unethical fundraising, and other charges.

A Return to the Spotlight

Terry largely disappeared from public sight in the early 2000s. But after a brief effort to launch a country-western singing career in Nashville, he returned to his former role as a vocal champion of conservative religious positions. As director of a new organization called the Society for Truth and Justice, he condemned abortion, homosexuality, same-sex marriage, right-to-die legislation, and the religion of Islam.

These efforts to re-establish himself as a relevant spokesman for the Christian right, however, were complicated by highly publicized rifts with the children from his first marriage. He publicly criticized both of his adopted daughters for becoming pregnant outside of marriage, and in 2004 Terry publicly disowned his adopted son after the young man revealed that he was a homosexual.

In 2005 Terry became involved in the national controversy over the fate of Terri Schiavo, a brain-damaged woman whose relatives engaged in a long legal battle over whether to remove her artificial life support systems. When these systems were finally removed at her husband's request, over the objections of her parents, Schiavo died soon afterward. Terry served as a spokesman for Schiavo's parents, Bob and Mary Schindler, during the final weeks of the legal battle over the woman's fate.

In 2006 Terry formally joined the Catholic Church. That same year, he lost a bitterly contested Republican primary election to incumbent James E. King, Jr., for a seat in the Florida state Senate. Since that time, he has continued to travel the country preaching his pro-life message and condemning supporters of abortion rights.

Sources:

Gorney, Cynthia. *Articles of Faith: A Frontline History of the Abortion Wars.* New York: Simon & Schuster, 2000.

Lacayo, Richard. "Crusading against the Pro-Choice Movement." *Time,* October 21, 1991.

Powell, Michael. "Family Values." *Washington Post,* April 22, 2004.

Terry, Randall A. *Accessory to Murder: The Enemies, Allies, and Accomplices to the Death of Our Culture.* Brentwood, TN: Wolgemuth & Hyatt, 1991.

Terry, Randall A. *Operation Rescue.* Springdale, PA: Whitaker House, 1988.

Henry Wade (1914-2001)
Dallas County District Attorney
Defendant in the Roe v. Wade *Case*

Henry Menasco Wade was born on November 11, 1914, in Rockwall, Texas. The son of a local judge, Wade developed an interest in the law at an early age. He excelled as a student throughout high school and college, and he graduated from the University of Texas Law School with top academic honors.

Wade passed the Texas bar exam, but instead of joining one of the Dallas law firms that extended job offers to him, he decided to join the Federal Bureau of Investigation (FBI). He spent several years as an FBI agent before beginning his legal career in earnest. In 1947 he became an assistant district attorney for Dallas County. Three years later Wade was elected district attorney for the county.

Prosecutor of Jack Ruby

As the head district attorney for Dallas County, Wade oversaw the prosecution of thousands of people accused of crimes every year. But two of these cases attracted national attention. The first of these cases came in 1963, after President John F. Kennedy was assassinated in Dallas on November 22 by Lee Harvey Oswald. Two days later, a Dallas nightclub owner named Jack Ruby killed Oswald when authorities were transferring the assassin from police headquarters to the county jail.

Wade's office sought the death penalty for Ruby, arguing that by killing Oswald he had "mocked American justice while the spotlight was on Dallas." Ruby was convicted and sentenced to death in 1964. An appeals court granted him a new trial, however, ruling that he did not receive a fair trial in Dallas, where emotions about the case ran extremely high. Ruby died of cancer in 1967 while awaiting re-trial.

Wade's prosecution of Ruby increased the district attorney's popularity in Dallas County, and his simple manner ensured that he remained a popular figure. But as the *New York Times* later observed, "Mr. Wade's cigar chewing, his drawl, his love of dominoes and his puttering around his farm near Dallas gave him an artfully deceiving image. His folksy manner masked a keen legal mind, a fiercely competitive streak, and a relentless faith in the efficacy of punishment."

Defendant in *Roe v. Wade* Case

Wade returned to the national spotlight in 1970, when Dallas County resident Norma McCorvey—under the fictitious name of Jane Roe—sued his office in order to gain the right to terminate her unwanted pregnancy. Wade was the "respondent" or defendant in the lawsuit because, as district attorney for Dallas County, he was officially responsible for enforcing a Texas state law prohibiting any abortions except in cases where the life of the mother was in danger.

Wade did not directly participate in the subsequent courtroom battle. Instead, he selected assistant district attorneys John Tolle and Robert Flowers to argue the case against Sarah Weddington and Linda Coffee, the attorneys representing McCorvey. On June 17, 1970, Wade's office lost the case when the Fifth Circuit Court ruled that Texas's abortion law violated the Ninth Amendment to the Constitution.

Wade, though, refused to accept defeat. Instead, he declared his intention to continue to enforce the state's anti-abortion law while his office appealed the verdict. "Apparently we're free to try them [doctors who perform abortion], so we'll still do that," he told reporters. This public defiance may have contributed to the U.S. Supreme Court's decision to hear the *Roe v. Wade* case rather than one of the many other abortion-related cases that were moving through the U.S. justice system in the early 1970s.

The legal battle continued until January 22, 1973, when the U.S. Supreme Court voted 7-2 to strike down the Texas abortion law. The Court ruled that the Texas statute violated constitutional rights to privacy. The majority opinion specifically asserted that the Constitution's First, Fourth, Ninth, and Fourteenth Amendments protected an individual's "zone of privacy" against intrusive state laws in such areas as marriage, parenting, and contraception, including "a woman's decision whether or not to terminate her pregnancy."

Wade had little involvement in the case once it went to the Supreme Court. After the landmark 1973 ruling legalized abortion throughout the United States, he stated that he had no strong feelings about abortion, either positive or negative. The media frenzy surrounding Wade faded once the

Court announced its decision in *Roe v. Wade*. He spent another 14 years as Dallas County district attorney. He finally retired in 1987, 36 years after first winning election, and joined a Dallas law firm. He died on March 1, 2001, at an assisted-living center in Dallas at the age of 86.

Sources:

Garrow, David J. *Liberty and Sexuality: The Right to Privacy and the Making of Roe v. Wade.* New York: Macmillan, 1994.

Saxon, Wolfgang. "Henry Wade, Prosecutor in National Spotlight, Dies at 86." *New York Times,* March 2, 2001.

Weddington, Sarah. *A Question of Choice.* New York: Putnam, 1992.

Sarah Weddington (1945-)
Attorney Who Won the 1973 Supreme Court Case Roe v. Wade

Sarah Ragle Weddington was born in Abilene, Texas, on February 5, 1945. Her parents were Herbert Doyle Ragle, a Methodist minister, and Lena Catherine Ragle, a teacher and girls' high school basketball coach. Independent-minded and ambitious, Weddington was heavily involved in school and church youth group activities. After graduating from high school, she attended McMurry College, a small Methodist school in Abilene. She graduated from McMurry at age 19 and gained admittance to the University of Texas Law School in Austin. During her years in Austin, however, her dream of a legal career sometimes seemed like an impossible goal.

Overcoming Gender Obstacles

Weddington's life in Austin was hectic and pressure-packed. In addition to taking a full course load of challenging law classes, she worked several jobs and became romantically involved with Ron Weddington, a fellow student. When she was a third-year law student at Texas, she discovered that she was pregnant. After discussing the situation with her boyfriend—who later became her husband—the couple decided to avoid the Texas state law prohibiting abortions (except ones where the life of the mother was endangered). They traveled to the Mexican border town of Piedras Negras. Abortion was illegal in Mexico as well, but it was far easier to find a competent doctor willing to perform the procedure in Piedras Negras.

After her abortion, Weddington returned to Austin, earned a law degree from the University of Texas School of Law in 1967, and married Ron Weddington. Weddington was one of only five women in her graduating class. She had an outstanding academic record, but when she went looking for a job, she found that most large Texas firms would not even consider hiring her because of her gender. Linda Coffee, a friend from Weddington's graduating

159

class, encountered the same hostile job market. To their great disgust, both women were forced to accept lesser jobs—Coffee with a small firm specializing in bankruptcy law, Weddington with the American Bar Association.

This rough beginning to Weddington's legal career increased the young lawyer's interest in women's rights. She became friends with staff members on *The Rag*, an Austin-based feminist underground newspaper. She also became involved in birth control counseling, including referring women with unwanted pregnancies to clean, safe abortion clinics in Mexico.

As Weddington's activities in these areas deepened, she began exploring whether it would be possible to mount an effective legal challenge to the Texas anti-abortion law. Her research soon convinced her to focus her attack on the constitutionality of the statute, which she believed violated a woman's right to privacy. In December 1969 she called Coffee and asked for help preparing the lawsuit. Coffee immediately signed up, and the two women began looking for a pregnant woman who could serve as a plaintiff in the case.

Walking Into History

In January 1970 Weddington and Coffee met Norma McCorvey, a single, pregnant woman from a troubled background who had been unable to end her unwanted pregnancy because of the Texas anti-abortion law. McCorvey agreed to be the plaintiff in their lawsuit, even though the young lawyers cautioned her that the case might not be resolved in time for her to obtain an abortion. To protect McCorvey's identity, the lawyers gave her the alias "Jane Roe."

In March 1970 Weddington and Coffee submitted the necessary legal papers in a federal court in Dallas. Two months later, Weddington entered the courtroom to make her oral presentation to the three-judge Fifth Circuit Court. Her legal experience up to that point amounted to little more than a few uncontested divorce cases. She was tremendously nervous, but she settled down and laid out the case for her anonymous client. When the hearing was over, she and her allies left the courtroom with no idea how the judges would rule. "It is the close calls that make it to trial," she later explained in her book *A Question of Choice*. "Most lawyers leave the courtroom knowing they will simply have to wait for the decision. That is just the way it is. We began to wait."

Three months later, the wait was over. On June 17, 1970, the Fifth Circuit Court sided with Weddington and Roe, ruling that Texas's abortion law violated the Ninth Amendment to the Constitution. Prosecuting attorney Henry

Wade, who had been on the losing end of the decision, immediately announced his intention to appeal the ruling. The legal fight was far from over.

The *Roe v. Wade* case reached the U.S. Supreme Court in May 1971. For the next year and a half, Weddington devoted her life to the case. Writing in *A Question of Choice,* she expressed her amazement at the chain of events:

> The little case that Linda and I had started as volunteer lawyers in response to questions from women at the referral project might well become the vehicle for protecting reproductive rights and freedom of choice for every American woman. The thought was overwhelming—and humbling. Reality set in as I thought of the responsibility of the case and the disastrous consequences and despair that would follow if we lost.

The legal battle continued until January 22, 1973, when the U.S. Supreme Court voted 7-2 to strike down the Texas abortion law. The Court ruled that the Texas statute violated Jane Roe's constitutional right to privacy. The majority opinion specifically asserted that the Constitution's First, Fourth, Ninth, and Fourteenth Amendments protected an individual's "zone of privacy" against intrusive state laws in such areas as marriage, parenting, and contraception, including "a woman's decision whether or not to terminate her pregnancy."

This landmark decision struck down anti-abortion laws across the country and established abortion as a fundamental right for American women. It also made Weddington the youngest person ever to win a case before the U.S. Supreme Court. She was overjoyed by the ruling, even though she later admitted that "I never thought I was walking into history when I started this case."

Looking back on the 1973 *Roe v. Wade* verdict in her book *A Question of Choice,* Weddington stated "the battle was never 'for abortion'—abortion was not what we wanted to encourage. The battle was for the basic right of women to make their own decisions. There was a basic question underlying the specific issue of abortion: Who is to control and define the lives of women? And our answer was: Not the government!"

Years of Public Service

Weddington's work on the *Roe* case made her well known across Texas and the rest of the country. This name recognition helped her gain election to the Texas House of Representatives in late 1972. She served three terms as a state congresswoman beginning in early 1973. One of her proudest legislative achievements stemmed from an incident in which a credit card company refused to issue her a credit card in her own name without her husband's signature. "So of course I ran for the [Texas state] legislature and passed the Equal Credit Bill, and then went back and got my credit card," she recalled.

In September 1974 Weddington and her husband divorced under friendly terms. Three years later, she joined the administration of President Jimmy Carter as general counsel of the U.S. Department of Agriculture. In 1978 she was appointed special assistant to Carter on women's issues and leadership outreach. In 1981 she returned to Texas, beginning a nine-year stint as a professor at Texas Woman's University.

The 1980s also brought Weddington a host of other career challenges and opportunities. From 1983 to 1985 she served as the first female director of the Texas Office of State-Federal Relations, and in 1986 she joined the faculty of the University of Texas at Austin.

In 1992 Weddington published *A Question of Choice,* which served as both a history of the *Roe v. Wade* case from her perspective as well as a call to preserve abortion rights for future generations of American women. Since that time, she has remained a steadfast supporter of abortion rights in the United States and around the world. Weddington has received awards from numerous progressive and women's organizations, and she has been featured frequently over the years in national newsmagazines, newspapers, and television programs. She is also a frequent speaker on leadership and women's issues.

Sources:

Faux, Marian. Roe v. Wade: *The Untold Story of the Landmark Supreme Court Decision That Made Abortion Legal.* New York: Macmillan, 1988.

Garrow, David J. *Liberty and Sexuality: The Right to Privacy and the Making of* Roe v. Wade. Berkeley: University of California Press, 1998.

Page, Cristina. *How the Pro-Choice Movement Saved America: Freedom, Politics, and the War on Sex.* New York: Basic Books, 2006.

Weddington, Sarah. *A Question of Choice.* New York: Putnam, 1992.

The Weddington Center. http://www.weddingtoncenter.com.

John C. Willke (1925-)
Pro-Life Activist
President of the National Right to Life
Committee from 1981 to 1991

John Charles Willke was born on April 5, 1925, in Maria Stein, Ohio. His parents were Gerald T. Willke, a physician, and Marie Wuennemann Willke. Raised in a devout Roman Catholic household, Willke developed a strong religious faith at an early age.

After graduating from high school, Willke studied at Xavier University in Cincinnati and Oberlin College in Oberlin, Ohio. He received his medical doctorate from the University of Cincinnati in 1948. That same year, he married Barbara Jean Hiltz. Willke and his wife, who worked as a registered nurse, eventually had six children together.

Willke started his own private practice in family medicine and obstetrics in the Cincinnati area in 1950. In 1952 he left his practice behind to serve in the U.S. Air Force Medical Corps. Two years later he completed his military service and returned home with the rank of captain.

Rising Prominence as Abortion Foe

Willke's Cincinnati practice thrived during the late 1950s and 1960s (he maintained his practice until the mid-1990s), and he eventually became a member of the senior attending staff at both Providence and Good Samaritan hospitals in Cincinnati. By 1970, he had also become known to many health professionals in the Cincinnati area for his staunch opposition to efforts to legalize abortion. That year, he and his wife Barbara founded Right to Life of Greater Cincinnati, the first local anti-abortion organization in the nation.

In 1971—a time when opponents of abortion were first organizing and mobilizing together to fight the threat of legalization—Jack and Barbara Willke published one of the most influential anti-abortion publications of the decade. *Handbook on Abortion*, which combined moral and religious arguments against abortion with pictures of aborted fetuses, became a basic tool of numerous pro-life organizations over the next several years.

In 1972 Willke traveled to Michigan to help defeat a ballot referendum that would have legalized abortion in the state during the first twenty weeks of pregnancy. During the weeks leading up to the referendum, Willke and his wife distributed a graphic color anti-abortion brochure called "Life and Death" all across the state. Their activism, combined with the efforts of Catholic leaders and other abortion opponents, was credited with swinging the sentiments of Michigan voters against the referendum. The "Life and Death" brochure was also distributed across North Dakota, where a similar referendum that would have legalized abortion in some circumstances went down to defeat in 1972.

Willke was deeply upset by the January 1973 Supreme Court decision in the *Roe v. Wade* case. This ruling struck down numerous state laws outlawing abortion and made the procedure legal across the United States. Willke and his wife devoted much of their time and energy to the pro-life cause in the years following the *Roe v. Wade* decision.

President of National Right to Life

In May 1973 Willke helped found the National Right to Life Committee, one of the most important and visible anti-abortion organizations to emerge following *Roe v. Wade*. In 1981 he became president of National Right to Life, and he served in that capacity for ten years before stepping down.

During his presidency, Willke worked hard to change the wording used in abortion debates to emphasize the humanity of the fetus. For instance, he suggested using terms like "unborn baby" instead of "embryo," and "tiny hands and feet" rather than "fetal tissue." Willke also returned again and again to his belief that embryos are people with legal rights from the moment of conception, since the 46 chromosomes that determine a person's separate and distinct genetic identity are all present in the fertilized egg. "Contained within the single cell who I once was, was the totality of everything I am today," he frequently declared.

Willke also maintained National Right to Life's reputation as an important force in national politics. "I believe that a political candidate who is in favor of abortion on demand is actively advocating the dismemberment and killing of every third baby conceived in America," he told *People Weekly* in

1984. "I must look at him or her and say, 'You beast. For this terrible thing you have disqualified yourself from holding public office.'"

For much of the 1980s and 1990s, Willke expressed his anti-abortion views on a daily radio program that was carried on stations all across the country. In 1985 he founded the International Right to Life Federation, and he continued to lead that organization as president into the 2000s. He also served as director of the Life Issues Institute, a Cincinnati-based organization devoted to fighting abortion, euthanasia, and embryonic stem cell research through education.

Willke's wife has supported him in all of these efforts. They have collaborated over the years to write numerous books and magazine articles on the abortion issue and sex education, as well as to produce videos, slide shows, and CDs on abortion and human sexuality. In 1997 they published a revised version of their 1971 *Handbook on Abortion*—often described as the Bible of the pro-life movement—entitled *Why Can't We Love Them Both?*

Sources:

Horstman, Barry M. "Jack and Barbara Willke: Willkes Still Battle Abortion." *Cincinnati Post,* June 4, 1999.

Stevens, Leonard A. *The Case of* Roe v. Wade. New York: Putnam, 1996.

Tribe, Laurence H. *Abortion: The Clash of Absolutes.* New York: Norton, 1990.

Willke, John C. *Handbook on Abortion.* Rev. ed. Cincinnati, OH: Hayes, 1975.

Willke, John C., and Daniel Maguire. "As the Abortion Issue Reaches a Political Flashpoint, Two Catholic Experts Clash in Debate." *People Weekly,* October 22, 1984.

PRIMARY SOURCES

The Foundations of Privacy in the U.S. Constitution

Throughout U.S. history, legal efforts to overturn state laws banning birth control and abortion have centered around the right to privacy. Opponents of such laws argue that people have the right to make decisions about personal matters, including whether or not to bear children, without interference from the government. Although privacy is not one of the specific rights guaranteed to American citizens under the U.S. Constitution, the activists who fought to legalize contraception and abortion claimed that implicit support for this strong right to privacy could be found in the Ninth and Fourteenth Amendments.

The Ninth Amendment is part of the Bill of Rights that was passed shortly after the Constitution took effect in 1789. It simply says that citizens may have rights and liberties that are not spelled out in the Constitution. The Fourteenth Amendment was passed in 1866, immediately following the Civil War. It was originally intended to secure the rights of citizenship for former African-American slaves, and Southern states were required to ratify it in order to rejoin the Union. The first section of the Amendment was later applied to reproductive rights. It guarantees citizens equal protection under the law and says that the government may not interfere with citizens' rights and liberties without due process of law.

Amendment 9

The enumeration in the Constitution, of certain rights, shall not be construed to deny or disparage others retained by the people.

Amendment 14

1. All persons born or naturalized in the United States, and subject to the jurisdiction thereof, are citizens of the United States and of the State wherein they reside. No State shall make or enforce any law which shall abridge the privileges or immunities of citizens of the United States; nor shall any State deprive any person of life, liberty, or property, without due process of law; nor deny to any person within its jurisdiction the equal protection of the laws.

Source: U.S. Constitution, Ninth Amendment and Fourteenth Amendment.

The Comstock Law Bans Birth Control and Abortion

On March 3, 1873, the U.S. Congress passed the Act for the Suppression of Trade in, and Circulation of, Obscene Literature and Articles for Immoral Use. This act was better known as the Comstock Law, after anti-obscenity crusader Anthony Comstock, who was a leading force behind the law. The Comstock Law made it illegal for anyone to sell, publish, or possess a wide variety of materials that Comstock and his supporters considered obscene. This included all printed information about sex and sexually transmitted diseases, as well as any drug or device that could be used for contraception or abortion. Following is an excerpt from the law:

Be it enacted.... That whoever, within the District of Columbia or any of the Territories of the United States, shall sell, or shall offer to sell, or to lend, or to give away, or in any manner to exhibit, or shall otherwise publish or offer to publish in any manner, or shall have in his possession, for any such purpose or purposes, an obscene book, pamphlet, paper, writing, advertisement, circular, print, picture, drawing or other representation, figure, or image on or of paper or other material, or any cast instrument, or other article of an immoral nature, or any drug or medicine, or any article whatever, for the prevention of conception, or for causing unlawful abortion, or shall advertise the same for sale, or shall write or print, or cause to be written or printed, any card, circular, book, pamphlet, advertisement, or notice of any kind, stating when, where, how, or of whom, or by what means, any of the articles in this section can be purchased or obtained, or shall manufacture, draw, or print, or in any wise make any of such articles, shall be deemed guilty of a misdemeanor, and on conviction thereof in any court of the United States, he shall be imprisoned at hard labor in the penitentiary for not less than six months nor more than five years for each offense, or fined not less than one hundred dollars nor more than two thousand dollars, with costs of court.

Source: Act of March 3, 1873, chapter 258, *Statutes at Large of the United States*, volume 17, page 598 (1873).

NOW Calls for the Repeal of Abortion Laws

The movement to reform or repeal state anti-abortion laws gained strength during the 1960s with the support of women's rights groups. The National Organization for Women (NOW) was founded in 1966 by the feminist author Betty Friedan. The following year, NOW members held a debate on abortion at their national meeting. They voted to promote legislation that would guarantee women the right to control their own reproductive decisions. To accomplish this goal, the organization developed the following set of proposals:

The following proposals are offered for purposes of discussion by the 1967 NOW Membership Conference:

1. Constitutional Amendment

There is perhaps no more fundamental human right, save the right to life itself, than the right to one's own physical person, a basic part of which is the right to determine whether or not one will give birth to another human being. An egg, a sperm, a zygote or a fetus is not a person or a human being and does not have "rights" as a person or a human being. Whatever "rights" these may have are necessarily because of biological fact completely dependent upon and subordinate to the human bodies which house them.

Constitutional rights are accorded to human beings solely in terms of *restrictions on governments*. It is the government's interference with the right of women to control their own reproductive process that we are concerned with here. All of the states have laws restricting this right of a woman to her own physical person. New York NOW has urged that that state adopt a constitutional provision prohibiting governmental interference with this right. The following suggested amendment to the United States Constitution would protect this right of women in all the states:

THE RIGHT OF A WOMAN TO PREVENT CONCEPTION AND WITH PROPER MEDICAL SAFEGUARDS TO TERMINATE HER PREGNANCY SHALL NOT BE DENIED OR ABRIDGED BY THE UNITED STATES OR BY ANY STATE.

Copyright © 1967 National Organization for Women. Reprinted with permission.

The effect of this amendment would be to nullify all existing state criminal abortion laws, leaving the question of whether or not to have an abortion a matter for the woman herself, rather than the government, to decide.

2. Revision of State Laws

Criminal abortion laws in 42 states prohibit the performance of abortions unless necessary to save the life of the pregnant woman. In the other eight states— Alabama, California, Colorado, Maryland, Mississippi, New Mexico, North Carolina, and Oregon—and in the District of Columbia, abortions are permitted in certain other additional circumstance, such as where pregnancy results from rape, incest, or where the physical or mental health of the woman is endangered.

Bills to make abortion laws restrictive were introduced in 28 state legislatures in 1967. The Colorado and North Carolina laws, enacted in 1967, are patterned after the American Law Institute's Model Penal Code.

They permit abortions where continuance of the pregnancy would gravely impair the physical or mental health of the woman, the child would be born with grave physical or mental defect, or the pregnancy resulted from rape, incest or other felonious intercourse. (It may be noted that the definition of "human being" in the ALI Model Penal Code criminal homicide provisions is "a person who has been born and is alive.")

In spite of the state criminal abortion laws, it is estimated that between 200,000 and over a million illegal abortions are performed in this country each year, and at least 4 out of 5 of them on married women.

Abortion is not a desirable method of birth control and other means should be made available to everyone who wishes to use them. However, criminal abortion laws clearly have proven to be ineffectual in eliminating the use of abortion as a means of birth control, and have driven women to unskilled practitioners, handicapped doctors in practicing their profession, and have made a mockery of the law.

State criminal abortion laws could, of course, simply be repealed or they could be replaced with statutes which give a pregnant woman a right of *civil* action against any government official who requires or attempts to require her to have an abortion or who prevents or attempts to prevent her from having an abortion. In other words, the statute would recognize her civil right to determine her own reproductive process by giving her a right to sue the particular agent of the state who deprives or attempts to deprive her of that right.

This kind of civil rights protection giving a right to sue for damages is similar to that provided in one of the post Civil War federal civil rights statutes (42 U.S.C. 1983):

"Every person who, under color of any statute, ordinance, regulation, custom, or usage, of any State or Territory, subjects, or causes to be subjected, any citizen of the United States or other person within the jurisdiction thereof to the deprivation of any rights, privileges, or immunities secured by the Constitution and laws, shall be liable to the party injured in an action at law, suit in equity, or other proper proceeding for redress."

Under such a replacement statute, a doctor would be free to perform an abortion without fear of any criminal prosecution. But if a state or local welfare official tried to force a woman to have (or not have) an abortion, she could sue him for damages or get a court order restraining him from pressuring her or cutting off her welfare funds if she refused to comply with his wishes.

The following is a proposed model state law to prevent governmental interference in a woman's reproductive process:

ANY PERSON WHO, UNDER COLOR OF ANY FEDERAL, STATE OR LOCAL LAW, REGULATION OR CUSTOM, REQUIRES OR ATTEMPTS TO REQUIRE ANY PREGNANT WOMAN IN THIS STATE TO HAVE AN ABORTION, OR PREVENTS OR ATTEMPTS TO PREVENT ANY PREGNANT WOMAN IN THIS STATE FROM HAVING AN ABORTION PERFORMED BY A LICENSED MEDICAL PRACTITIONER, SHALL BE LIABLE TO SUCH WOMAN IN AN ACTION AT LAW, SUIT IN EQUITY, OR OTHER PROPER PROCEEDING FOR REDRESS.

SECTION (*reference to criminal abortion law*) OF (*state statutes*) IS HEREBY REPEALED.

It is not the function of government to determine who shall and who shall not give birth to a child. The first paragraph of the above model law, with the deletion of the words "in this state" might also be appropriate for a federal law.

Source: National Organization for Women. "The Right of a Woman to Determine Her Own Reproductive Process." Proposal from the National Organization for Women Membership Conference, 1967.

Justice Harry A. Blackmun Announces the Court's Decision

The U.S. Supreme Court announced its decision in the case of Roe v. Wade *on January 22, 1973. Justice Harry Blackmun wrote the majority opinion, which is excerpted below. The ruling declared the Texas abortion law in question unconstitutional. In the process, the Court invalidated all other state abortion laws and made abortion legal throughout the United States.*

MR. JUSTICE BLACKMUN delivered the opinion of the Court.

This Texas federal appeal and its Georgia companion, *Doe v. Bolton*, present constitutional challenges to state criminal abortion legislation. The Texas statutes under attack here are typical of those that have been in effect in many States for approximately a century. The Georgia statutes, in contrast, have a modern cast and are a legislative product that, to an extent at least, obviously reflects the influences of recent attitudinal change, of advancing medical knowledge and techniques, and of new thinking about an old issue.

We forthwith acknowledge our awareness of the sensitive and emotional nature of the abortion controversy, of the vigorous opposing views, even among physicians, and of the deep and seemingly absolute convictions that the subject inspires. One's philosophy, one's experiences, one's exposure to the raw edges of human existence, one's religious training, one's attitudes toward life and family and their values, and the moral standards one establishes and seeks to observe, are all likely to influence and to color one's thinking and conclusions about abortion. In addition, population growth, pollution, poverty, and racial overtones tend to complicate and not to simplify the problem.

Our task, of course, is to resolve the issue by constitutional measurement, free of emotion and of predilection. We seek earnestly to do this, and, because we do, we have inquired into, and in this opinion place some emphasis upon, medical and medical-legal history and what that history reveals about man's attitudes toward the abortion procedure over the centuries....

[Sections I-IV of the opinion lay out the facts of the *Roe v. Wade* case: the Texas law at issue; the claims of the plaintiffs; and lower court decisions. Blackmun then addresses the question of legal standing. The Court finds that Jane Roe "had standing to undertake this litigation, that she presented a justiciable controversy, and that the termination of her 1970 pregnancy has not rendered her case moot." But the Court finds that the two other parties in the lawsuit, Dr. James Hallford and John and Mary Doe, lack standing and dismisses their parts of the case.]

V

The principal thrust of appellant's [Roe's] attack on the Texas statutes is that they improperly invade a right, said to be possessed by the pregnant woman, to choose to terminate her pregnancy. Appellant would discover this right in the concept of personal "liberty" embodied in the Fourteenth Amendment's Due Process Clause; or in personal, marital, familial, and sexual privacy said to be protected by the Bill of Rights or its penumbras, or among those rights reserved to the people by the Ninth Amendment. Before addressing this claim, we feel it desirable briefly to survey, in several aspects, the history of abortion, for such insight as that history may afford us, and then to examine the state purposes and interests behind the criminal abortion laws.

VI

It perhaps is not generally appreciated that the restrictive criminal abortion laws in effect in a majority of States today are of relatively recent vintage. Those laws, generally proscribing abortion or its attempt at any time during pregnancy except when necessary to preserve the pregnant woman's life, are not of ancient or even of common-law origin. Instead, they derive from statutory changes effected, for the most part, in the latter half of the 19th century.

[Blackmun examines the history of abortion, touching on ancient attitudes and English common law. In the United States, he finds that most states did not enact laws to restrict or ban abortion until after the Civil War. State abortion laws proliferated in the late 19th and early 20th centuries, Blackmun notes, until "by the end of the 1950's, a large majority of the jurisdictions banned abortion, however and whenever performed, unless done to save or preserve the life of the mother."]

In the past several years, however, a trend toward liberalization of abortion statutes has resulted in adoption, by about one-third of the States, of less stringent laws, most of them patterned after the ALI Model Penal Code.... It is thus apparent that at common law, at the time of the adoption of our Constitution, and throughout the major portion of the 19th century, abortion was viewed with less disfavor than under most American statutes currently in effect. Phrasing it another way, a woman enjoyed a substantially broader right to terminate a pregnancy than she does in most States today. At least with respect to the early stage of pregnancy, and very possibly without such a limitation, the opportunity to make this choice was present in this country well into the 19th century. Even later, the law continued for some time to treat less punitively an abortion procured in early pregnancy.

[Blackmun then outlines the historical positions of the American Medical Association, the American Public Health Association, and the American Bar Association on abortion.]

VII

Three reasons have been advanced to explain historically the enactment of criminal abortion laws in the 19th century and to justify their continued existence.

It has been argued occasionally that these laws were the product of a Victorian social concern to discourage illicit sexual conduct. Texas, however, does not advance this justification in the present case, and it appears that no court or commentator has taken the argument seriously. The appellants and amici ["friends of the court," or parties that filed amicus curiae briefs in the case] contend, moreover, that this is not a proper state purpose at all and suggest that, if it were, the Texas statutes are overbroad in protecting it since the law fails to distinguish between married and unwed mothers.

A second reason is concerned with abortion as a medical procedure. When most criminal abortion laws were first enacted, the procedure was a hazardous one for the woman. This was particularly true prior to the development of antisepsis. Antiseptic techniques, of course, were based on discoveries by Lister, Pasteur, and others first announced in 1867, but were not generally accepted and employed until about the turn of the century. Abortion mortality was high. Even after 1900, and perhaps until as late as the development of antibiotics in the 1940's, standard modern techniques such as dilation and curettage were not nearly so safe as they are today. Thus, it has been argued that a State's real concern in enacting a criminal abortion law was to protect the pregnant woman, that is, to restrain her from submitting to a procedure that placed her life in serious jeopardy.

Modern medical techniques have altered this situation. Appellants and various amici refer to medical data indicating that abortion in early pregnancy, that is, prior to the end of the first trimester, although not without its risk, is now relatively safe. Mortality rates for women undergoing early abortions, where the procedure is legal, appear to be as low as or lower than the rates for normal childbirth. Consequently, any interest of the State in protecting the woman from an inherently hazardous procedure, except when it would be equally dangerous for her to forgo it, has largely disappeared. Of course, important state interests in the areas of health and medical standards do remain.

The State has a legitimate interest in seeing to it that abortion, like any other medical procedure, is performed under circumstances that insure maximum safety for the patient. This interest obviously extends at least to the performing physician and his staff, to the facilities involved, to the availability of after-care, and to adequate provision for any complication or emergency that might arise. The prevalence of high mortality rates at illegal "abortion mills" strengthens, rather than weakens, the State's interest in regulating the conditions under which abortions are performed. Moreover, the risk to the woman increases as her pregnancy continues. Thus, the State retains a definite interest in protecting the woman's own health and safety when an abortion is proposed at a late stage of pregnancy.

The third reason is the State's interest—some phrase it in terms of duty—in protecting prenatal life. Some of the argument for this justification rests on the theory that a new human life is present from the moment of conception. The State's interest and general obligation to protect life then extends, it is argued, to prenatal life. Only when the life of the pregnant mother herself is at stake, balanced against the life she carries within her, should the interest of the embryo or fetus not prevail. Logically, of course, a legitimate state interest in this area need not stand or fall on acceptance of the belief that life begins at conception or at some other point prior to live birth. In assessing the State's interest, recognition may be given to the less rigid claim that as long as at least potential life is involved, the State may assert interests beyond the protection of the pregnant woman alone.

Parties challenging state abortion laws have sharply disputed in some courts the contention that a purpose of these laws, when enacted, was to protect prenatal life. Pointing to the absence of legislative history to support the contention, they claim that most state laws were designed solely to protect the woman. Because medical advances have lessened this concern, at least with respect to abortion in early pregnancy, they argue that with respect to such abortions the laws can no longer be justified by any state interest. There is some scholarly support for this view of original purpose. The few state courts called upon to interpret their laws in the late 19th and early 20th centuries did focus on the State's interest in protecting the woman's health rather than in preserving the embryo and fetus. Proponents of this view point out that in many States, including Texas, by statute or judicial interpretation, the pregnant woman herself could not be prosecuted for self-abortion or for cooperating in an abortion performed upon her by another. They claim that adoption of the "quickening" distinction through received common law and state statutes tacitly recognizes the greater health hazards inherent in late abortion and impliedly repudiates the theory that life begins at conception.

It is with these interests, and the weight to be attached to them, that this case is concerned.

VIII

The Constitution does not explicitly mention any right of privacy. In a line of decisions, however, going back perhaps as far as *Union Pacific Railroad Co. v. Botsford* (1891), the Court has recognized that a right of personal privacy, or a guarantee of certain areas or zones of privacy, does exist under the Constitution. In varying contexts, the Court or individual Justices have, indeed, found at least the roots of that right in the First Amendment; in the Fourth and Fifth Amendments; in the penumbras of the Bill of Rights; in the Ninth Amendment; or in the concept of liberty guaranteed by the first section of the Fourteenth Amendment. These decisions make it clear that only personal rights that can be deemed "fundamental" or "implicit in the concept of ordered liberty" ... are included in this guarantee of personal privacy. They also make it clear that the right has some extension to activities relating to marriage; procreation; contraception; family relationships; and child rearing and education.

This right of privacy, whether it be founded in the Fourteenth Amendment's concept of personal liberty and restrictions upon state action, as we feel it is, or, as the District Court determined, in the Ninth Amendment's reservation of rights to the people, is broad enough to encompass a woman's decision whether or not to terminate her pregnancy. The detriment that the State would impose upon the pregnant woman by denying this choice altogether is apparent. Specific and direct harm medically diagnosable even in early pregnancy may be involved. Maternity, or additional offspring, may force upon the woman a distressful life and future. Psychological harm may be imminent. Mental and physical health may be taxed by child care. There is also the distress, for all concerned, associated with the unwanted child, and there is the problem of bringing a child into a family already unable, psychologically and otherwise, to care for it. In other cases, as in this one, the additional difficulties and continuing stigma of unwed motherhood may be involved. All these are factors the woman and her responsible physician necessarily will consider in consultation.

On the basis of elements such as these, appellant and some amici argue that the woman's right is absolute and that she is entitled to terminate her pregnancy at whatever time, in whatever way, and for whatever reason she alone chooses. With this we do not agree. Appellant's arguments that Texas either has no valid interest at all in regulating the abortion decision, or no interest strong enough to support any limitation upon the woman's sole determination, are unpersuasive. The Court's decisions recognizing a right of privacy also acknowledge that some state regulation in areas protected by that right is appropriate. As noted above, a State may properly assert important interests in safeguarding health, in maintaining medical standards, and in protecting potential life. At some point in pregnancy, these respective interests become sufficiently compelling to sustain regulation of the factors that govern the abortion decision. The privacy right involved, therefore, cannot be said to be absolute. In fact, it is not clear to us that the claim asserted by some amici that one has an unlimited right to do with one's body as one pleases bears a close relationship to the right of privacy previously articulated in the Court's decisions. The Court has refused to recognize an unlimited right of this kind in the past.

We, therefore, conclude that the right of personal privacy includes the abortion decision, but that this right is not unqualified and must be considered against important state interests in regulation.

We note that those federal and state courts that have recently considered abortion law challenges have reached the same conclusion. A majority, in addition to the District Court in the present case, have held state laws unconstitutional, at least in part, because of vagueness or because of overbreadth and abridgment of rights.... Others have sustained state statutes.... Although the results are divided, most of these courts have agreed that the right of privacy, however based, is broad enough to cover the abortion decision; that the right, nonetheless, is not absolute and is subject to some limitations; and that at some point the state interests as to protection of health, medical standards, and prenatal life, become dominant. We agree with this approach.

Where certain "fundamental rights" are involved, the Court has held that regulation limiting these rights may be justified only by a "compelling state interest," and that legislative enactments must be narrowly drawn to express only the legitimate state interests at stake.

In the recent abortion cases, cited above, courts have recognized these principles. Those striking down state laws have generally scrutinized the State's interests in protecting health and potential life, and have concluded that neither interest justified broad limitations on the reasons for which a physician and his pregnant patient might decide that she should have an abortion in the early stages of pregnancy. Courts sustaining state laws have held that the State's determinations to protect health or prenatal life are dominant and constitutionally justifiable.

IX

The District Court held that the appellee [Wade] failed to meet his burden of demonstrating that the Texas statute's infringement upon Roe's rights was necessary to support a compelling state interest, and that, although the appellee presented "several compelling justifications for state presence in the area of abortions," the statutes outstripped these justifications and swept "far beyond any areas of compelling state interest." Appellant and appellee both contest that holding. Appellant, as has been indicated, claims an absolute right that bars any state imposition of criminal penalties in the area. Appellee argues that the State's determination to recognize and protect prenatal life from and after conception constitutes a compelling state interest. As noted above, we do not agree fully with either formulation.

A. The appellee and certain amici argue that the fetus is a "person" within the language and meaning of the Fourteenth Amendment. In support of this, they outline at length and in detail the well-known facts of fetal development. If this suggestion of personhood is established, the appellant's case, of course, collapses, for the fetus' right to life would then be guaranteed specifically by the Amendment. The appellant conceded as much on reargument. On the other hand, the appellee conceded on reargument that no case could be cited that holds that a fetus is a person within the meaning of the Fourteenth Amendment.

The Constitution does not define "person" in so many words. Section 1 of the Fourteenth Amendment contains three references to "person." The first, in defining "citizens," speaks of "persons born or naturalized in the United States." The word also appears both in the Due Process Clause and in the Equal Protection Clause. "Person" is used in other places in the Constitution.... But in nearly all these instances, the use of the word is such that it has application only postnatally. None indicates, with any assurance, that it has any possible pre-natal application.

All this, together with our observation, supra, that throughout the major portion of the 19th century prevailing legal abortion practices were far freer than they are today, persuades us that the word "person," as used in the Fourteenth Amendment, does not include the unborn.... This conclusion, however, does not of itself fully answer the contentions raised by Texas, and we pass on to other considerations.

B. The pregnant woman cannot be isolated in her privacy. She carries an embryo and, later, a fetus, if one accepts the medical definitions of the developing young in the human uterus. The situation therefore is inherently different from marital intimacy, or bedroom possession of obscene material, or marriage, or procreation, or education, with which [previous cases] were respectively concerned. As we have intimated above, it is reasonable and appropriate for a State to decide that at some point in time another interest, that of health of the mother or that of potential human life, becomes significantly involved. The woman's privacy is no longer sole and any right of privacy she possesses must be measured accordingly.

Texas urges that, apart from the Fourteenth Amendment, life begins at conception and is present throughout pregnancy, and that, therefore, the State has a compelling interest in protecting that life from and after conception. We need not resolve the difficult question of when life begins. When those trained in the respective disciplines of medicine, philosophy, and theology are unable to arrive at any consensus, the judiciary, at this point in the development of man's knowledge, is not in a position to speculate as to the answer....

In areas other than criminal abortion, the law has been reluctant to endorse any theory that life, as we recognize it, begins before live birth or to accord legal rights to the unborn except in narrowly defined situations and except when the rights are contingent upon live birth. For example, the traditional rule of tort law denied recovery for prenatal injuries even though the child was born alive. That rule has been changed in almost every jurisdiction. In most States, recovery is said to be permitted only if the fetus was viable, or at least quick, when the injuries were sustained, though few courts have squarely so held. In a recent development, generally opposed by the commentators, some States permit the parents of a stillborn child to maintain an action for wrongful death because of prenatal injuries. Such an action, however, would appear to be one to vindicate the parents' interest and is thus consistent with the view that the fetus, at most, represents only the potentiality of life. Similarly, unborn children have been recognized as acquiring rights or interests by way of inheritance or other devolution of property, and have been represented by guardians ad litem. Perfection of the interests involved, again, has generally been contingent upon live birth. In short, the unborn have never been recognized in the law as persons in the whole sense.

X

In view of all this, we do not agree that, by adopting one theory of life, Texas may override the rights of the pregnant woman that are at stake. We repeat, however, that the State does have an important and legitimate interest in preserving and protecting the health of the pregnant woman, whether she be a resident of the State or a nonresident who seeks medical consultation and treatment there, and that it has still another important and legitimate interest in protecting the potentiality of human life. These interests are separate and distinct. Each grows in substantiality as the woman approaches term and, at a point during pregnancy, each becomes "compelling."

With respect to the State's important and legitimate interest in the health of the mother, the "compelling" point, in the light of present medical knowledge, is at approximately the end of the first trimester. This is so because of the now-established medical fact ... that until the end of the first trimester mortality in abortion may be less than mortality in normal childbirth. It follows that, from and after this point, a State may regulate the abortion procedure to the extent that the regulation reasonably relates to the preservation and protection of maternal health. Examples of permissible state regulation in this area are requirements as to the qualifications of the person who is to perform the abortion; as to the licensure of that person; as to the facility in which the procedure is to be performed, that is, whether it must be a hospital or may be a clinic or some other place of less-than-hospital status; as to the licensing of the facility; and the like.

This means, on the other hand, that, for the period of pregnancy prior to this "compelling" point, the attending physician, in consultation with his patient, is free to determine, without regulation by the State, that, in his medical judgment, the patient's pregnancy should be terminated. If that decision is reached, the judgment may be effectuated by an abortion free of interference by the State.

With respect to the State's important and legitimate interest in potential life, the "compelling" point is at viability. This is so because the fetus then presumably has the capability of meaningful life outside the mother's womb. State regulation protective of fetal life after viability thus has both logical and biological justifications. If the State is interested in protecting fetal life after viability, it may go so far as to proscribe abortion during that period, except when it is necessary to preserve the life or health of the mother.

Measured against these standards, Art. 1196 of the Texas Penal Code, in restricting legal abortions to those "procured or attempted by medical advice for the purpose of saving the life of the mother," sweeps too broadly. The statute makes no distinction between abortions performed early in pregnancy and those performed later, and it limits to a single reason, "saving" the mother's life, the legal justification for the procedure. The statute, therefore, cannot survive the constitutional attack made upon it here.

This conclusion makes it unnecessary for us to consider the additional challenge to the Texas statute asserted on grounds of vagueness.

XI

To summarize and to repeat:

1. A state criminal abortion statute of the current Texas type, that excepts from criminality only a life-saving procedure on behalf of the mother, without regard to pregnancy stage and without recognition of the other interests involved, is violative of the Due Process Clause of the Fourteenth Amendment.

(a) For the stage prior to approximately the end of the first trimester, the abortion decision and its effectuation must be left to the medical judgment of the pregnant woman's attending physician.

(b) For the stage subsequent to approximately the end of the first trimester, the State, in promoting its interest in the health of the mother, may, if it chooses, regulate the abortion procedure in ways that are reasonably related to maternal health.

(c) For the stage subsequent to viability, the State in promoting its interest in the potentiality of human life may, if it chooses, regulate, and even proscribe, abortion except where it is necessary, in appropriate medical judgment, for the preservation of the life or health of the mother.

2. The State may define the term "physician," as it has been employed in the preceding paragraphs of this Part XI of this opinion, to mean only a physician currently licensed by the State, and may proscribe any abortion by a person who is not a physician as so defined.

In *Doe v. Bolton,* procedural requirements contained in one of the modern abortion statutes are considered. That opinion and this one, of course, are to be read together.

This holding, we feel, is consistent with the relative weights of the respective interests involved, with the lessons and examples of medical and legal history, with the lenity of the common law, and with the demands of the profound problems of the present day. The decision leaves the State free to place increasing restrictions on abortion as the period of pregnancy lengthens, so long as those restrictions are tailored to the recognized state interests. The decision vindicates the right of the physician to administer medical treatment according to his professional judgment up to the points where important state interests provide compelling justifications for intervention. Up to those points, the abortion decision in all its aspects is inherently, and primarily, a medical decision, and basic responsibility for it must rest with the physician. If an individual practitioner abuses the privilege of exercising proper medical judgment, the usual remedies, judicial and intra-professional, are available.

XII

Our conclusion that Art. 1196 is unconstitutional means, of course, that the Texas abortion statutes, as a unit, must fall. The exception of Art. 1196 cannot be struck down separately, for then the State would be left with a statute proscribing all abortion procedures no matter how medically urgent the case.

Although the District Court granted appellant Roe declaratory relief, it stopped short of issuing an injunction against enforcement of the Texas statutes. The Court has recognized that different considerations enter into a federal court's decision as to declaratory relief, on the one hand, and injunctive relief, on the other. We are not dealing with a statute that, on its face, appears to abridge free expression....

We find it unnecessary to decide whether the District Court erred in withholding injunctive relief, for we assume the Texas prosecutorial authorities will give full credence to this decision that the present criminal abortion statutes of that State are unconstitutional.

The judgment of the District Court as to intervenor Hallford is reversed, and Dr. Hallford's complaint in intervention is dismissed. In all other respects, the judgment of the District Court is affirmed. Costs are allowed to the appellee.

It is so ordered.

Source: Roe v. Wade, 410 U.S. 113 (1973).

Justice William H. Rehnquist Dissents

Two of the Supreme Court's nine justices disagreed with the majority opinion in Roe v. Wade *and expressed their objections to the ruling in dissenting opinions. Justice William H. Rehnquist, who went on to serve as chief justice from 1986 until his death in 2005, was one of the dissenters. Rehnquist's dissent, which is excerpted below, focuses mainly on technical issues of law. He disputes Jane Roe's legal standing in the case, for instance, and argues that the constitutional right to privacy does not apply to abortion. Rehnquist also joined Justice Byron R. White's dissenting opinion.*

MR. JUSTICE REHNQUIST, dissenting.

The Court's opinion brings to the decision of this troubling question both extensive historical fact and a wealth of legal scholarship. While the opinion thus commands my respect, I find myself nonetheless in fundamental disagreement with those parts of it that invalidate the Texas statute in question, and therefore dissent.

I

The Court's opinion decides that a State may impose virtually no restriction on the performance of abortions during the first trimester of pregnancy. Our previous decisions indicate that a necessary predicate for such an opinion is a plaintiff who was in her first trimester of pregnancy at some time during the pendency of her law-suit. While a party may vindicate his own constitutional rights, he may not seek vindication for the rights of others.... The Court's statement of facts in this case makes clear, however, that the record in no way indicates the presence of such a plaintiff. We know only that plaintiff Roe at the time of filing her complaint was a pregnant woman; for aught that appears in this record, she may have been in her last trimester of pregnancy as of the date the complaint was filed.

Nothing in the Court's opinion indicates that Texas might not constitutionally apply its proscription of abortion as written to a woman in that stage of pregnancy. Nonetheless, the Court uses her complaint against the Texas statute as a fulcrum for deciding that States may impose virtually no restrictions on medical abortions performed during the first trimester of pregnancy. In deciding such a hypothetical lawsuit, the Court departs from the longstanding admonition that it should never "formulate a rule of constitutional law broader than is required by the precise facts to which it is to be applied...."

II

Even if there were a plaintiff in this case capable of litigating the issue which the Court decides, I would reach a conclusion opposite to that reached by the Court. I have difficulty in concluding, as the Court does, that the right of "privacy" is involved in this case. Texas, by the statute here challenged, bars the performance of a medical abortion by a licensed physician on a plaintiff such as Roe. A transaction resulting in an operation such as this is not "private" in the ordinary usage of that word. Nor is the "privacy" that the Court finds here even a distant relative of the freedom from searches and seizures protected by the Fourth Amendment to the Constitution, which the Court has referred to as embodying a right to privacy....

If the Court means by the term "privacy" no more than that the claim of a person to be free from unwanted state regulation of consensual transactions may be a form of "liberty" protected by the Fourteenth Amendment, there is no doubt that similar claims have been upheld in our earlier decisions on the basis of that liberty. I agree with the statement of MR. JUSTICE STEWART in his concurring opinion that the "liberty," against deprivation of which without due process the Fourteenth Amendment protects, embraces more than the rights found in the Bill of Rights. But that liberty is not guaranteed absolutely against deprivation, only against deprivation without due process of law. The test traditionally applied in the area of social and economic legislation is whether or not a law such as that challenged has a rational relation to a valid state objective.... The Due Process Clause of the Fourteenth Amendment undoubtedly does place a limit, albeit a broad one, on legislative power to enact laws such as this. If the Texas statute were to prohibit an abortion even where the mother's life is in jeopardy, I have little doubt that such a statute would lack a rational relation to a valid state objective.... But the Court's sweeping invalidation of any restrictions on abortion during the first trimester is impossible to justify under that standard, and the conscious weighing of competing factors that the Court's opinion apparently substitutes for the established test is far more appropriate to a legislative judgment than to a judicial one.

The Court eschews the history of the Fourteenth Amendment in its reliance on the "compelling state interest" test.... But the Court adds a new wrinkle to this test by transposing it from the legal considerations associated with the Equal Protection Clause of the Fourteenth Amendment to this case arising under the Due Process Clause of the Fourteenth Amendment. Unless I misapprehend the consequences of this transplanting of the "compelling state

187

interest test," the Court's opinion will accomplish the seemingly impossible feat of leaving this area of the law more confused than it found it.... The decision here to break pregnancy into three distinct terms and to outline the permissible restrictions the State may impose in each one, for example, partakes more of judicial legislation than it does of a determination of the intent of the drafters of the Fourteenth Amendment.

The fact that a majority of the States reflecting, after all, the majority sentiment in those States, have had restrictions on abortions for at least a century is a strong indication, it seems to me, that the asserted right to an abortion is not "so rooted in the traditions and conscience of our people as to be ranked as fundamental...." Even today, when society's views on abortion are changing, the very existence of the debate is evidence that the "right" to an abortion is not so universally accepted as the appellant would have us believe.

To reach its result, the Court necessarily has had to find within the scope of the Fourteenth Amendment a right that was apparently completely unknown to the drafters of the Amendment. As early as 1821, the first state law dealing directly with abortion was enacted by the Connecticut Legislature.... By the time of the adoption of the Fourteenth Amendment in 1868, there were at least 36 laws enacted by state or territorial legislatures limiting abortion. While many States have amended or updated their laws, 21 of the laws on the books in 1868 remain in effect today. Indeed, the Texas statute struck down today was, as the majority notes, first enacted in 1857 and "has remained substantially unchanged to the present time."

There apparently was no question concerning the validity of this provision or of any of the other state statutes when the Fourteenth Amendment was adopted. The only conclusion possible from this history is that the drafters did not intend to have the Fourteenth Amendment withdraw from the States the power to legislate with respect to this matter.

III

Even if one were to agree that the case that the Court decides were here, and that the enunciation of the substantive constitutional law in the Court's opinion were proper, the actual disposition of the case by the Court is still difficult to justify. The Texas statute is struck down in toto, even though the Court apparently concedes that at later periods of pregnancy Texas might impose these selfsame statutory limitations on abortion. My understanding of past practice is that a statute found to be invalid as applied to a particular plaintiff, but not unconstitutional as a whole, is not simply "struck down" but is, instead, declared unconstitutional as applied to the fact situation before the Court....

For all of the foregoing reasons, I respectfully dissent.

Source: *Roe v. Wade,* 410 U.S. 113 (1973) (Rehnquist, J., dissenting).

Justice Byron R. White Dissents

The second dissenting opinion in the Supreme Court's 7-2 Roe v. Wade *decision came from Justice Byron R. White. Appointed to the Court in 1962 by President John F. Kennedy, White was widely viewed as a moderate jurist who resisted broad interpretations of the Constitution. In his dissent, which also applies to the companion case* Doe v. Bolton *from Georgia, White argues that the Court exceeded its authority and invented a new right for pregnant women that had no constitutional basis.*

MR. JUSTICE WHITE, with whom MR. JUSTICE REHNQUIST joins, dissenting.

At the heart of the controversy in these cases are those recurring pregnancies that pose no danger whatsoever to the life or health of the mother but are, nevertheless, unwanted for any one or more of a variety of reasons—convenience, family planning, economics, dislike of children, the embarrassment of illegitimacy, etc. The common claim before us is that, for any one of such reasons, or for no reason at all, and without asserting or claiming any threat to life or health, any woman is entitled to an abortion at her request if she is able to find a medical advisor willing to undertake the procedure.

The Court, for the most part, sustains this position: during the period prior to the time the fetus becomes viable, the Constitution of the United States values the convenience, whim, or caprice of the putative mother more than the life or potential life of the fetus; the Constitution, therefore, guarantees the right to an abortion as against any state law or policy seeking to protect the fetus from an abortion not prompted by more compelling reasons of the mother.

With all due respect, I dissent. I find nothing in the language or history of the Constitution to support the Court's judgment. The Court simply fashions and announces a new constitutional right for pregnant mothers and, with scarcely any reason or authority for its action, invests that right with sufficient substance to override most existing state abortion statutes. The upshot is that the people and the legislatures of the 50 States are constitutionally disentitled to weigh the relative importance of the continued existence and development of the fetus, on the one hand, against a spectrum of possible impacts on the mother, on the other hand. As an exercise of raw judicial power, the Court perhaps has authority to do what it does today; but, in my view, its judgment is an improvident and extravagant exercise of the power of judicial review that the Constitution extends to this Court.

190

The Court apparently values the convenience of the pregnant mother more than the continued existence and development of the life or potential life that she carries. Whether or not I might agree with that marshaling of values, I can in no event join the Court's judgment because I find no constitutional warrant for imposing such an order of priorities on the people and legislatures of the States. In a sensitive area such as this, involving as it does issues over which reasonable men may easily and heatedly differ, I cannot accept the Court's exercise of its clear power of choice by interposing a constitutional barrier to state efforts to protect human life and by investing mothers and doctors with the constitutionally protected right to exterminate it. This issue, for the most part, should be left with the people and to the political processes the people have devised to govern their affairs.

It is my view, therefore, that the Texas statute is not constitutionally infirm because it denies abortions to those who seek to serve only their convenience, rather than to protect their life or health. Nor is this plaintiff, who claims no threat to her mental or physical health, entitled to assert the possible rights of those women whose pregnancy assertedly implicates their health. This, together with *United States v. Vuitch,* 402 U.S. 62 (1971), dictates reversal of the judgment of the District Court.

Likewise, because Georgia may constitutionally forbid abortions to putative mothers who, like the plaintiff in this case, do not fall within the reach of ... its criminal code, I have no occasion, and the District Court had none, to consider the constitutionality of the procedural requirements of the Georgia statute as applied to those pregnancies posing substantial hazards to either life or health. I would reverse the judgment of the District Court in the Georgia case.

Source: Roe v. Wade, 410 U.S. 113 (1973) (White, J., dissenting).

Anna Quindlen Describes Her Conflicting Feelings about Abortion

In this 1986 piece from the New York Times, Pulitzer Prize-winning columnist Anna Quindlen recalls the evolution of her views on abortion. Although she describes herself as pro-choice, she also acknowledges feelings of doubt and ambivalence about the divisive issue. Quindlen concludes that "the issue of abortion is difficult for all thoughtful people."

I t was always the look on their faces that told me first. I was the freshman dormitory counselor and they were the freshmen at a women's college where everyone was smart. One of them could come into my room, a golden girl, a valedictorian, an 800 verbal score on the SAT's, and her eyes would be empty, seeing only a busted future, the devastation of her life as she knew it. She had failed biology, messed up the math; she was pregnant.

That was when I became pro-choice.

It was the look in his eyes that I will always remember, too. They were as black as the bottom of a well, and in them for a few minutes I thought I saw myself the way I had always wished to be—clear, simple, elemental, at peace. My child looked at me and I looked back at him in the delivery room, and I realized that out of a sea of infinite possibilities it had come down to this: a specific person, born on the hottest day of the year, conceived on a Christmas Eve, made by his father and me miraculously from scratch.

—◄≡≡█∫█≡≡►—

Once I believed that there was a little blob of formless protoplasm in there and a gynecologist went after it with a surgical instrument, and that was that. Then I got pregnant myself—eagerly, intentionally, by the right man, at the right time—and I began to doubt. My abdomen still flat, my stomach roiling with morning sickness, I felt not that I had protoplasm inside but instead a complete human being in miniature to whom I could talk, sing, make promises. Neither of these views was accurate; instead, I think, the reality is something in the middle. And that is where I find myself now, in the middle, hating the idea of abortions, hating the idea of having them outlawed.

From the *New York Times*, March 13, 1986. Copyright © The New York Times. All Rights Reserved. Used by permission and protected by the Copyright Laws of the United States. The printing, copying, redistribution, or retransmission of the material without express written permission is prohibited.

For I know it is the right thing in some times and places. I remember sitting in a shabby clinic far uptown with one of those freshmen, only three months after the Supreme Court had made what we were doing possible, and watching with wonder as the lovely first love she had had with a nice boy unraveled over the space of an hour as they waited for her to be called, degenerated into sniping and silences. I remember a year or two later seeing them pass on campus and not even acknowledge one another because their conjoining had caused them so much pain, and I shuddered to think of them married, with a small psyche in their unready and unwilling hands.

I've met 14-year-olds who were pregnant and said they could not have abortions because of their religion, and I see in their eyes the shadows of 22-year-olds I've talked to who lost their kids to foster care because they hit them or used drugs or simply had no money for food and shelter. I read not long ago about a teenager who said she meant to have an abortion but she spent the money on clothes instead; now she has a baby who turns out to be a lot more trouble than a toy. The people who hand out those execrable little pictures of dismembered fetuses at abortion clinics seem to forget the extraordinary pain children may endure after they are born when they are unwanted, even hated or simply tolerated.

I believe that in a contest between the living and the almost living, the latter must, if necessary, give way to the will of the former. That is what the fetus is to me, the almost living. Yet these questions began to plague me—and, I've discovered, a good many other women—after I became pregnant. But they became even more acute after I had my second child, mainly because he is so different from his brother. On two random nights 18 months apart the same two people managed to conceive, and on one occasion the tumult within turned itself into a curly-haired brunet with merry black eyes who walked and talked late and loved the whole world, and on another it became a blond with hazel Asian eyes and a pug nose who tried to conquer the world almost as soon as he entered it.

If we were to have an abortion next time for some reason or another, which infinite possibility becomes, not a reality, but a nullity? The girl with the blue eyes? The improbable redhead? The natural athlete? The thinker? My husband, ever at the heart of the matter, put it another way. Knowing that he is finding two children somewhat more overwhelming than he expected, I asked if he would want me to have an abortion if I accidentally became pregnant again right away. "And waste a perfectly good human being?" he said.

Coming to this quandary has been difficult for me. In fact, I believe the issue of abortion is difficult for all thoughtful people. I don't know anyone who has had an abortion who has not been haunted by it. If there is one thing I find intolerable about most of the so-called right-to-lifers, it is that they try to portray abortion rights as something that feminists thought up on a slow Saturday over a light lunch. That is nonsense. I also know that some people who support abortion rights are most comfortable with a monolithic position because it seems the strongest front against the smug and sometimes violent opposition.

—◆—

But I don't feel all one way about abortion anymore, and I don't think it serves a just cause to pretend that many of us do. For years I believed that a woman's right to choose was absolute, but now I wonder. Do I, with a stable home and marriage and sufficient stamina and money, have the right to choose abortion because a pregnancy is inconvenient right now? Legally I do have that right; legally I want always to have that right. It is the morality of exercising it under those circumstances that makes me wonder.

Technology has foiled us. The second trimester has become a time of resurrection; a fetus at six months can be one woman's late abortion, another's premature, viable child. Photographers now have film of embryos the size of a grape, oddly human, flexing their fingers, sucking their thumbs. Women have amniocentesis to find out whether they are carrying a child with birth defects that they may choose to abort. Before the procedure, they must have a sonogram, one of those fuzzy black-and-white photos like a love song heard through static on the radio, which shows someone is in there.

I have taped on my VCR a public television program in which somehow, inexplicably, a film is shown of a fetus in utero scratching its face, seemingly putting up a tiny hand to shield itself from the camera's eye. It would make a potent weapon in the arsenal of anti-abortionists. I grow sentimental about it as it floats in the salt water, part fish, part human being. It is almost living, but not quite. It has almost turned my heart around, but not quite turned my head.

Source: Quindlen, Anna. "Hers." *New York Times*, March 13, 1986, p. C2.

Robert H. Bork Defends the Pro-Life Position

Robert H. Bork, a conservative law professor and federal judge, was nominated for a seat on the U.S. Supreme Court by President Ronald Reagan in 1987. By this time, Bork had emerged as an outspoken critic of the 1973 Roe v. Wade *decision. He described the Court's ruling in the case as unconstitutional and made no secret of his desire to overturn it. Bork's views on abortion became the main focus of the Senate confirmation hearings on his nomination, which turned into a bitter, highly publicized battle between pro-choice and pro-life advocates. In the end, Bork's nomination was defeated in the Senate by a 58-42 vote.*

Bork went on to publish several books promoting his conservative judicial philosophy and political views. The essay below, "Inconvenient Lives," is adapted from his best-known work, Slouching Towards Gomorrah: Modern Liberalism and American Decline. *It offers a point-by-point explanation and defense of the pro-life position on abortion.*

Judging from the evidence, Americans do not view human life as sacrosanct. We engage in a variety of activities, from driving automobiles to constructing buildings, that we know will cause deaths. But the deliberate taking of the life of an individual has never been regarded as a matter of moral indifference. We debate the death penalty, for example, endlessly. It seems an anomaly, therefore, that we have so easily accepted practices that are the deliberate taking of identifiable individual lives. We have turned abortion into a constitutional right; one state has made assisted suicide a statutory right and two federal circuit courts, not to be outdone, have made it a constitutional right; campaigns to legalize euthanasia are underway. It is entirely predictable that many of the elderly, ill, and infirm will be killed, and often without their consent. This is where radical individualism has taken us.

When a society revises its attitude toward life and death, we can see the direction of its moral movement. The revision of American thought and practice about life questions began with abortion, and examination of the moral confusion attending that issue helps us understand more general developments in public morality.

The necessity for reflection about abortion does not depend on, but is certainly made dramatic by, the fact that there are approximately a million

---

Copyright © 1996 First Things. Reprinted with permission.

and a half abortions annually in the United States. To put it another way, since the Supreme Court's 1973 decision in *Roe v. Wade,* there have been perhaps over thirty million abortions in the United States. Three out of ten conceptions today end in the destruction of the fetus. These facts, standing alone, do not decide the issue of morality, but they do mean that the issue is hugely significant.

The issue is also heated, polarizing, and often debated on both sides in angry, moralistic terms. I will refrain from such rhetoric because for most of my life I held a position on the subject very different from the one I now take. For years I adopted, without bothering to think, the attitude common among secular, affluent, university-educated people who took the propriety of abortion for granted, even when it was illegal. The practice's illegality, like that of drinking alcohol during Prohibition, was thought to reflect merely unenlightened prejudice or religious conviction, the two being regarded as much the same. From time to time, someone would say that it was a difficult moral problem, but there was rarely any doubt how the problem should be resolved. I remember a woman at Yale saying, without any disagreement from those around her, that "The fetus isn't nothing, but I am for the mother's right to abort it." I probably nodded. Most of us had a vague and unexamined notion that while the fetus wasn't nothing, it was also not fully human. The slightest reflection would have suggested that non-human or semi-human blobs of tissue do not magically turn into human beings.

Qualms about abortion began to arise when I first read about fetal pain. There is no doubt that, after its nervous system has developed to a degree, the fetus being dismembered or poisoned in the womb feels excruciating pain. For that reason, many people would confine abortion to the early stages of pregnancy but have no objection to it then. There are, on the other hand, people who oppose abortion at any stage and those who regard it as a right at any stage up to the moment of birth. But in thinking about abortion—especially abortion at any stage—it is necessary to address two questions. Is abortion always the killing of a human being? If it is, is that killing done simply for convenience? I think there can be no doubt that the answer to the first question is, yes; and the answer to the second is, almost always.

The question of whether abortion is the termination of a human life is a relatively simple one. It has been described as a question requiring no more than a knowledge of high school biology. There may be doubt that high school biology courses are clear on the subject these days, but consider what we know. The male sperm and the female egg each contains twenty-three chromosomes. Upon fertilization, a single cell results containing forty-six chromosomes, which is what all humans have, including, of course, the mother and the father. But the new organism's forty-six chromosomes are in a different combination from those of either parent; the new organism is unique. It is not an organ of the mother's body but a different individual. This cell produces specifically human proteins and enzymes from the beginning. Its chromosomes will heavily influence its destiny until the day of its death, whether that death is at the age of ninety or one month after conception.

The cell will multiply and develop, in accordance with its individual chromosomes, and, when it enters the world, will be recognizably a human baby. From single-cell fertilized egg to baby to teenager to adult to old age to death is a single process of one individual, not a series of different individuals replacing each other. It is impossible to draw a line anywhere after the moment of fertilization and say before this point the creature is not human but after this point it is. It has all the attributes of a human from the beginning, and those attributes were in the forty-six chromosomes with which it began. Francis Crick, the Nobel laureate and biophysicist, is quoted as having estimated that "the amount of information contained in the chromosomes of a single fertilized human egg is equivalent to about a thousand printed volumes of books, each as large as a volume of the Encyclopedia Britannica." Such a creature is not a blob of tissue or, as the Roe opinion so felicitously put it, a "potential life." As someone has said, it is a life with potential.

It is impossible to say that the killing of the organism at any moment after it originated is not the killing of a human being. Yet there are those who say just that by redefining what a human being is. Redefining what it means to be a human being will prove dangerous in contexts other than abortion. One of the more primitive arguments put forward is that in the embryonic stage, which lasts about two months after conception, the creature does not look human. One man said to me, "Have you ever seen an embryo? It looks like a guppy." A writer whose work I greatly respect refers to "the patently inhuman fetus of four weeks." A cartoonist made fun of a well-known anti-abortion doctor by showing him pointing to the microscopic dot that is the zygote and saying, "We'll call him Timmy." It is difficult to know what the appearance of Timmy has to do with the humanity of the fetus. I suspect appearance is made an issue because the more recognizably a baby the fetus becomes, the more our emotions reject the idea of destroying it. But those are uninstructed emotions, not emotions based on a recognition of what the fetus is from the beginning.

Other common arguments are that the embryo or fetus is not fully sentient, or that it cannot live outside the mother's womb, or that the fetus is not fully a person unless it is valued by its mother. These seem utterly insubstantial arguments. A newborn is not fully sentient, nor is a person in an advanced stage of Alzheimer's disease. There are people who would allow the killing of the newborn and the senile, but I doubt that is a view with general acceptance. At least not yet. Equally irrelevant to the discussion is the fact that the fetus cannot survive outside the womb. Neither can a baby survive without the nurture of others, usually the parents. Why dependency, which lasts for years after birth, should justify terminating life is inexplicable. No more apparent is the logic of the statement that a fetus is a person only if the mother values its life. That is a tautology: an abortion is justified if the mother wants an abortion.

In discussing abortion, James Q. Wilson wrote, "The moral debate over abortion centers on the point in the development of the fertilized ovum when it has acquired those characteristics that entitle it to moral respect." He did not, apparently, think the cell resulting from conception was so entitled. Wilson gave an example of moral respect persisting in difficult circumstances: "An elderly man who has been a devoted husband and father but who now lies comatose in a vegetative state barely seems to be alive, . . . yet we experience great moral anguish in deciding whether to withdraw his life support." In response, my wife was moved to observe, "But suppose the doctor told us that in eight months the man would recover, be fully human, and live a normal life as a unique individual. Is it even conceivable that we would remove his life-support system on the ground that his existence, like that of the fetus, is highly inconvenient to us and that he does not look human at the moment? There would be no moral anguish but instead a certainty that such an act would be a grave moral wrong."

It is certainly more likely that we would refuse to countenance an abortion if a sonogram showed a recognizable human being than if only a tiny, guppy-like being appeared. But that is an instinctive reaction and instinctive reactions are not always the best guide to moral choice. Intellect must play a role as well. What if biology convinces us that the guppy-like creature or the microscopic fertilized egg has exactly the same future, the same capacity to live a full human life, as does the fetus at three months or at seven months or the infant at birth? "It is difficult to see," my wife added, "that the decision in the imagined case of the comatose elderly man who in time will recover is different from the abortion decision." In both cases, it is only a matter of time. The difference is that the death of the elderly man would deprive him of a few years of life while the aborted embryo or fetus loses an entire lifetime.

The issue is not, I think, one of appearance, sentience, or anything other than prospective life that is denied the individual by abortion. In introductory ethics courses, there used to be a question put: If you could obtain a hundred million dollars by pressing a button that would kill an elderly Chinese mandarin whom you had never seen, and if nobody would know what you had done, would you press the button? That seems to me the same issue as the abortion decision, except that the unborn child has a great deal longer to live if you don't press that particular button. Most of us, I suspect, would like to think we would not kill the mandarin. The characteristics of appearance, sentience, ability to live without assistance, and being valued by others cannot be the characteristics that entitle you to sufficient moral respect to be allowed to go on living. What characteristic does, then? It must lie in the fact that you are alive with the prospect of years of life ahead. That characteristic the unborn child has.

That seems to me an adequate ground to reject the argument made by Peter Singer last year in the London *Spectator* that supports not only abortion but infanticide. He writes that it is doubtful that a fetus becomes conscious until well after the time most abortions are performed and even if it is conscious, that would not put the fetus at a level of awareness comparable to that of "a dog, let alone a chimpanzee. If on the other hand it is self-awareness, rather than mere consciousness, that grounds a right to life, that does not arise in a human being until some time after birth."

Aware that this line leaves out of account the potential of the child for a full human life, Singer responds that "in a world that is already over-populated, and in which the regulation of fertility is universally accepted, the argument that we should bring all potential people into existence is not persuasive." That is disingenuous. If overpopulation were a fact, that would hardly justify killing humans. If overpopulation were taken to be a justification, it would allow the killing of any helpless population, preferably without the infliction of pain.

Most contraceptive methods of regulating fertility do not raise the same moral issue as abortion because they do not permit the joining of the sperm and the egg. Until the sperm and the egg unite, there is no human being.

Singer goes on to make the unsubstantiated claim that "just as the human being develops gradually in a physical sense, so too does its moral significance gradually increase." That contention is closely allied to the physical appearance argument and is subject to the same rebuttal. One wonders at measuring moral significance by physique. If a person gradually degenerated physically, would his moral significance gradually decline?

Many who favor the abortion right understand that humans are being killed. Certainly the doctors who perform and nurses who assist at abortions know that. So do nonprofessionals. Otherwise, abortion would not be smothered in euphemisms. Thus, we hear the language of "choice," "reproductive rights," and "medical procedures." Those are oddly inadequate terms to describe the right to end the life of a human being. It has been remarked that "pro-choice" is an odd term since the individual whose life is at stake has no choice in the matter. These are ways of talking around the point that hide the truth from others and, perhaps, from one's self. President Clinton speaks of keeping abortion "safe, legal, and rare." Why rare, if it is merely a choice, a medical procedure without moral problems?

That there are severe moral problems is becoming clear even to many who favor abortion. That is probably why, as Candace C. Crandall observed last year in the *Women's Quarterly,* "the morale of the pro-choice side of the abortion stalemate has visibly collapsed." The reason: "Proponents of abortion rights overcame Americans' qualms about the procedure with a long series of claims about the benefits of unrestricted abortion on demand. Without exception, those claims have proved false." The proponents claimed that *Roe v. Wade* rescued women from death during unsafe, back-alley abortions, but it was the availability of antibiotics beginning in the 1940s and improved medical techniques that made abortion safe well before *Roe.* It was argued that abortion on demand would guarantee that every child was a wanted child, would keep children from being born into poverty, reduce illegitimacy rates, and help end child abuse. Child poverty rates, illegitimacy rates, and child abuse have all soared. We heard that abortion should be a decision between a woman and her doctor. The idea of a woman and her personal physician deliberating about the choice is a fantasy: women are going to specialized abortion clinics that offer little support or counseling. (Crandall does not address the point, but it is difficult to see that bringing a doctor in for consultation would change the nature of the decision about taking human life.) She does note, however, that many women use abortion for birth control.

Crandall says she sympathizes with abortion-rights advocates. But on her own showing, it is difficult to see why. No anti-abortion advocate could make it clearer that human lives are being destroyed at the rate of 1.5 million a year for convenience.

The author Naomi Wolf, who favors the right to abort, has challenged the feminists whose rhetoric seeks to disguise the truth that a human being is killed by abortion. In a 1995 article in the *New Republic,* she asks for "an abortion-rights movement willing publicly to mourn the evil—necessary evil though it may be—that is abortion." But she asks a question and gives an answer about her support for abortion rights that is troublesome: "But how, one might ask, can I square a recognition of the humanity of the fetus, and the moral gravity of destroying it, with a pro-choice position? The answer can only be found in the context of a paradigm abandoned by the left and mis-used by the right: the paradigm of sin and redemption."

That seems an odd paradigm for this problem. It is one thing to have sinned, atoned, and sought redemption. It seems quite another to justify planning to sin on the ground that you also plan to seek redemption after-ward. That justification seems even stranger for repeat abortions, which Wolf says are at least 43 percent of the total. Sin plus redemption falls short as a resolution of her dilemma. If that were an adequate resolution, it would seem to follow, given the humanity of the fetus, that infanticide, the killing of the elderly, indeed any killing for convenience, would be licensed if atonement and redemption were planned in advance.

Nor is it clear why the evil is necessary. It is undeniable that bearing and rearing a child sometimes places a great burden on a woman or a family. That fact does not, however, answer the question whether the burden justifies destroying a human life. In most other contexts, we would say such a burden is not sufficient justification. The fact is, in any event, that the burden need not be borne. Putting the child up for adoption is an alternative. The only drawback is that others will know the woman is pregnant. If that is the reason to choose abortion, then the killing really is for convenience.

But it is clear, in any event, that the vast majority of all abortions are for convenience. In those cases, abortion is used as merely one more technique of birth control. A 1987 survey of the reasons given by women for having abortions made by researchers with the Alan Guttmacher Institute, which is very much pro-abortion, demonstrated this fact. The following table shows the percentage of women who gave the listed reasons.

Reason	Total Percentage
Woman is concerned about how having a baby could change her life	76
Woman can't afford baby now	68
Woman has problems with relationship or wants to avoid single parenthood	51
Woman is unready for responsibility	31
Woman doesn't want others to know she has had sex or is pregnant	31
Woman is not mature enough or is too young to have a child	30
Woman has all the children she wanted, or has all grown-up children	26
Husband or partner wants woman to have abortion	23
Fetus has possible health problem	13
Woman has health problem	7
Woman's parents want her to have abortion	7
Woman was victim of rape or incest	1
Other	6

It is clear that the overwhelming number of abortions were for birth control unrelated to the health of the fetus or the woman. Moreover, of those who were concerned about a possible health problem of the fetus, only 8 percent said that a physician had told them that the fetus had a defect or was abnormal. The rest were worried because they had taken medication, drugs, or alcohol before realizing they were pregnant, but did not apparently obtain a medical confirmation of any problem. Of those aborting because of their own health, 53 percent said a doctor had told them their condition would be made worse by being pregnant. Some of the rest cited physical problems, and 11 percent gave a mental or emotional problem as the reason. Only 1 percent cited rape or incest.

The survey noted that "some 77 percent of women with incomes under 100 percent or between 100 and 149 percent of the poverty level said they were having an abortion because they could not afford to have a child, compared with 69 percent of those with incomes between 150 and 199 percent and 60 percent of those with incomes at or above 200 percent of the poverty level." The can't-afford category thus included a great many women who, by most reckonings, could afford to have a baby and certainly could have put the baby up for adoption.

This demonstration that abortion is almost always a birth control technique rather than a response to a serious problem with the mother's or the fetus' health must have been a considerable embarrassment to the pro-abortion forces. Perhaps for that reason no survey by them seems to have been reported since. More recent statistics by anti-abortion groups, however, bear out the conclusions to be drawn from the Guttmacher Institute study. The reasons most women give for having an abortion are "social": a baby would affect their educations, jobs, lives, or they felt unable to handle it economically, their partners did not want babies, etc.

Perhaps the most instructive episode demonstrating the brutalization of our culture by abortion was the fight over "partial-birth abortions." These abortions are usually performed late in the pregnancy. The baby is delivered feet first until only the head remains within the mother. The aborting physician inserts scissors into the back of the infant's skull and opens the blades to produce a hole. The child's brains are then vacuumed out, the skull collapses, and the rest of the newly made corpse is removed. If the head had been allowed to come out of the mother, killing the baby then would be the criminal act of infanticide.

When it was proposed to outlaw this hideous procedure, which obviously causes extreme pain to the baby, the pro-abortion forces in Congress and elsewhere made false statements to fend off the legislation or to justify an anticipated presidential veto. Planned Parenthood and the National Abortion and Reproductive Rights Action League stated that the general anesthesia given the mother killed the fetus so that there is no such thing as a partial-birth abortion. Physicians promptly rebutted the claim. Local anesthesia, which is most often used in these abortions, has no effect on the baby and general anesthesia not only does not kill the baby, it provides little or no painkilling effect to the baby. The vice president of the Society for Obstetric Anesthesia and Perinatology said the claim was "crazy," noting that "anesthesia does not kill an infant if you don't kill the mother." Two doctors who perform partial-birth abortions stated that the majority of fetuses aborted in this fashion are alive until the end of the procedure.

Other opponents of a ban on partial-birth abortions claimed that it was used only when necessary to protect the mother's life. Unfortunately for that argument, the physician who is the best-known practitioner of these abortions stated in 1993 that 80 percent of them are "purely elective," not necessary to save the mother's life or health. Partial-birth understates the matter. The baby is outside the mother except for its head, which is kept in the mother only to avoid a charge of infanticide. Full birth is inches away and could easily be accomplished.

No amount of discussion, no citation of evidence, can alter the opinions of radical feminists about abortion. One evening I naively remarked in a talk that those who favor the right to abort would likely change their minds if they could be convinced that a human being was being killed. I was startled at the anger that statement provoked in several women present. One of them informed me in no uncertain terms that the issue had nothing to do with the humanity of the fetus but was entirely about the woman's freedom. It is here that radical egalitarianism reinforces radical individualism in supporting the abortion right. Justice Harry Blackmun, who wrote *Roe* and who never offered the slightest constitutional defense of it, simply remarked that the decision was a landmark on women's march to equality. Equality, in this view, means that if men do not bear children, women should not have to either. Abortion is seen as women's escape from the idea that biology is destiny, to escape from the tyranny of the family role.

Discussions about life and death in one area influence such decisions in others. Despite assurances that the abortion decision did not start us down a slippery and very steep slope, that is clearly where we are, and gathering speed. The systematic killing of unborn children in huge numbers is part of a general disregard for human life that has been growing for some time. Abortion by itself did not cause that disregard, but it certainly deepens and legitimates the nihilism that is spreading in our culture and finds killing for convenience acceptable. We are crossing lines, at first slowly and now with rapidity: killing unborn children for convenience; removing tissue from live fetuses; contemplating creating embryos for destruction in research; considering taking organs from living anencephalic babies; experimenting with assisted suicide; and contemplating euthanasia. Abortion has coarsened us. If it is permissible to kill the unborn human for convenience, it is surely permissible to kill those thought to be soon to die for the same reason. And it is inevitable that many who are not in danger of imminent death will be killed to relieve their families of burdens. Convenience is becoming the theme of our culture. Humans tend to be inconvenient at both ends of their lives.

Source: Bork, Robert H. "Inconvenient Lives." *First Things,* December 1996. This article was adapted from *Slouching Towards Gomorrah* by Robert H. Bork (New York: Regan Books, 1996).

The Democratic Party Platform Supports Reproductive Choice

The 1973 Roe v. Wade *decision launched a national debate over abortion that led to significant changes in the American political system. Beginning with the election of Ronald Reagan in 1980, the Republican Party defined itself as pro-life, and the Democratic Party defined itself as pro-choice. The following excerpt from the 2004 Democratic National Platform presents the Democratic Party's official position on abortion.*

Because we believe in the privacy and equality of women, we stand proudly for a woman's right to choose, consistent with *Roe v. Wade*, and regardless of her ability to pay. We stand firmly against Republican efforts to undermine that right. At the same time, we strongly support family planning and adoption incentives. Abortion should be safe, legal, and rare.

Source: *Strong at Home, Respected in the World: The 2004 Democratic National Platform for America.* Washington, D.C.: Democratic National Convention Committee, 2004. Available online at http://www.democrats.org/a/2005/09/the_2004_democr.php.

Copyright © 2004 Democratic National Convention Committee, Inc. Reprinted with permission.

The Republican Party Platform Opposes Abortion

The Republican Party first adopted a pro-life position during the 1980 presidential campaign, which resulted in the election of abortion opponent Ronald Reagan. The following excerpt from the 2004 Republican National Platform expresses the party's official support for the passage of a constitutional amendment banning abortion, the appointment of federal judges who oppose abortion, and the denial of federal funding to organizations that provide abortion services.

We must keep our pledge to the first guarantee of the Declaration of Independence. That is why we say the unborn child has a fundamental individual right to life which cannot be infringed. We support a human life amendment to the Constitution and we endorse legislation to make it clear that the 14th Amendment's protections apply to unborn children. Our purpose is to have legislative and judicial protection of that right against those who perform abortions. We oppose using public revenues for abortion and will not fund organizations which advocate it. We support the appointment of judges who respect traditional family values and the sanctity of innocent human life.

We oppose abortion, but our pro-life agenda does not include punitive action against women who have an abortion. We salute those who provide alternatives to abortion and offer adoption services, and we commend Congressional Republicans for expanding assistance to adopting families and for removing racial barriers to adoption.

Source: Republican Platform Committee. *A Safer World and a More Hopeful America: The 2004 Republican Party Platform.* Washington, D.C.: Republican National Committee, 2004. Available online at http://www.gop.com/media/2004platform.pdf.

Copyright © Republican National Committee. Reprinted with permission.

The War That Never Ends: Abortion in America

The following article appeared in The Economist *in January 2003, in anticipation of the thirtieth anniversary of the Supreme Court ruling in* Roe v. Wade. *It recounts the history of the abortion debate in the United States and explores the reasons that the issue remained so bitter and divisive thirty years after abortion became legal. The authors conclude that "it would be hard to design a way of legalizing abortion that could be better calculated to stir up controversy" than the* Roe *decision. They also predict that the abortion issue will continue to dominate American political and social life for the foreseeable future.*

Anniversaries don't get much more controversial than this. On January 22nd, America will mark the thirtieth anniversary of the Supreme Court decision that declared abortion a constitutional right. Anti-abortionists will march in Washington in their thousands, carrying gruesome photographs. Supporters of abortion rights will retort that *Roe v. Wade,* the decision in question, was one of the great milestones in the long march for women's rights—a heroic decision that has saved thousands of women from death by coat-hanger or back-street butchery. The two sides will end the day even more polarized than ever.

Since 1973, about 75 countries have liberalized their abortion laws (the most recent being Switzerland and Nepal last year). In most countries, that was enough to settle the debate. Not in America.

The Supreme Court's ruling immediately created a furious backlash. State legislatures passed laws restricting the rights of minors to obtain abortions, usually by requiring the consent of one or both parents. In 1976 Henry Hyde, an Illinois congressman, sponsored legislation eliminating Medicaid funding for abortions except in extreme cases (such as rape, incest or where a woman's life was endangered by her pregnancy). Some extremists took to blowing up clinics and shooting abortion doctors (who, in turn, took to coming to work wearing bullet-proof vests).

There are no signs that the debate is quieting down. One of George [W.] Bush's first actions on coming to office was to reinstate a rule barring overseas recipients of American development funds from using their own money to

"The War That Never Ends: Abortion in America." Copyright © 2003 by The Economist Newspaper Group. Reproduced with permission.

advocate or provide abortions. The day after the 2002 mid-term elections, Trent Lott, then poised to resume the leadership of the Senate, promised to ban partial-birth abortion, a late-term and particularly grisly procedure. The battle over abortion reaches the obscurest sides of life. The Center for Reproductive Law and Policy has filed lawsuits against the states of Florida and Louisiana for allowing the sale of "choose life" license plates but not "pro-choice" ones.

Why does abortion remain so much more controversial in America than in the other countries that have legalized it? The fundamental reason is the way the Americans went about legalization. European countries did so through legislation and, occasionally, referenda. This allowed abortion opponents to vent their objections and legislators to adjust the rules to local tastes. Above all, it gave legalization the legitimacy of majority support.

Most European countries provide abortion free. But they have also hedged the practice with all sorts of qualifications. They justify abortion on the basis of health rather than rights. Many European countries impose a 12-week limit (America, by contrast, allows abortion up to about 24 weeks and beyond, and many abortion-rights advocates seem to oppose any restrictions). Frances Kissling, head of Catholics for a Free Choice, also points out that the Europeans have been careful to preserve a patina of disapproval. Even in England, the country with the most liberal abortion laws in Europe, women have to get permission from two doctors.

America went down the alternative route of declaring abortion a constitutional right. (The only other country that has done anything comparable is South Africa.) A seven-to-two majority of justices struck down state abortion laws on the grounds that reproductive rights are included in a fundamental right to privacy which—rather like freedom of speech and freedom of religion—is guaranteed by the constitution.

It would be hard to design a way of legalizing abortion that could be better calculated to stir up controversy. Abortion opponents were furious about being denied their say. Abortion supporters had to rely on the precarious balance of power on the Supreme Court. Legalization did not have the legitimacy of majority support. Instead, it rested on a highly controversial interpretation of the constitution (abortion rights are clearly not enshrined in the constitution in the same plain way that free speech is). By going down the legislative road, the Europeans managed to neutralize the debate; by relying on the hammer-blow of a Supreme Court decision, the Americans institutionalized it.

A second reason is the continued importance of religion in American life. The Pew Global Attitudes Project recently revealed that six in ten (59%) of Americans say that religion plays a "very important" role in their lives. This is roughly twice the percentage of self-avowed religious people in Canada (30%) and an even higher proportion when compared with Japan and Europe. To find comparable numbers, you need to look at developing countries.

When Americans say "very important," they mean it. America, in Robert Fogel's phrase, is in the middle of a "fourth great awakening" to religion. Churches that insist on passionate commitment to Christ are growing at the expense of more moderate congregations. Religious organizations also provide many of the social services that the state provides in Europe.

One result of America's religiosity is its relative conservatism about sex. Thirteen states still have anti-sodomy laws. The Bush administration favors sex education based on abstinence. Many of the noisiest opponents of abortion also oppose easy access to contraception. Puritanical America has higher rates of both abortion and unwanted pregnancy than many European countries with more liberal attitudes to sex education.

The third reason why abortion is so controversial is the American fondness for arguing about fundamentals. Europeans routinely turn moral issues into technical ones—and then hand them over to technocratic elites. America is a country of fundamentalists, thanks to its constitutional tradition, its legal culture and perhaps its Puritan heritage. For Americans, abortion can never be just about health. It has to be a clash of absolutes: the right to choose versus the right to life. Add to that the openness of the American political system, which makes it impossible to hand controversial questions over to technocratic elites, and you have the making of an endless argument about fundamentals.

The Party Divide

Roe v. Wade did as much as anything to make American politics what it is today. Up until the 1960s, politics was defined by a combination of economic class and the legacy of the civil war. The Republicans, like Europe's conservative parties, were rooted in the business and professional elites; the Democrats were rooted in the trade unions, the urban political machines and ethnic minorities, mostly Irish and Italian. White southerners of all classes also voted Democratic (a legacy of Republican opposition to slavery). Those most opposed to abortion—Catholics and southerners—were almost all Democrats.

But from the mid-1960s onwards values started to trump class. Abortion was not the first issue that redefined politics: that honor goes to civil rights. But it was certainly one of the most powerful. *Roe* helped to drive millions of northern Catholics and southern evangelicals into the Republican Party. (Republicans dubbed [1972 Democratic presidential nominee] George McGovern the triple-A candidate: amnesty, acid and abortion.) It also persuaded Catholics and evangelicals to put aside their long-standing enmity in order to form a common front. The term "moral majority" was first used by Paul Weyrich, an arch-traditional Catholic, in a presentation to Jerry Falwell, a leading evangelical.

American politics is now deeply colored by both religion and abortion. Regularity of church attendance is a much more reliable predictor of voting intentions than income. Anti-abortion groups such as the Family Research Council (FRC) and Focus on the Family are among the most powerful components of the Republican coalition. The Democratic Party is so intertwined with NARAL Pro-Choice America, the rebranded National Abortion Rights Action League, that all the party's prospective presidential candidates have been invited to dine at its headquarters on January 21st to celebrate the anniversary.

There are still pro-choice Republicans (like Colin Powell) and anti-abortion Democrats. But they are swimming against the tide. Some 84% of state Democratic platforms support abortion (the rest have no position), while 88% of state Republican platforms oppose it (none support it). The Republican Party threw away its chance of wresting the governorship of California from the hugely unpopular Gray Davis when it chose an anti-abortion candidate, Bill Simon, over Richard Riordan, the popular former mayor of Los Angeles.

The abortion debate is also responsible for one of the most obvious confusions in the political debate. Republicans usually oppose government regulation in the name of free choice. Grover Norquist, the head of Americans for Tax Reform, even goes so far as to call the Republicans the "leave-us-alone coalition." But on the most sensitive subject of all—reproductive rights—conservatives are now on the side of government control. The Democrats are no more coherent: a party that will do anything to protect a woman's right to choose an abortion will not support her right to choose a public school for her child.

Roe has left the American legal system hopelessly politicized. The Democrats destroyed Robert Bork's chances of sitting on the Supreme Court in part because of his presumed views on abortion. Abortion politics are even poisoning the appointment of lower-level judges (despite the fact that they have almost no discretion over abortion), creating ever more vacancies on the bench and denying many eminent lawyers the promotion they deserve. The Senate confirmed 95% of Ronald Reagan's circuit-court nominees in his first two years, and 86% of Bill Clinton's; so far, it has confirmed 53% of Mr. Bush's.

The abortion debate has more practical implications, too. The number of doctors willing to practice this branch of medicine is declining, in part because of fear of violence. It took years for RU486, the "abortion pill" that is common in Europe, to make it to the United States. Mr. Bush, sensitive to pressure from the Christian right, severely restricted embryonic stem-cell research in the United States, a decision that some scientists think could cost America its lead in a vital area of research.

Abortion politics have also had a marked influence on foreign policy. Since the 1970s, America has introduced strict rules governing the distribution of family-planning assistance to developing countries. In 1973 Jesse Helms, an intractable former senator from North Carolina, introduced an amendment to the Foreign Assistance Act prohibiting the use of federal money to support abortions overseas. In 1984 the Reagan administration imposed the "Mexico City Policy" prohibiting overseas NGOs [non-governmental organizations] from receiving American funds if they performed or promoted abortions, even if they did so with their own money. (This has since become the subject of much symbolism: one of the first things Mr. Clinton did on coming to office was to abolish this rule, and one of the first things Mr. Bush did was to reimpose it.) In December last year the head of the American delegation caused a stir at a United Nations conference in Bangkok when he declared that America "supports the sanctity of life from conception to natural death."

A Future of Stalemate

Where is abortion politics going? The abortion-rights camp believes that their position is as perilous as it has been for 30 years. This is the first time since 1973 that the president, the leader of the Senate and the leader of the House have all been opposed to abortion.

Many anti-abortionists are also quietly convinced that they are winning the battle for people's minds. They have highlighted rare practices like "partial-birth abortion" that most people find repugnant: the name in itself is a propaganda coup. They are busy building what they call a "coalition of the vulnerable," arguing that, if people are prepared to dispose of inconvenient fetuses, they will start disposing of inconvenient old people, sick people and poor people. According to a Gallup poll, the proportion of the public who believe that abortion should be legal in all cases has gone down from 34% in 1992 to 24%.

Anti-abortionists have also relentlessly whittled away at abortion rights. Every year new legislation restricting abortion is introduced in statehouses across the country. A long queue of anti-abortion bills is awaiting consideration in Congress. The Child Custody Protection Act makes it a crime for anybody other than the parent to transport a minor across state lines in order to have an abortion. The Unborn Victims of Violence Act (which is similar to bills introduced in many states) creates a new offense: killing or injuring a fetus during the commission of a federal crime. The Bush administration has made fetuses eligible for the State Children's Health Insurance Program, and directed the Advisory Commission on Human Research Protection to consider embryos as "human research subjects" on a par with children.

Abortion foes are also convinced that science is on their side. Medical advances are making it possible for younger and younger fetuses to survive outside their mothers' bodies. Modern sonograms are so powerful that they can delineate tiny fingers and toes. Parents-to-be take photographs of their future offspring and keep them along with their other baby pictures. Ken Connor, the head of the FRC, says that three-dimensional ultrasounds are "windows on the womb" that undo the logic of Roe v. Wade. "People recognize immediately that an unborn child is a child."

There are several problems with this argument. The biggest is that most Americans want to preserve abortion rights. They don't celebrate abortion. They recoil at partial-birth abortion. But they want no return to the back streets. Their attitude was perfectly captured by Mr. Clinton when he said that he wanted abortion to remain "safe, legal and rare." Support for the status quo is strongly reinforced by the fact that Roe v. Wade is now 30 years old. Most women of child-bearing age have grown up with Roe as the law of the land.

Scientific advances also cut both ways. The morning-after pill can be used to induce abortion almost immediately after conception. Stem cells offer the potential of curing Parkinson's disease. The anti-abortion movement's insistence that a tiny clump of cells constitutes life just as much as a 24-week-old fetus makes it look both extreme and uncaring. Several leading

213

Republicans, including Utah's Orrin Hatch, have broken with the anti-abortion movement over embryonic stem-cell research.

Abortion is now better regulated than ever before. Many of the restrictions on abortion rights imposed by anti-abortionists have had the paradoxical effect of making the practice more acceptable. More than half of all abortions are now performed in the first eight weeks of pregnancy, up from under 40% in 1973, and 89% in the first 12 weeks. A report just released by the Alan Guttmacher Institute also shows abortions at an all-time low of 21.3 per 1,000 women aged 15-44, compared with the 1980-81 peak of 29.3.

Lastly, Republican presidents are terrified of pushing the abortion issue too far. They are happy to throw a few bones to the religious right (which is why development aid is such a convenient target). But they realize that challenging the central principle of *Roe* would doom them with moderate voters—particularly women. In his confirmation hearings, John Ashcroft, the attorney-general, was following White House instructions when he described *Roe* as "the settled law of the land." "The Supreme Court's decisions on this have been multiple, they have been recent, and they have been emphatic," he said.

Emphatic indeed. The court reaffirmed *Roe*'s central principle—that states cannot ban abortions—as recently as 1992, by a five-to-four majority, in the case of *Planned Parenthood v. Casey*. In doing so, it cited the need for stability in the law. In 2000, the same majority struck down Nebraska's ban on partial-birth abortion. And even if the court should revisit the case, there is little chance that it will reverse itself and make abortion illegal. The most that anti-abortion justices such as Antonin Scalia argue for is taking the decision away from the Supreme Court and handing it back to the legislatures. The betting is that almost all legislatures would uphold the right to abortion.

Is there any chance that the opposite will happen—and that abortion will become as uncontroversial in the United States as it is in Europe? Not really. The last 30 years of abortion politics have seen the creation of two pressure groups with a vested interest in keeping the debate as fierce as possible. Ken Connor of the FRC is thoroughly connected to the Republican establishment. And the best way for Kate Michelman, the head of NARAL Pro-Choice America, to shake the liberal money trees is to insist that *Roe* is on the verge of being overturned. There is no chance of America becoming "European" in its attitude to abortion.

There is also no truth in the predictions that abortion is about to be banned. The practice has become too much of a safety-net for middle-class women to be marginalized, let alone removed. Debates will flicker on the margins as opponents of abortion grapple with the potential of stem-cell research to cure terrible diseases, and as supporters grapple with the full horror of what it means to abort a fetus at 28 weeks. But, for the most part, the prospect is stalemate.

Roe v. Wade may have liberated many women; yet it has also trapped America in an irresolvable clash of absolutes. The one safe prediction is that the issue will continue to shape the war between left and right for years to come—and that the fortieth anniversary of *Roe v. Wade* will be just as acrimonious as the thirtieth.

Source: "The War That Never Ends: Abortion in America." *The Economist* (U.S.), January 18, 2003.

IMPORTANT PEOPLE, PLACES, AND TERMS

Abortifacient
A substance that induces or causes an abortion

Abortion
The intentional termination of a pregnancy at any time before birth

Akron v. Akron Center for Reproductive Health
A 1983 Supreme Court ruling that struck down a series of Ohio abortion restrictions

Alito, Samuel (1950-)
Justice of the Supreme Court appointed in 2006

AMA
Acronym for the American Medical Association

American Medical Association
A professional organization for doctors that was formed in 1847

***Amicus Curiae* Brief**
A document submitted for judges' consideration by an interested party, or "friend of the court," in a lawsuit

Barnum Law
Connecticut state law prohibiting the distribution and use of contraceptives

Barnum, Phineas T. (1810-1891)
Circus showman, politician, and social reformer who led the anti-birth control movement in Connecticut

Blackmun, Harry A. (1908-1999)
Justice of the Supreme Court who wrote the majority opinion in *Roe v. Wade*

Bork, Robert H. (1927-)
Supreme Court nominee whose outspoken pro-life views led the Senate to vote against his confirmation in 1987

Brennan, William (1906-1997)
Justice of the Supreme Court who joined the majority opinion in *Roe v. Wade*

Breyer, Stephen G. (1938-)
Justice of the Supreme Court appointed in 1994

Brief
A written document that presents arguments for judges to consider in a lawsuit

Burger, Warren E. (1907-1995)
Chief justice of the Supreme Court who issued a concurring opinion in *Roe v. Wade*

Carhart v. Gonzales
A 2007 Supreme Court decision that upheld the federal Partial-Birth Abortion Ban Act

Carhart v. Stenberg
A 2000 Supreme Court decision that struck down a Nebraska law prohibiting partial-birth abortion

Casey, Robert (1932-2000)
Pro-life Pennsylvania governor who was named as the defendant in *Planned Parenthood v. Casey*

Class Action
A type of lawsuit that represents the interests of an entire class of people (for example, all pregnant women) rather than an individual

Coffee, Linda (1942-)
Attorney who, with Sarah Weddington, represented plaintiff Jane Roe and helped prepare *Roe v. Wade* for the Supreme Court

Comstock Act
An 1873 federal law that prohibited birth control, abortion, and all printed materials considered immoral or obscene

Comstock, Anthony (1844-1915)
Social reformer who crusaded against obscenity, birth control, and abortion

Conception
The point at which a sperm fertilizes an egg to begin a pregnancy

Concurring Opinion
A separate opinion issued by a Supreme Court justice who agrees with the majority decision

Contraceptive
A substance or device used to prevent pregnancy; also known as birth control

Defendant
The person or group that presents a defense against legal charges in a lawsuit

Dissenting Opinion
A separate opinion issued by a Supreme Court justice who disagrees with the majority opinion

Doe v. Bolton
Case concerning a Georgia abortion law that the Supreme Court heard as a companion case to Roe v. Wade

Douglas, William O. (1898-1980)
Justice of the Supreme Court who issued a concurring opinion in Roe v. Wade

Eisenstadt v. Baird
A 1972 Supreme Court decision that legalized the use of contraception by unmarried people

Embryo
Medical term for an unborn human from conception to the eighth week of development

FACE
Acronym for the Freedom of Access to Clinic Entrances Act

Feminist
An activist in the women's liberation movement or strong supporter of women's rights

Fetus
> Medical term for an unborn human from eight weeks after conception until birth

Finkbine, Sherri (1932-)
> TV personality whose decision to abort a deformed fetus received extensive news coverage in 1962

Flowers, Robert
> Assistant district attorney who defended Henry Wade and the Texas abortion law in the 1972 reargument of *Roe v. Wade* before the Supreme Court

Floyd, Jay
> Assistant district attorney who defended Henry Wade and the Texas abortion law in the 1971 initial argument of *Roe v. Wade* before the Supreme Court

Fourteenth Amendment
> A part of the Constitution that grants all citizens equal protection under the law and requires all laws to be clearly written

Freedom of Access to Clinic Entrances (FACE) Act
> A 1994 federal law intended to protect abortion clinics, staff, and patients from harassment and violence by pro-life protesters

Gag Rule
> A 1988 federal policy that prohibited doctors at publicly funded clinics from engaging in any abortion-related activities, including counseling and referrals

Ginsburg, Ruth Bader (1933-)
> Justice of the Supreme Court appointed in 1993

Griswold, Estelle (1900-1981)
> Activist in the movement to legalize birth control and plaintiff in *Griswold v. Connecticut*

Griswold v. Connecticut
> A 1965 Supreme Court ruling that legalized the use of birth control by married couples and established a constitutional right to privacy in reproductive decisions

Harris v. McRae
A 1980 Supreme Court decision that upheld the Hyde Amendment's ban on federal funding for abortion

Hill, Paul (1954-2003)
Radical anti-abortion activist who murdered an abortion provider and his escort outside a Florida clinic in 1994

Hyde Amendment
A federal policy that banned government-funded programs like Medicaid from providing abortions

Injunction
A court order that halts enforcement of a law

Intact Dilation and Extraction
An abortion method that involves pulling the fetus into the birth canal; known by critics as partial-birth abortion

Kennedy, Anthony (1936-)
Justice of the Supreme Court appointed in 1987

Kissling, Frances (1943-)
Pro-Choice activist and president of Catholics for a Free Choice from 1973–2007

Maher v. Roe
A 1976 Supreme Court decision that allowed states to ban public funding for abortion

Majority Opinion
The document that explains a final decision reached by the Supreme Court

Marshall, Thurgood (1908-1993)
Justice of the Supreme Court who joined the majority opinion in *Roe v. Wade*

McCorvey, Norma (1947-)
Real name of plaintiff Jane Roe in *Roe v. Wade*

Michelman, Kate (1942-)
Pro-choice activist and leader of the National Abortion Rights Action League

Miscarriage
The unintentional termination of a pregnancy at any time before birth

NARAL
Acronym for the National Abortion Rights Action League (originally National Association for the Repeal of Abortion Laws, now NARAL Pro-Choice America)

National Abortion Rights Action League
Organization dedicated to ensuring access to safe, legal abortion in the United States

National Organization for Women
A group formed in 1966 to fight for greater rights and opportunities for women

National Organization for Women v. Joseph Scheidler
A 1994 Supreme Court decision that allowed pro-choice groups to sue pro-life protesters under federal laws intended to help victims of organized crime

National Right to Life Committee
An organization founded in 1973 and dedicated to ending abortion in the United States

Ninth Amendment
An article that says U.S. citizens possess certain rights and liberties that may not be explicitly stated in the Constitution

NOW
Acronym for the National Organization for Women

O'Connor, Sandra Day (1930-)
First female justice of the Supreme Court, appointed in 1981

Operation Rescue
A pro-life group that used direct-action techniques, like blockading clinic entrances, to prevent abortions

Partial-Birth Abortion

An abortion method that involves pulling the fetus into the birth canal; also known as intact dilation and extraction

Partial-Birth Abortion Ban Act

A 2003 federal law that prohibited the use of any abortion method that was performed with part of the fetus extending outside of the mother's body

Plaintiff

A person who initiates a lawsuit

Planned Parenthood League of Connecticut

Organization that led the fight to overturn the state's anti-birth control laws

Planned Parenthood v. Casey

A 1992 Supreme Court decision that upheld a series of Pennsylvania abortion restrictions and established the "undue burden" standard, but also reaffirmed *Roe v. Wade*

Planned Parenthood v. Danforth

A 1976 Supreme Court decision that overturned a series of state restrictions aimed at limiting access to abortion

Powell, Lewis F., Jr. (1907-1998)

Justice of the Supreme Court who joined the majority opinion in *Roe v. Wade*

PPLC

Acronym for the Planned Parenthood League of Connecticut

Precedent

A previous legal ruling

Privacy

A right, not explicitly stated in the U.S. Constitution, that protects some aspects of citizens' personal lives from intrusion by government

Pro-Choice

A person or group that supports legalized abortion

Pro-Life

A person or group that opposes legalized abortion

Quickening
The stage of pregnancy (around four months from conception) when the expectant mother first detects movement of the fetus

Rehnquist, William H. (1924-2005)
Justice of the Supreme Court who issued a dissenting opinion in *Roe v. Wade*

Roberts, John (1955-)
Chief Justice of the Supreme Court appointed in 2005

Roe, Jane
False name chosen to protect the privacy of Norma McCorvey, the plaintiff in *Roe v. Wade*

Roe v. Wade
A 1973 Supreme Court decision that legalized abortion in the United States

RU 486
A drug, approved for use in the United States in 2000, that causes a miscarriage to occur when taken in early pregnancy; also known as the "abortion pill"

Rubella
A disease, also known as German measles, that carries a risk of birth defects when contracted during pregnancy

Rust v. Sullivan
A 1991 Supreme Court decision that upheld the "gag rule," a federal ban on abortion counseling at publicly funded clinics

Sanger, Margaret (1879-1966)
Leader in the movement to legalize birth control

Scalia, Antonin (1936-)
Justice of the Supreme Court appointed in 1986

Scheidler, Joseph (1927-)
Pro-life leader known for using confrontational tactics

Souter, David H. (1939-)
Justice of the Supreme Court appointed in 1990

Stare Decisis
>The idea that courts should respect precedents in order to promote stability in the law

Stevens, John Paul (1920-)
>Justice of the Supreme Court appointed in 1975

Stewart, Potter (1915-1985)
>Justice of the Supreme Court who issued a concurring opinion in *Roe v. Wade*

Supreme Court
>A nine-member court that is the ultimate authority on American law under the U.S. Constitution

Terry, Randall (1959-)
>Pro-life activist and founder of Operation Rescue

Thalidomide
>A drug that poses a high risk of birth defects when taken during pregnancy

Therapeutic Abortion
>An abortion that is performed in order to protect the mother's physical or mental health

Thomas, Clarence (1948-)
>Justice of the Supreme Court appointed in 1991

Thornburgh v. American College of Obstetricians and Gynecologists
>A 1986 Supreme Court decision that invalidated a series of Pennsylvania abortion restrictions

Trimester
>A period of time equal to approximately one-third of a typical nine-month pregnancy, or about three months

Trimester Formula
>The legal guideline established in *Roe v. Wade* to determine when state abortion restrictions were permissible

Undue Burden Standard
A legal guideline to determine whether state abortion restrictions are permissible; it replaced the trimester formula outlined in *Roe v. Wade*

Wade, Henry (1914-2001)
Dallas County district attorney who was named as the defendant in *Roe v. Wade*

Webster v. Reproductive Health Services
A 1989 Supreme Court ruling that upheld a series of Missouri abortion restrictions and came within one vote of overturning *Roe v. Wade*

Weddington, Sarah (1945-)
Attorney who represented plaintiff Jane Roe and argued *Roe v. Wade* before the Supreme Court

White, Byron R. (1917-2002)
Justice of the Supreme Court who issued a dissenting opinion in *Roe v. Wade*

Willke, John C. (1925-)
Pro-Life activist and a founder of the National Right to Life Committee

Women's Liberation Movement
A social reform movement of the 1960s and 1970s that sought equal rights and opportunities for women in American society

CHRONOLOGY

1821

Connecticut becomes the first state to outlaw abortion. *See p. 6.*

1854

Texas passes a law—later challenged in *Roe v. Wade*—making abortion illegal except when necessary to save the life of the mother. *See p. 37.*

1869

The Roman Catholic Church abandons the concept of "quickening" and declares that human life begins at the moment of conception. *See p. 10.*

1873

March 3—The U.S. Congress passes the Comstock Act, outlawing birth control, abortion, and the distribution of materials considered immoral or obscene. *See p. 12.*

1916

Margaret Sanger opens the first birth control clinic in the United States. *See p. 15.*

1928

Supreme Court Justice Louis Brandeis first argues that the Constitution supports a citizen's right to privacy. *See p. 22.*

1953

Estelle Griswold becomes executive director of the Planned Parenthood League of Connecticut. *See p. 22.*

1955

Planned Parenthood medical director Mary S. Calderone organizes a conference, "Abortion in America," that draws public attention to the abortion-reform movement.

1959

The American Law Institute recommends the reform of all state abortion laws. *See p. 28.*

1962

Children's TV host Sherri Finkbine's decision to abort a deformed fetus brings national attention to the abortion-reform issue. *See p. 26.*

1965

June 7—The Supreme Court decision in *Griswold v. Connecticut* legalizes birth control and establishes a constitutional right to privacy in reproductive decisions. *See p. 25.*

A national epidemic of rubella (German measles), which carries a risk of birth defects when contracted during pregnancy, increases public support for abortion reform. *See p. 27.*

1966

Feminist Betty Friedan forms the National Organization for Women (NOW). *See p. 33.*

1967

The American Medical Association calls for the reform of state abortion laws. *See p. 29.*

Abortion-reform measures are considered in 28 state legislatures. *See p. 30.*

A group of ministers in New York form the Clergy Consultation Service to provide abortion referrals. *See p. 33.*

1968

Planned Parenthood calls for the repeal of all anti-abortion laws. *See p. 33.*

1969

Abortion-rights activist Lawrence Lader forms the National Association for the Repeal of Abortion Laws (NARAL). *See p. 33.*

Feminists begin holding "speak outs" to raise awareness of illegal abortions. *See p. 31.*

1970

January—Attorneys Sarah Weddington and Linda Coffee convince pregnant Dallas resident Norma McCorvey to serve as the anonymous plaintiff in a legal case challenging Texas anti-abortion laws, which becomes known by the legal shorthand *Roe v. Wade. See p. 40.*

New York, Hawaii, and Washington become the first states to legalize abortion. *See p. 35.*

May 23—The case of *Roe v. Wade* is argued before the Fifth Circuit Court in Dallas, Texas. *See p. 42.*

June 17—The Fifth Circuit Court finds the 1854 Texas abortion law unconstitutional. *See p. 42.*

1971

May 21—The U.S. Supreme Court announces that it will hear the case of *Roe v. Wade. See p. 44.*

September—Supreme Court justices John Marshall Harlan and Hugo Black retire due to failing health. *See p. 46.*

December 13—Down to seven members, the Supreme Court hears initial arguments in *Roe v. Wade. See p. 47.*

Pro-life activist John C. Willke publishes his influential *Handbook on Abortion. See p. 34.*

1972

President Richard Nixon nominates Lewis Powell and William Rehnquist to fill the vacancies on the Supreme Court. *See p. 51.*

The Equal Rights Amendment passes Congress and goes to the states for ratification. *See p. 79.*

October 12—The full Supreme Court hears rearguments in the case of *Roe v. Wade.* *See p. 52.*

November 22—Justice Harry Blackmun sends a draft of the majority opinion to his colleagues for comments. *See p. 54.*

1973

January 20—President Richard Nixon is inaugurated for a second term in office. *See p. 56.*

January 22—The Supreme Court decision in *Roe v. Wade* legalizes abortion throughout the United States. *See p. 60.*

May 14—The National Right to Life Committee is formed. *See p. 64.*

August—Pro-life groups demonstrate growing power by organizing a boycott of an abortion-related episode of the CBS television series "Maude." *See p. 66.*

1974

August 9—President Nixon resigns and Vice President Gerald Ford takes office.

1975

Upon the retirement of Justice William O. Douglas, President Ford adds Justice John Paul Stevens to the Supreme Court. *See p. 74.*

1976

Pro-life Democrat Jimmy Carter is elected president of the United States. *See p. 72.*

The Supreme Court overturns state abortion restrictions in *Planned Parenthood v. Danforth. See p. 69.*

The Supreme Court allows states to ban public funding for abortion in *Maher v. Roe. See p. 69.*

Republican Congressman Henry Hyde leads a successful effort to ban federal Medicaid funding for abortion. *See p. 69.*

1977

An arson attack against a Planned Parenthood clinic in Minnesota is the first incidence of anti-abortion violence. *See p. 83.*

1979

The Reverend Jerry Falwell founds a conservative Christian organization called the Moral Majority. *See p. 64.*

1980

Republican Ronald Reagan is elected president on a pro-life platform. *See p. 74.*

The Supreme Court upholds the Hyde Amendment in *Harris v. McRae*. *See p. 70.*

1981

Upon the retirement of Justice Potter Stewart, President Reagan appoints Sandra Day O'Connor as the first female Supreme Court justice. *See p. 74.*

1982

The Equal Rights Amendment fails to be ratified by the required 38 states. *See p. 79.*

1983

On the tenth anniversary of *Roe v. Wade*, Reagan publishes a pro-life essay entitled "Abortion and the Conscience of the Nation." *See p. 74.*

1984

Dr. Bernard Nathanson produces and narrates the pro-life documentary film *The Silent Scream,* which shows ultrasound footage of a fetus during an abortion. *See p. 82.*

1986

Upon the retirement of Chief Justice Warren Burger, Reagan elevates Justice William Rehnquist to the position and appoints Antonin Scalia to the vacant seat. *See p. 75.*

1987

Upon the retirement of Lewis Powell, Reagan nominates Robert Bork to the Supreme Court, but Bork is denied confirmation in the Senate due to his pro-life views. *See p. 75.*

Reagan successfully appoints Anthony Kennedy to the Supreme Court. *See p. 78.*

Pro-life activist Randall Terry founds Operation Rescue. *See p. 83.*

1988

Congress passes the "gag rule" prohibiting doctors at federally funded clinics from providing abortion counseling and referrals. *See p. 94.*

1989

April 9—An estimated 600,000 pro-choice activists take part in the March for Women's Lives in Washington, D.C. *See p. 88.*

April 26—The Supreme Court hears arguments in *Webster v. Reproductive Health Services. See p. 88.*

July 3—In its *Webster* decision, the Supreme Court upholds a number of Missouri abortion restrictions and comes within one vote of overturning *Roe v. Wade. See p. 89.*

1990

Upon the retirement of Justice William Brennan, President George H.W. Bush appoints David H. Souter to the Supreme Court. *See p. 94.*

1991

The Supreme Court upholds the "gag rule" in *Rust v. Sullivan. See p. 94.*

Upon the retirement of Justice Thurgood Marshall, Bush appoints Clarence Thomas to the Supreme Court. *See p. 95.*

1992

April 22—The Supreme Court hears oral arguments in *Planned Parenthood v. Casey.* *See p. 96.*

June 29—In its *Casey* ruling, the Supreme Court upholds a series of Pennsylvania abortion restrictions but also reaffirms *Roe v. Wade. See p. 97.*

November—Pro-choice Democrat Bill Clinton is elected president of the United States. *See p. 102.*

Shortly after taking office, Clinton lifts the "gag rule." *See p. 102.*

1993

March 10—Michael Griffin kills Dr. David Gunn, the nation's first murder of an abortion provider by a pro-life activist. *See p. 103.*

June—Upon the retirement of Justice Byron White, Clinton appoints Ruth Bader Ginsburg to the Supreme Court. *See p. 103.*

Congress expands the Hyde Amendment to allow federal funding for abortions in cases of rape or incest. *See p. 102.*

1994

July 29—Paul Hill murders a doctor and his escort outside a Florida clinic. *See p. 104.*

Upon the retirement of Justice Harry Blackmun, Clinton appoints Stephen G. Breyer to the Supreme Court. *See p. 103.*

Responding to a wave of violence targeting abortion clinics, Congress passes the Freedom of Access to Clinic Entrances (FACE) Act. *See p. 106.*

In *NOW v. Joseph Scheidler,* the Supreme Court allows pro-choice groups to sue pro-life protesters under federal laws intended to help victims of organized crime. *See p. 107.*

1996

Congress passes a bill banning partial-birth abortions, but Clinton vetoes it.

1998

Abortion provider Dr. Barnett Slepian is killed by a sniper at his home in Amherst, New York. *See p. 108.*

2000

In *Carhart v. Stenberg,* the Supreme Court strikes down a Nebraska law banning partial-birth abortion. *See p. 114.*

September 28—The Food and Drug Administration (FDA) approves the sale and use of the abortion drug RU 486 in the United States. *See p. 111.*

November—George W. Bush is elected president of the United States. *See p. 112.*

2003

The U.S. Congress passes the Partial-Birth Abortion Ban Act. *See p. 115.*

2004

President George W. Bush is elected to a second term in office. *See p. 112.*

2005

Upon the death of Chief Justice William Rehnquist, Bush appoints John Roberts to lead the Supreme Court. *See p. 113.*

2006

Upon the retirement of Justice Sandra Day O'Connor, Bush appoints Samuel Alito to the Supreme Court. *See p. 113.*

The FDA approves over-the-counter distribution of the Plan B emergency contraceptive (also known as the "morning-after pill"). *See p. 112.*

2007

April 18—In *Carhart v. Gonzales,* the Supreme Court upholds the federal Partial-Birth Abortion Ban Act. *See p. 116.*

SOURCES FOR FURTHER STUDY

CNN Interactive. "CNN Special Reports: *Roe v. Wade,*" 1998. Available online at http://www.cnn.com/SPECIALS/1998/roe.wade. This CNN special report, prepared for the twenty-fifth anniversary of the Supreme Court decision, features statistics on abortion, a timeline of the abortion debate, profiles of participants in the legal case, and links to audio and written transcripts of oral arguments.

Craig, Barbara Hinkson, and David M. O'Brien. *Abortion and American Politics.* Chatham, NJ: Chatham House, 1993. This book provides a comprehensive account of the political and legal battles over abortion in the United States in the two decades after the 1973 *Roe v. Wade* decision.

Hull, N.E.H., and Peter Charles Hoffer. Roe v. Wade: *The Abortion Rights Controversy in American History.* Lawrence: University Press of Kansas, 2001. This book examines the historical, legal, and social context of the *Roe v. Wade* decision, as well as its impact on America's political landscape.

Oyez: U.S. Supreme Court Media. Available online at http://www.oyez.org. This award-winning Web site provides a wealth of information about the Supreme Court, including biographies of justices, a searchable database of cases, transcripts of oral arguments, and full text of decisions.

PBS. "The Supreme Court: *Roe v. Wade* (1973)." Available online at http://www.pbs.org/wnet/supremecourt/rights/landmark_roe.html. Based on a PBS television series, this site explores the history of the U.S. Supreme Court. Features include biographies, interviews, landmark cases, and lesson plans.

Stevens, Leonard A. *The Case of Roe v. Wade.* New York: Putnam, 1996. This book provides a readable history of the landmark case for middle- and high-school students.

Tribe, Laurence H. *Abortion: The Clash of Absolutes.* New York: W.W. Norton, 1990. Written by a liberal constitutional scholar, this book describes the evolution of the abortion debate in the United States.

Weddington, Sarah. *A Question of Choice.* New York: Putnam, 1992. In this personal autobiography, the attorney who argued *Roe v. Wade* before the U.S. Supreme Court shares her memories of the case.

BIBLIOGRAPHY

Books

Balkin, Jack. *What* Roe v. Wade *Should Have Said.* New York: New York University Press, 2006.

Blanchard, Dallas A. *The Anti-Abortion Movement and the Rise of the Religious Right.* New York: Twayne, 1994.

Bork, Robert H. *Slouching Towards Gomorrah: Modern Liberalism and American Decline.* New York: Regan Books, 1996.

Butler, J. Douglas, ed. *Abortion, Medicine, and the Law.* New York: Facts on File, 1986.

Craig, Barbara Hinkson, and David M. O'Brien. *Abortion and American Politics.* Chatham, NJ: Chatham House, 1993.

Faux, Marian. Roe v. Wade: *The Untold Story of the Supreme Court Decision That Made Abortion Legal.* New York: Macmillan, 1988.

Garrow, David J. *Liberty and Sexuality: The Right to Privacy and the Making of* Roe v. Wade. Berkeley: University of California Press, 1994.

Greenhouse, Linda. *Becoming Justice Blackmun.* New York: Times Books, 2006.

Hull, N.E.H., and Peter Charles Hoffer. Roe v. Wade: *The Abortion Rights Controversy in American History.* Lawrence: University Press of Kansas, 2001.

Hull, N.E.H., William James Hoffer, and Peter Charles Hoffer. *The Abortion Rights Controversy in America: A Legal Reader.* Chapel Hill, NC: University of North Carolina Press, 2004.

McCorvey, Norma, with Andy Meisler. *I Am Roe.* New York: HarperCollins, 1994.

"Roe v. Wade." In *Great American Court Cases.* 4 vols. Farmington Hills, MI: Gale Group, 1999.

Rose, Melody. *Safe, Legal, and Unavailable: Abortion Politics in the United States.* Washington, D.C.: CQ Press, 2007.

Rubin, Eva R. *The Abortion Controversy: A Documentary History.* Westport, CT: Greenwood Press, 1994.

Rudy, Kathy. *Beyond Pro-Life and Pro-Choice: Moral Diversity in the Abortion Debate.* Boston: Beacon, 1996.

Solinger, Rickie. *Pregnancy and Power: A Short History of Reproductive Politics in America.* New York: New York University Press, 2005.

Steinem, Gloria. *Outrageous Acts and Everyday Rebellions.* 2nd ed. New York: Henry Holt, 1995.

Stevens, Leonard A. *The Case of* Roe v. Wade. New York: Putnam, 1996 (juvenile).

Tribe, Laurence H. *Abortion: The Clash of Absolutes.* New York: W.W. Norton, 1990.

Weddington, Sarah. *A Question of Choice.* New York: Putnam, 1992.

Periodicals

"Abortion: Prohibition Is Not Prevention," *Time,* October 29, 2007, p. 14.

"The America We Seek: A Statement of Pro-Life Principle and Concern," *First Things,* May 1996, p. 40.

Arthur, Kate. "Television's Most Persistent Taboo," *New York Times,* July 18, 2004.

Bork, Robert H. "Inconvenient Lives," *First Things,* December 1996, p. 9.

Campo-Flores, Arian. "An Abortion Foe's End," *Newsweek,* September 8, 2003, p. 52.

Chesler, Ellen. "Public Triumphs, Private Rights," *Ms.,* Summer 2005.

Coyle, Marcia. "Shift to the Right Seen as Long-Term Reality," *Connecticut Law Tribune,* August 6, 2007.

Feldhahn, Shaunti, and Diane Glass. "Morning-After Pill: Friend or Foe of Women?" *Indianapolis Business Journal,* October 2, 2006, p. B13.

Freifeld, K. "Rights Eroding, *Roe* Lawyer Says," *Newsday,* June 30, 1992, p.86.

Glendon, Mary Ann. "A World without *Roe:* How Different Would It Be?" *New Republic,* February 20, 1989, p. 19.

"*Gonzales v. Carhart:* An Important Step Forward," *National Right to Life News,* May 2007, p. 10.

Greenhouse, Linda. "Documents Reveal the Evolution of a Justice," *New York Times,* March 4, 2004.

Greenhouse, Linda. "The Blackmun Papers," *New York Times,* March 5, 2004.

Gross, Judy. "Web of Life Issues Tangled in Florida," *National Catholic Reporter,* September 26, 2003, p. 12.

Hayes, Kathleen. "Fully Pro-Life," *Soujourners,* November 1989, p. 22.

Hittinger, Russell. "Abortion before *Roe,*" *First Things,* October 1994, p. 14.

Hoffman, Jan. "TV Shouts 'Baby,' and Barely Whispers 'Abortion,'" *New York Times,* May 31, 1992.

Kennedy, John W. "Killings Distort Pro-Life Message," *Christianity Today,* September 12, 1994, p. 56.

Kinsley, Michael. "Why Not Kill the Baby-Killers?" *Time,* August 15, 1994, p. 64.

Kissling, Frances. "Is There Life after *Roe?*" *Conscience,* Winter 2004-2005.

Krol, John Cardinal. "Statement by Two Cardinals," *New York Times,* January 23, 1972, p. 20.

Lowery, Nick. "Byron White Balanced Brains, Sports, Character," *USA Today,* April 17, 2002.

Mauro, Tony. "Unanimous Court Sidesteps Abortion Issue," *Legal Intelligencer,* January 19, 2006.

Nelson, Sarah. "The Partial-Birth Abortion Ban: Effects on Women's Right," *Women's Health Activist,* July-August 2007, p. 8.

Quindlen, Anna. "Bedroom v. Courtroom," *Newsweek,* November 14, 2005, p. 70.

Quindlen, Anna. "Hers," *New York Times,* March 13, 1986, p. C2.

Quindlen, Anna. "One Vote," *New York Times,* July 1, 1992, p. A23.

"*Roe:* 25 Years Later," *First Things,* January 1998, p. 9.

Rosenberg, Debra. "In *Roe*'s Shadow," *Newsweek,* January 27, 2003, p. 58.

Savage, Dan. "Can I Get a Little Privacy?" *New York Times,* November 16, 2005.

Savage, David G. "*Roe* Ruling: More Than Its Author Intended," *Los Angeles Times,* September 14, 2005.

Steinfels, Margaret O'Brien. "What Women Have Lost," *Commonweal,* October 21, 1994, p. 20.

Tell, David. "Planned Un-Parenthood: *Roe v. Wade* at Thirty," *Weekly Standard,* January 27, 2003.

"Vengeance: Possible Reasons for Increasing Violence against Abortion Clinics," *The Economist (U.S.),* January 7, 1995, p. A21.

"The War That Never Ends: Abortion in America," *The Economist (U.S.),* January 18, 2003.

Weddington, Sarah. "January 22, 1973: Getting the Right to Choose," *Time,* March 31, 2003, p. A54.

Online

Alan Guttmacher Institute. "Facts on Induced Abortion in the United States," May 2006. Available online at http://www.guttmacher.org/pubs/fb_induced_abortion.html.

CNN Interactive. "CNN Special Reports: *Roe v. Wade,*" 1998. Available online at http://www.cnn.com/SPECIALS/1998/roe.wade.

Feminists for Life. "The Feminist Case against Abortion," September 13, 1999. Available online at http://www.feministsforlife.org/news/commonw.htm.

Hill, Paul. "Defending the Defenseless," August 2003. Available online at http://www.armyofgod.com/PHillonepage.html.

National Right to Life Committee. "Abortion History Timeline." Available online at http://www.nrlc.org/abortion/timeline1.html, and "Abortion in the United States: Statistics and Trends." Available online at http://www.nrlc.org/abortion/facts/abortionstats.html.

Oyez: U.S. Supreme Court Media. Available online at http://www.oyez.org.

PBS. "The Supreme Court: *Roe v. Wade* (1973)." Available online at http://www.pbs.org/wnet/supremecourt.

PBS Online NewsHour. "The Blackmun Tapes," March 4, 2004. Available online at http://www.pbs.org/newshour/bb/law/jan-june04/blackmun_3-04.html.

Physicians for Reproductive Choice and Health. "Physicians Denounce Supreme Court Ruling on Abortion," April 18, 2007. Available online at http://www.prch.org/press/pr/04_18_07.shtml.

Planned Parenthood. "Before *Roe*." Available online at http://www.plannedparenthood.org/news-articles-press.

Planned Parenthood. "Fact Sheet: Medical and Social Health Benefits Since Abortion Was Made Legal in the U.S." December 2006.

Schlafly, Phyllis. "*Roe v. Wade* at 25," January 28, 1998. Available online at http://www.eagleforum.org/column/1998/jan98/98-01-28.html.

Voices of Choice. Available online at http://www.voicesofchoice.org.

PHOTO AND ILLUSTRATION CREDITS

Cover and Title Page photo: William Philpott/Reuters/Landov.

Chapter One: Prints and Photographs Division, Library of Congress, LC-USZ62-84946 (p. 9); Associated Press (p. 14); New York World-Telegram and the Sun Newspaper Photograph Collection, Prints and Photographs Division, Library of Congress: LC-USZ62-118518 (p. 16), LC-USZ62-113629 (p. 18).

Chapter Two: Time & Life Pictures/Getty Images: Lee Lockwood (p. 25), J.R. Eyerman (p. 29); Photoprint by Bachrach, Prints and Photographs Division, Library of Congress, LC-USZ62-77521 (p. 26); New York World-Telegram and the Sun Newspaper Photograph Collection, Prints and Photographs Division, Library of Congress, LC-USZ62-122632 (p. 32).

Chapter Three: Courtesy: Jimmy Carter Library (p. 37); Getty Images: Greg Gibson/AFP (p. 40), Shelly Katz/Time & Life Pictures (p. 43); Photographer Warren K. Leffler, U.S. News & World Report Magazine Photograph Collection. Prints and Photographs Division, Library of Congress, LC-DIG-ppmsca-03411 (p. 46); Color negative by Robert S. Oakes, Prints and Photographs Division, Library of Congress, LC-DIG-cph-3b07878 (p. 48), LC-DIG-cph-3b07875 (p. 49).

Chapter Four: Cartoon by Bill Garner, The Washington Times, Courtesy of the Supreme Court of the United States (p. 55); Prints and Photographs Division, Library of Congress, LC-DIG-cph-3b07883 (p. 60). Michael L. Abramson/Time & Life Pictures/Getty Images (p. 62); Photograph by Bernard Gotfryd, Prints and Photographs Division, The Library of Congress, LC-DIG-ppmsca-12454 (p. 65); U.S. News & World Report Magazine Photograph Collection, Prints and Photographs Division, Library of Congress: Photograph by Warren K. Leffler, LC-DIG-ppmsca-09733 (p. 68), Photograph by Thomas J. O'Halloran, LC-DIG-ppmsca-09742 (p. 71).

Chapter Five: Photograph by Dane Penland, Smithsonian Institution, Courtesy of the Supreme Court of the United States (p. 75); Courtesy: Ronald Reagan Library (p. 78); Getty Images: Darren McCollester (p. 82), Robert Sherbow/Time & Life Pictures (p. 87); Brian Snyder/Reuters/Newscom (p. 84); Photograph by Joe Lavenburg, National Geographic Society, Courtesy of the Supreme Court of the United States (p. 90).

Chapter Six: Photograph by Dane Penland, Smithsonian Institution, Courtesy of the Supreme Court of the United States (p. 97); Robert Sherbow/Time & Life Pictures/

Getty Images (p. 99); Prints and Photographs Division, Library of Congress, LC-USZ62-113158 (p. 102); Khue Bui/Associated Press (p. 107).

Chapter Seven: Ron Edmonds/Associated Press (p. 111); Photo reprinted with permission of the National Organization for Women (p. 113); White House photo by Eric Draper (p. 115); Alex Wong/Getty Images (p. 121).

Biographies: Color negative by Robert S. Oakes, Prints and Photographs Division, Library of Congress, LC-DIG-cph-3b07876 (p. 125); Getty Images: CNP (p. 129), Cynthia Johnson/Time & Life Pictures (p. 134), Chris Kleponis/AFP (p. 138), Alex Wong/Getty for Meet the Press (p. 143), Tim Boyles (p. 152), Shelly Katz/Time & Life Pictures (p. 156); Photograph by Underwood & Underwood, Prints and Photographs Division, Library of Congress, LC-DIG-cph-3a30477 (p. 146); Harry Cabluck/Associated Press (p. 159); Courtesy: Life Issues Institute (p. 163).

INDEX